Cross-examination
in Criminal Trials

To Anthony

Cross-examination in Criminal Trials

Second edition

Marcus Stone MA LLB
Advocate
formerly Sheriff of Glasgow
and Strathkelvin at Glasgow

Butterworths
London, Boston, Dublin, Durban, Edinburgh, Kuala Lumpur,
San Juan, Singapore, Sydney, Toronto, Wellington
1995

United Kingdom	Butterworths a Division of Reed Elsevier (UK) Ltd, Halsbury House, 35 Chancery Lane, LONDON WC2A 1EL and 4 Hill Street, EDINBURGH EH2 3JZ
Australia	Butterworths, SYDNEY, MELBOURNE, BRISBANE, ADELAIDE, PERTH, CANBERRA and HOBART
Canada	Butterworths Canada Ltd, TORONTO and VANCOUVER
Ireland	Butterworth (Ireland) Ltd, DUBLIN
Malaysia	Malayan Law Journal Sdn Bhd, KUALA LUMPUR
New Zealand	Butterworths of New Zealand Ltd, WELLINGTON and AUCKLAND
Puerto Rico	Butterworth of Puerto Rico, Inc, SAN JUAN
Singapore	Butterworths Asia, SINGAPORE
South Africa	Butterworths Publishers (Pty) Ltd, DURBAN
USA	Butterworth Legal Publishers, CARLSBAD, California and SALEM, New Hampshire

A CIP Catalogue record for this book is available from the British Library.

First edition 1988

ISBN 0 406 00622 9

Printed in England by Clays Ltd, St Ives plc

Foreword to the second edition

Until I was asked to write this foreword, I had not realised just how much time had passed since the first edition. September 1988 may not be even a decade ago but, in terms of advocacy training both sides of the border, it is an epoch ago. In the foreword to the first edition, I wrote:

> It is incredible that it has taken so long for the legal profession, here and abroad, to acknowledge that it is possible—and, even, desirable—to teach the skills of advocacy …

In the last four to five years a remarkable change has occurred. In England and in Scotland, the Bar (and solicitors) have addressed in a practical way the critical importance of providing professional advocacy training to those who are starting in the professions—and those beyond. Advocacy is taught as a performance skill, but not in a vacuum.

Advocacy is about cases, it is about people, about how they think, about how they react to events and about how they remember. It is about preparation. It is about planning and about executing the plan. So, teaching advocacy as a performance skill is only part of the process. Unless the student advocate—and we are *all* student advocates until the day we retire from the Bar—learns and understands the elements upon which he or she can practise the performance skill, it is little more than a series of tricks or ploys, a shell without substance.

That is where the work that Marcus Stone has done on cross-examination, which he has now brought up to date, is so vitally important. The individual lessons which he seeks to convey are essential reading, but the reading must be with the clear understanding that Marcus is not writing about abstractions, he is writing about practical matters. Time and again, he will be found saying that what he is talking about are real problems encountered by real advocates in real cases and about their practical solutions. Take, just as an example, what he says in Chapter 3, entitled 'The reliability of evidence'. Having made the point that all evidence is potentially flawed simply by the process of human observation and recall, he says:

The subject of how errors in evidence are caused should really be a branch of applied psychology. While some use may be made of academic findings, they are generally inadequate for the task. *Theoretical psychology has little to offer to advocates.* The approach taken here is *mainly a commonsense one*, with a view to application in court. [My emphasis added.]

The administration of justice—and the legal professions at the heart of it—are the subjects of intense debate in virtually every jurisdiction. Delays, costs, structure, principles: all these have come under scrutiny. That much of the criticism seems to practitioners and judges not to be about the real world may be the inevitable reaction of the criticised but, whether it is fair or not, which of us really doubts that we have been extraordinarily slow in recognising a responsibility to explain what we do (and why) and to ensure that we are seen to be doing everything we can do to do it better. There is no greater service that any of us can perform, not just for our own professions but for the increasingly unconsidered freedoms of our societies, than to make ourselves and those who will follow us, better advocates. Marcus Stone has provided that service in his, now, two editions of this book. We—and those whose service is our justification—are enormously in his debt.

36 Essex Street   *Michael Hill, Q.C.*
London WC2R 3AS

February 1995

Preface to the second edition

In the United Kingdom and overseas, the response to the first edition has been gratifying. Reviews and other books have approved of the analysis contained in this work. It has contributed to advocacy training programmes.

In 1990, an edition published in Italian, in Milan, appears to have played a significant role in the new adversarial criminal procedure in Italy.

It appears, therefore, that the book meets a widespread demand. But the practice of advocacy is hardly affected by legal developments. Why then has the need for a second edition emerged? After a period of six years, scope for improvement has been seen to an extent which justified a new edition.

The whole book has been thoroughly revised. Much of it has been rewritten in order to increase clarity and balance. New insights have been added. Examples have been provided. The text has been considerably expanded. But the essential aim of the book is unchanged, namely to provide practitioners and those entering practice with a proper foundation for developing their personal skills in cross-examination. This consists of a comprehensive and realistic analysis of its role and significance as an integral part of a criminal trial. This insight is the basis for individual judgment in selecting tactics and techniques, in the particular context.

This is the only possible approach if advocacy is to be a profession and not just an expression of the superior natural ability of gifted amateurs. Yet until recently this professional approach was absent in legal education and training.

Now, because of changes in the two branches of the legal profession and their relationships, advocacy training is in vogue. It will only be effective to the extent that it is based on sound analysis and understanding. The aim of this second edition is to provide this at a time when the need is crucial.

Edinburgh   *Marcus Stone*
January 1995

Foreword to the first edition

Even in these days of undemonstrative advocacy, there are some great cross-examiners whose every word and movement command attention and frequently create tension. There are some pretty awful ones as well. Not all the latter are to be found amongst the young and inexperienced, just as not all the former are senior and supposedly leading advocates. The worst cross-examination I have ever heard was by a silk who manfully, almost single-handed, managed to secure the conviction of his client in the teeth of no evidence by getting him to stand up in the dock whilst he asked the frightened eyewitness, who had hardly lifted his eyes from the floor since he had come into court, 'That's not the man who pointed the gun at you, is it?'—with the inevitable result.

That which distinguishes the best cross-examiners from the rest is the confidence which they inspire in their knowledgeable audience that they obviously know what they are doing and why and have thought about how to achieve their objective. They do not cross-examine on a wish and a prayer; they are not pursuing the merely desirable at the expense of the necessary; they have decided what is attainable; they understand how witnesses work and the fallibility of human recollection and accuracy under stress and they have that inexplicable sixth sense which enables them to 'feel' the witness long before the tribunal can recognise what is happening.

It is unlikely that anyone has ever taught them their skills. They have learnt by observation of their elders and their contemporaries, and those skills upon which they so greatly depend have been long in coming.

It is incredible that it has taken so long for the legal profession, here and abroad, to acknowledge that it is possible—and, even, desirable—to teach the skills of advocacy; and regrettable that, even now, so much of the teaching is unstructured, frequently idiosyncratic and, in many cases, an uncomfortable reflection of the blind leading the blind.

So far as I am aware, Marcus Stone is the first person in the United Kingdom to essay a comprehensive study of cross-examination, to identify the skills that are involved and to explain them and, above all, to place them in the context of the whole trial process. The latter is so important; cross-examination, particularly a successfully destructive cross-examination, can too frequently become an end in itself, with the triumphant advocate forgetting the purpose of the whole operation.

The most crucial lesson which this book teaches, in various ways but all the way through, is encapsulated at the beginning of chapter 8: 'a cross-examiner must know what he can do, how he can do it, and the probable effects of doing it ...'. With cross-examination, as with every other element of his tasks, the advocate must be the master of his field, not a mere wandering, semi-informed hopeful, striking here, striking there, wishing but seldom achieving. And his field includes understanding and compassion for human weaknesses. There is more than an echo of Birkett's exposition of the good advocate in this book. In his Presidential Address to the Holdsworth Club in 1945, Birkett said:

> It is well, if the advocate is possessed of a quick mind, alert to seize the unexpected opportunity, to adapt himself to the sudden changes which occur in the conduct of a case .... But more important than the quick mind is the understanding heart, the insight into human nature, the natural sympathy with all sorts and conditions of men, the intuitive recognition of what the particular situation demands.

The lesson that understanding witnesses and why they may depart from total accuracy and recall is needed, is vitally important to the cross-examiner. Even genuine human recollection is fallible. Marcus Stone sets out to teach that lesson to the aspiring advocate: a cynical old hand would wish that some judges and even more magistrates would learn that lesson as well.

As he takes us through cross-examination, its purpose(s), its place in the trial process, the material upon which it works, the rules by which it must be conducted, its relationship with examination-in-chief, its different techniques and its problems, Marcus Stone does more than instruct the beginner. He has made at least one senior think again about what he is doing and why—and how he can do it better. Almost every page is illuminated by his long and varied experience, by his learning, by his insight and by his love of his profession. The only pity (for an English barrister) is that it has taken a Scot to do this—even if he is a friend.

The Temple
September 1988

Michael Hill, Q.C.

Preface to the first edition

It is remarkable that on the crucial subject of cross-examination pen has not been put to paper, whereas impressive-looking volumes flaunt dubious knowledge, or even ignorance, of less important human affairs.

Everyone sees advocacy, the art of persuasion in court, as a profession. Nearly all criminal trials turn on issues of fact, where cross-examination is the essence of adversarial confrontation. Yet although advocates may not know the elements of the art, they are turned out as qualified for professional practice. University courses in criminal law, procedure and evidence ignore the central fact-finding process and do not develop the skill which is required, especially in cross-examination. Post-graduate training in advocacy is still elementary and unsystematic.

Fact-finding depends on whether evidence is held to be truthful, untruthful, accurate or mistaken. This field and the techniques of presenting, testing and challenging evidence, require study. Practitioners deal with it every day, but it is alien to the academic teaching of law. If advocacy is a profession, and not just an activity for amateurs or born geniuses, it should be an integral part of legal training and qualification.

So far as skill in cross-examination is concerned, a barrier is the lack of any specialised, systematic and comprehensive textbook on the subject in British legal literature. Isolated and anecdotal chapters on the topic in a few books on advocacy do not meet the need. It is the aim of this work to do so.

Its objective is to provide a foundation for developing practical skill in cross-examination. Like so many skills, this one depends on natural aptitude, learning the techniques, practical experience in applying them and noting the results.

In anticipation of objections, it is stressed that this book is not in competition with either natural ability nor experience in the courts, both of which are essential. It offers a base for maximising them.

The view that ability in cross-examination is just a natural gift, and that there is nothing to learn, is untenable. Of course innate talent may settle whether a pianist, pilot or advocate will surpass ordinary proficiency and attain levels of virtuosity—but not straight from school without training or experience! Moreover, if advocacy is just a matter of aptitude, how does a professional differ from a gifted amateur? Often, what counts is not what is inherited, but how it is used—a matter of motivation and effort.

Of course, personal qualities affect style but all styles are found in successful advocates.

Would even a genius in cross-examination agree that he was as good at the start as at the end of a long and successful career? If not, what did he learn in between? This book sets out to provide some of the answers. Most advocates absorb such information naturally over a long period. The present material is the result of studying many thousands of witnesses under cross-examination, throughout 40 years at the bar and on the bench.

But court experience is not enough per se. Some advocates never seem to learn. Experience just reinforces their poor methods. Even for able advocates, experience is enhanced if it is based on clear insight into what goes on, not just intuitive leaps at witnesses. If advocacy is not calculating, what is?

If cross-examination is a mystique, beyond explanation or learning, this is odd. Other complex intellectual processes can be analysed, e g logic, semantics, psychotherapy, the art of negotiation and so on. Also, advocates and courts analyse the significance of cross-examination constantly. But the best answer to such mysticism is the validity of the present analysis.

Cross-examination is seen here not in isolation, but as an integral part of advocacy and of the whole trial process, distinguishing its constructive and destructive functions. Challenging the witness or the evidence are considered separately, in detail. Emphasis is placed on the importance of contradicting evidence by other evidence in support of destructive cross-examination.

The context of the trial is explained, including the nature of the real issues of fact, how errors arise in testimony, and the various forms of deception which play a major role in criminal trials. A full account is given of examination-in-chief and re-examination, with recommendations for speeches in relation to cross-examination.

Questions of law, including the rules of evidence, being outwith the subject, are omitted. There are many excellent books on the law of evidence which may be consulted for full statements of the law where required.

Simply by reading a book one cannot learn to become a good cross-examiner any more than one can learn to swim. Practice and experience are required. But a sound analysis is a basis for intelligent and directed development of skill by practice. Various techniques and tactics may be tried out, and maximum benefit can be derived from experience, by reflecting on the results.

Efficiency is the immediate goal for a cross-examiner. In the vast majority of trials, especially in summary trials, virtuosity in cross-examination would offer little or no advantage over the professional competence which is attainable by any advocate of reasonable aptitude.

The development of skill would including a growing understanding of witnesses, increasing familiarity with recurrent problems and patterns of evidence and their weaknesses, a better grasp of typical court situations, more insight into the probable views taken by courts of different kinds of evidence, and practice in using a variety of techniques in different circumstances.

The text covers cross-examination by either the prosecution or defence counsel or solicitors in both jury trials and summary trials. Obviously, it also applies, substantially, to civil courts, although no reference is made to this.

Cross-examination is based on processes in human nature which are not confined to any jurisdiction. The present material applies to any adversarial system of criminal procedure, i e all criminal courts conducted in the English language.

This book is intended mainly but not exclusively for those who are preparing for or are engaged in criminal advocacy. At the outset, guidance is essential, but even experienced advocates should benefit from a systematic analysis of the whole field of cross-examination.

Lay magistrates rarely have court experience on appointment and gain it only slowly by intermittent service on the bench. This book should increase their insight into the trial process and assist them in fact-finding.

For police officers who are regularly subjected to rigorous cross-examination, the analysis should add to their grasp of the process. It will also enable them to foresee challenges to evidence which they are assembling, and when reinforcement is desirable.

Mysteries should be removed by the text for many persons connected with the courts, other than lawyers, e g expert witnesses, doctors, psychiatrists, forensic scientists, psychologists, social workers or journalists. Their roles should become more meaningful by a better appreciation of the context.

Since technicalities, especially of the law, are avoided, the book is suitable for general readers who are interested in the subject of the criminal process for its own sake. They may also develop a personal interest in it if they become involved as jurors, witnesses or otherwise.

Edinburgh   *Marcus Stone*
August 1988

Acknowledgments

In a book like this, where the text, but not the subject, is innovative, the opinions of distinguished readers are invaluable. Even a lack of comment may suggest that some hazard has been avoided. But when encouragement and detailed advice are added, gratitude must be even greater.

I again thank His Honour Judge McLean and Peter G B McNeil, QC, PhD for their contributions to the first edition—both for their valuable comments and for what they omitted (though the responsibility for any inadequacies is mine alone!).

I must also once again thank Michael Hill, QC, for contributing a foreword to this edition as he did to the last.

Contents

CHAPTER 1

Cross-examination: preliminary

Cross-examination is not an isolated technique or skill. It operates in a context. To make the most of cross-examination, this context must be understood. It includes the rules of evidence, professional ethics, other ways of questioning witnesses, speeches, and the overall presentation of the case. In this chapter, the relationship of cross-examination to the other aspects of the trial process is outlined briefly. This subject is developed in more detail later.

I THE RULES OF EVIDENCE

An advocate on his feet should know, instantly, which way he can go. This is no time to consult law books.

Mastery of the rules of evidence, especially those which regulate admissibility, is essential. But this mastery is only a precondition of ability as an advocate. Cross-examination as a persuasive skill starts where the law of evidence stops. The techniques and tactics of cross-examination are based on human nature, not law. Accordingly, they apply in all English-speaking courts, whatever their legal framework. For the rules of evidence relating to cross-examination in any country, reference should be made to standard texts. Where rules of English courts are mentioned here, this is only to illustrate points of practice in cross-examining—not to state the law. No case decisions are cited.

II PROFESSIONAL ETHICS

An advocate's conduct is controlled by express professional codes, judicial dicta, tradition and practice. Some leading principles are stated here. The ethics of advocacy impose restrictions on cross-examination; winning at all costs is unacceptable. Impropriety in court may be the subject of objection, criticism, reprimand, exclusion of evidence, or worse. Impropriety discovered after the trial may also have repercussions.

The ethics of advocacy are designed to maintain personal integrity in an adversarial conflict. An advocate's duty is to present his case as forcefully as he can, without becoming personally identified with it, or forming or expressing any opinion about it. Nevertheless, it is acceptable for an advocate to conduct a case in a way which suggests that he believes in it. This is part of his persuasive function. Such role-playing is taken for granted in other fields, from the dignified formality of the judge, to the tactful bedside manner of the doctor.

By the nature of things, the case presented by one side will usually be based on inaccurate or false evidence. This is not the advocate's responsibility, so long as his instructions are to the effect that his case is genuine.

A fundamental principle, from which others flow, is that an advocate must not knowingly mislead or deceive the court. This is the limit of his accountability for the accuracy of his case or the evidence which he leads. It means that he must only assert facts responsibly on the basis of his information, not invention. He must not challenge, or try to disprove, facts which he knows to be accurate.

All advocates have the above duties, but they are more exacting in the case of a prosecutor. His official position obliges him to disclose any material evidence which may help the defence. He should present his case with the aim of assisting the court to reach a true verdict, and not just to win. His cross-examination, especially of the accused, should be fair and reasonable, and based on his information both for and against guilt.

A prosecutor should never exaggerate or distort his case to secure a conviction. Where he can competently attack an accused's character, he should only do this if it is necessary. He should not do it merely to create prejudice.

The defence have more latitude. They need not disclose adverse evidence in order to assist the Crown. In cross-examination, the defence advocate must not suggest facts without grounds, eg that someone else was the offender. He may test Crown evidence for accuracy, or reliability, but he must not challenge it as inaccurate, eg by denying the crime, unless this is based on his information.

Obviously, an advocate must not devise a defence. His duty depends on what he is told. Normally, a defence advocate is not given any incriminating information. Presumably guilty clients keep this to themselves. The advocate is therefore free to contest anything which differs from what he was told.

If however an advocate is embarassed by his client's confidential disclosures, he might withdraw or, in many cases, he could still conduct a 'legal' type of defence independently of the facts, where this has some prima facie basis in law, eg by objecting to the admissibility of crucial evidence or by making a submission that there is no case to answer.

III EXAMINATION-IN-CHIEF

Leading evidence-in-chief is linked with cross-examining an opponent's witnesses. Expectations about what cross-examination alone can achieve should be realistic. Defence attacks on Crown evidence seldom destroy it outright. But it may weaken it and expose the evidence as unreliable and unsafe. Better still, the weakened evidence may be overcome by contradictory evidence-in-chief led by the cross-examiner.

Another important link between examination-in-chief and cross-examination is the desirability of anticipating and forestalling challenge, when leading one's own evidence.

These topics will be developed in the chapter on examination-in-chief.

IV RE-EXAMINATION

Since re-examination should only be undertaken to repair damage or to explain something which has become unclear, as a result of cross-examination, the links are obvious. This will be amplified in the appropriate chapter.

V SPEECHES

Final speeches, of course, summarise the effects of cross-examination. But there are other specific links.

As will be seen, it is often a good idea to refrain from asking an opponent's witness a final and conclusive question, after a chain of questions has brought his evidence to a critical point. This avoids retraction or qualification of anything favourable which has already been achieved.

Again, when inconsistency in evidence has been exposed by cross-examination, eg self-contradiction by any witness, or the emergence of a conflict between witnesses who support the same story, it is often best to end cross-examination at that point. The tactic is not to give the witnesses a chance to explain the inconsistency. The opponent may try to do it, but he is the person with the difficulty. The final speech is the stage where unexplained inconsistencies may be highlighted.

VI THE ROLE OF CROSS-EXAMINATION

A cross-examiner's practical decisions should be based on a realistic grasp of what he can hope to achieve. Exaggerated or mistaken views of the role of cross-examination can be a handicap in practice.

A The adversarial system

The adversarial system of court procedure consists of a conflict between the prosecution and the defence, unlike a state-directed enquiry into facts. The parties decide what evidence to collect, present, agree or dispute. The court's role is limited to judgment. The advocate's partiality contributes to impartial justice. The Bar and Bench co-operate to this end.

Less dynamic procedure could be imagined, where the evidence of witnesses is not challenged directly by adversaries, but is simply compared and assessed by the court rather like the Eurovision Song Contest. This would be less effective. Mere competition between contradictory assertions is not enough. It is best that parties test each other's cases by head-on confrontation. This occurs when the opposing points of view meet in cross-examination. This is the cutting edge of advocacy. In this way, in forming sound judgments, the court is assisted by contentious advocacy, which directly tests evidence for accuracy, and exposes errors, gaps or lies.

B Variety of views

A whole spectrum of views on the role and value of cross-examination can be found in legal literature; quotations may be found to support any kind of evaluation. These views are open to the criticism that they are only personal impressions whose acceptability must be qualified by their variety and disagreement.

The following classical antithesis of idealistic and cynical views, will suffice to show the range.

Wigmore was enthusiastic about cross-examination:

> ... it is beyond any doubt the greatest legal engine ever invented for the discovery of truth ... The fact of this unique and irresistible power remains, and is the reason for our faith in its merits ... cross-

examination, not trial by jury, is the great and permanent contribution of the Anglo-American system of law to improved methods of trial procedure.   [John Henry Wigmore *Evidence* (3rd edn) para 1367]

Archbishop Whately was less impressed:

...I think that the kind of skill by which the cross-examiner succeeds in alarming, misleading or bewildering an honest witness may be characterised as the most, or one of the most, base and depraved of all possible employments of intellectual power.
[Archbishop Whately *Elements of Rhetoric* p 165]

These, and many less extreme views, err in looking at cross-examination in isolation, rather than as an integral part of a complex process. When it is so seen, its role in the criminal trial emerges more clearly.

C   Cross-examination in context

The context in which cross-examination occurs includes the real situation which is under enquiry, as well as the trial process as a whole.

The reality underlying the trial is at least significant, and may be crucial, in determining the outcome. Certainly, the aim of the system of justice is to discover this, not to provide a forum for intellectual combat, where winning is all. Cross-examination is intended to contribute to fact-finding, not concealment or distortion of facts.

In theory, the truth ought to determine success. Cross-examination is not designed to destroy true or accurate evidence. In practice, it may be suggested that truth, in the mouths of most witnesses, is often fairly robust under attack. The context in which cross-examination operates also includes the whole trial process. However significant cross-examination may be, it rarely determines the verdict by itself. Its effect depends on its complex interaction with a number of other factors. This will be discussed in relation to various techniques in different situations, but two aspects may be mentioned here.

Cross-examination has an important constructive function. Here the advocate seeks positive and favourable evidence to build up his case, from the opponent's witness. Concessions from opponents' witnesses can have a strong impact. Yet they are rarely a substitute for the evidence-in-chief led by the cross-examiner. Positive evidence elicited in cross-examination normally supplements, reinforces and highlights the main body of positive evidence which a party leads himself. Presumably there is nothing 'base or depraved' in this activity.

The destructive function of cross-examination is to weaken or destroy the evidence of the opponent's witness. Where this succeeds, it is normally the result of a combination of factors, not one devastating blow. A cross-examiner may succeed in weakening evidence by showing that it is unreliable and unsafe. But he may go further and establish contrary facts, by evidence which he leads himself.

So in order to win his case, if Whately's 'depraved' advocate managed to shake an honest witness, he would still need the support of perjured evidence from his own witnesses, which survived cross-examination and defeated his opponent's evidence. One would hope that the opponent, in cross-examining, was not as inept as the first advocate was depraved.

The interactions of cross-examination with other factors will be developed in the text to follow. The scenario which Whately condemns, is hardly the norm. It is rather a reflection of popular mythology and stereotypes. The complex process of a criminal trial has many built-in checks to offset the kind of situation which he describes. The truth is not so fragile as Whately claims. But although his image of cross-examination is exaggerated it cannot be wholly dismissed. It is necessary to face up to the significance of presentation and tactics in criminal trials.

VII PRESENTATION AND TACTICS

The above analysis of the role of cross-examination, must be supplemented by consideration of the psychology of presentation and tactics.

This approach was first developed by the Sophists in the classical age of Greek rhetoric. The true facts were regarded as almost irrelevant. The advocate's role was to create some kind of make-believe theatre which persuaded the court to accept the view presented. What it decided was the truth.

This approach has persisted, and is more prevalent in the USA than in the UK. It would mean that within the limits set by law, ethics and the advocate's information, he puts on a show which is designed to secure acceptance of his version of the facts. What is stressed here is skill in presentation, rather than the role played by the true facts in moulding the trial process.

Certainly while a criminal trial is concerned with truth, it is not a free enquiry into the facts. The time for discovery is over. A limited decision, based on the evidence available, is all that is possible.

On this restricted material the arts of advocacy are exercised. It increases the importance of presentation. In a sense, the verdict expresses a preference for one version of the facts over the other although this is not the legal image.

Again, on any view, advocac is not an exact science. The effect of any particular approach cannot be guaranteed. There are too many variables.

This book is designed to be helpful to the practitioner, not to reach theoretical conclusions about whether an objective approach, or a presentational approach, to advocacy is more effective. On any view, presentation plays a role in every case, and advocates must be proficient in the relevant skills. They may make a difference. Guidance as to presentation and tactics is given throughout the text.

Defence tactics may vary according to their overall approach. An acquittal may be obtained without establishing whether Crown evidence about crucial facts is false, mistaken or incomplete. It is enough to persuade the court that essential Crown evidence is too unreliable or unsafe for conviction.

In this way the defence benefits from the legal burden on the Crown to prove guilt beyond reasonable doubt. The Crown may fail to do so because the prosecution evidence is too weak, or because of the skills of the respective advocates.

But defence advocates usually try to do more than this, by striving to prove that Crown evidence is untruthful or mistaken. Doing this would generally require contradictory evidence.

Although, by law, the defence are not obliged to prove anything or lead evidence, they usually do so, in order to present an alternative account which, if true, would result in an acquittal. The defence would succeed if this were proved or merely if it threw enough doubt on the Crown case.

The more the defence takes the form of a continuous and believable human story, the more persuasive it will be. The prosecution will also present a connected story. In this way, advocates come closest to putting on a show albeit on the basis of their respective information. This theatrical approach has to be kept in mind and adopted where appropriate.

CHAPTER 2

The anatomy of a criminal trial

I Introduction
II Alternative defences
III Commission of crime
IV Identity

I INTRODUCTION

In nearly all criminal trials, the essential question is one of fact, not law. Despite the wide variety of criminal situations, issues of fact often fall into recognisable patterns. An analysis of these is given here, as a guide to the areas where cross-examiners may expect to find material errors or lies, viz in relation to disputed facts.

II ALTERNATIVE DEFENCES

By law, for conviction, the prosecutor has the burden of proving what he states in the indictment or information, viz (1) that the crime was committed (including any necessary knowledge or intent), and (2) that it was the accused who committed it. But the burden is less in practice. The real issue is generally restricted to whichever one of these two Crown requirements the defence choose to dispute. This is, of course, not a matter of law. For convenience, it may be called the 'rule of alternative defences'.

Irrespective of innocence or guilt, the logical and practical implication of denying one of the two foundations of the Crown case is to limit the defence to that one issue. This is explained below.

The defence, who create the issue, know what it is when they make their selection. But for tactical reasons, usually of little importance, they rarely admit undisputed facts formally, as they could do, to make evidence unnecessary. But assuming that the supporting evidence is sufficient, these uncontested facts are easily proved, as a rule. This is seen in one trial after another.

The prosecutor usually discovers the real issues from pre-trial disclosure of the defence case in committal proceedings, depositions, statements, interviewing witnesses, exchange of information or discussion. Otherwise, the issues soon become obvious in the trial, from opening speeches, when made, or defence cross-examination of Crown witnesses. Later, the defence may also lead evidence and present arguments to the same effect.

The 'rule of alternative defences' follows from the fact that few defences take the purely legal form of simply testing Crown evidence, objecting to admissibility of evidence, or contending that there is no case to answer. The defence usually put forward some version of the facts contradicting one or other of the two assertions in the Crown case.

Although a defendant need not testify and, if he refrains from doing so, comment is restricted, it may be assumed that he will give evidence to support a positive version of the disputed facts, which contradicts the Crown version. Any other defence evidence may then be expected to coincide with the accused's testimony, in whole or in part.

Most crimes, whether serious or not, occur at specific times and places. For simplicity, this may be taken as typical, although some crimes consist of a course of conduct over a period, eg fraud or child neglect.

An accused who testifies that he was not at the scene of the crime, whether or not he pleads alibi, cannot personally deny that the crime was committed, and it is not to be expected that he would call other defence witnesses to do so.

Without such information, a defence advocate could not dispute the crime either (although he could of course test the evidence). Thus, the only real issue would be that of the accused's identity as the offender.

An accused who, in evidence, denies that the crime was committed, places himself at the locus, and thereby concedes the issue of his identification so far as presence is concerned; often this will be conclusive in establishing that he was the offender—especially if no others are involved. Then, only the crime will be in issue.

If other persons were there, an accused who admits that he was at the scene of the crime, may claim that one or more of them committed the crime, and that he was not involved. This would then raise a special kind of question of relating his admitted identity to observed actions. This would be the only issue.

In all these examples, which cover nearly every situation, the 'rule of alternative defences' is found to apply; ie the defence is either that the crime was not committed, or that it was not committed by the accused; but both contentions cannot be put forward, for the reasons given.

The 'rule' is not absolute of course. Exceptions may be encountered in unusual circumstances. One illustration of this would be where an accused admitted his presence at the locus, while denying that he was involved in the incident under enquiry which, in any event, he claims, did not constitute a crime, eg if he was a non-participating member of a crowd of football fans charged with disorderly conduct. Here, both the crime and identity are in dispute, but this rarely occurs.

Cross-examiners should know that in almost every trial either party's evidence may be mistaken or untruthful but only on one question, viz whether the crime was committed, or whether the accused was the offender, but not on both issues. However, even closer guidance may be given.

III COMMISSION OF CRIME

Though absolute rules cannot be stated, pointers can be given to the kinds of crime most likely to be disputed, viz those involving transient facts, because proof depends on eyewitness evidence, unsupported by evidence of enduring facts.

Thus, an intangible crime, or one containing an essential but intangible element, is likely to be contested.

On the basis of tangibility, crimes may be analysed into result-crimes, conduct-crimes, and object-crimes.

A Result-crimes

An act which must have a specific physical result to be criminal is a result-crime, eg murder requires death caused by the attack. Most serious crimes come within this class, eg crimes of violence causing injury; sexual crimes involving intercourse; dishonest transfer of property; criminal damage to property; and road traffic offences causing death, injury or accident.

The physical results of such crimes are usually lasting and indisputable, eg the victim's fractured skull, or the vandalised police van.

Such facts, even if they no longer exist at the time of the trial, would have endured for long enough to provide abundant and cogent evidence.

Even an audacious liar might shrink from denying that a headless body riddled with bullets was the result of a murder, or that medical evidence of sexual violation was unsound. Cross-examiners are unlikely to find that evidence about such physical consequences or the assertion of a non-existent fact, require challenge. Lies or errors about the incident involving the denial of a real fact, or the assertion of a non-existent fact, are not normally found in result-crimes.

A result-crime may include an essential but intangible element, where the Crown must prove that the act was done with a certain quality of knowledge or intention. Sometimes, this may be inferred from the act or the result, e g where the owner of a starved dog is charged with cruelty. At other times, the act or the result may give no clue to the mental state, e g in a question of whether taking the wrong coat from a cloakroom was theft or absent-mindedness.

So no dispute is likely if the crime can be proved by the act and the result, but disputes about some intangible quality, viz a mental state, are likely to give rise to lies or errors, for which cross-examiners should be ready.

B   Conduct-crimes

A conduct-crime is one committed by a forbidden act alone. It needs no physical result, and may be wholly intangible, eg menacing someone with a knife, disorderly conduct in public, driving while disqualified, intimidating witnesses, or some forms of indecency based on mens rea alone.

Attempts to commit result-crimes, e g murder, assault, theft, or arson, which stop before they cause the forbidden effect, may be regarded as conduct-crimes for present purposes.

Here, proof must depend on eyewitness evidence, which is usually in sharp conflict; no traces remain after the event to point one way or another.

Evidence of ambiguous acts or of impressions based on suspicion, if admitted, is open to error arising from bias, eg misinterpreting neutral conduct.

Evidence of conduct-crimes is vulnerable to errors and lies, because it often consists of assertion and counter-assertion by eyewitnesses. Here, there is ample scope for cross-examination.

Whether conduct-crimes were committed is commonly the real issue. As they are proved by eyewitnesses, who must have seen the offender, the issue of identity is often eliminated, e g if the witnesses knew the accused personally, or if he is arrested at the time. In any event, if an accused contests such a crime, he almost always places himself at the locus.

C   Object-crimes

Object-crimes are committed by virtue of the offender's forbidden relationship to some object. They differ from result-crimes in producing no result, and from conduct-crimes because more than an act, i e the object, is required.

Examples are possessing prohibited drugs, a weapon in a public place, a firearm without a certificate, obscene publications for sale, or stolen property.

Such crimes may involve both tangible and intangible facts in various combinations. The intangible facts are those most likely to be in issue, and to give rise to mistakes or lies, with opportunity for cross-examination.

Examples may be an accused's state of knowledge about an object, or the circumstances of possession.

The relevant objects would be produced as exhibits in the trial. Sometimes their nature is not in doubt, eg a piece of cannabis resin. In other cases, the nature of the exhibit could be the issue, eg whether a magazine was obscene, or whether an article was an offensive weapon.

Because of the wide variety of object-crimes, it cannot be said, generally, whether the commission of the crime or the implication of the accused is likely to be the real issue, but for both to be issues would be exceptional.

IV   IDENTITY

Identification evidence for the Crown may be, and for the defence usually is, direct. Crown circumstantial evidence is considered in the next chapter.

For the reasons given, the issue of identity is common where a result-crime is charged, and uncommon in a charge of a conduct-crime. In object-crimes, the issue will vary according to circumstances.

Three types of defence based on identity are possible, according to whether the accused claims that he was not at the locus of the crime, whether he pleads alibi, or whether he admits that he was at the locus, but did not commit the crime.

A   Accused not at locus

The defence may simply deny that the accused was at the locus when the crime was committed. He need not give or lead evidence, or say where he was at that time, ie plead alibi. If he did testify, he might claim, not unreasonably, that he had forgotten, or was unsure of, where he was, although he certainly was not at the locus of the crime.

The target of defence cross-examination would be the reliability or credibility of the prosecution evidence. But since the defendant may be expected to know the truth, the prosecutor would cross-examine him on the basis that he was lying.

B Alibi

The defence that the accused was absent from the locus at the time of the crime may be supported by proof that he was at a specified place, with other defence witnesses, ie an alibi.

Crown witnesses, especially if they are independent, and unconnected with each other, are likely to be cross-examined on the basis that their visual identifications are mistaken. Less commonly, malicious lying about the accused's implication may be imputed to those who are alleged to be motivated, eg police witnesses or accomplices.

Since defence witnesses supporting the alibi usually know the accused, mistaken identification may be unlikely, unless conditions were difficult. They, and the accused, are likely to be cross-examined as untruthful, on the assumption that the real situation must be known to them.

Alibi witnesses may of course be correct in identifying the accused as being where they say, but they could be mistaken or untruthful about when that happened. False alibis are sometimes planned by falsifying the date of a real event.

A prosecutor might cross-examine them to the effect that the accused could have been with them—but not when the crime was committed.

Challenging alibi evidence as false is common. Destroying it does not per se prove the opposite case, viz presence at the locus, or that the accused committed the crime, eg a false alibi may be intended to boost a weak, but genuine, defence.

C Accused at locus: uninvolved

An accused may admit that he was at the locus of a crime, having been recognised or arrested there, yet he may deny any part in a crime which another committed. A conflict of direct evidence is typical. The responsibility of one person for another's acts is a different question, ie one of substantive law. Here, the alternatives are mere presence, which is not a crime, unless, per se, it contributes to the criminal situation, or criminal acts carried out personally. In this rather special issue of relating admitted identity to criminal acts, errors in observing facts rather than errors of visual identification may occur.

In confusing events involving several persons, generalised evidence may not discriminate sufficiently between individuals, or discussion may influence the evidence of observers. Many opportunities arise for cross-examination concerning eyewitness errors or lies, or false denials by the accused.

This guide to where a cross-examiner may look for mistakes or lies is followed in the next two chapters by an analysis of such inaccurate evidence.

CHAPTER 3

The reliability of evidence

I INTRODUCTION

The subject of this chapter is the reliability of evidence, ie the extent to which it is acceptable as being free from mistake. In the next chapter, the credibility of evidence will be considered, ie the extent to which it is acceptable as truthful.

The reliability of evidence is a question of great importance in courts. The law cannot stop errors in evidence from occurring altogether, but it tries to minimise them so far as rules and procedures can do this. However, mistakes are involuntary. No offence is committed by a genuine error, however serious its consequences.

The oath, and penalties for offences relating to testimony, may make witnesses more careful in marginal situations where they have some doubt about their evidence, but these provisions cannot guarantee accuracy.

Pre-trial police procedure governing confessions or the identification of suspects, is regulated by statute and related codes of practice. These rules are designed to minimise errors as well as impropriety. But success depends very much on the integrity and conduct of police officers in informal situations which are hard to control.

The law also tries to prevent mistakes by means of rules of evidence which exclude unreliable forms of testimony, and by requiring corroboration, or warnings to be given to juries, in circumstances where evidence may be unreliable.

Despite these, and other measures, the possibility that evidence is mistaken always exists. As Bentham said, 'Witnesses are the eyes and ears of justice'. Trust in honest witnesses is the foundation of any system of justice, but it is necessary to reckon with the universal fallibility of observation and memory. This creates a risk that mistaken or dubious evidence may be accepted, or that accurate evidence may be rejected as mistaken or unreliable. Again, accurate evidence may be incomplete, and the omissions may distort the picture. Total and perfect recall of any incident is not to be expected.

In showing the limitations of testimony, and in exposing errors, cross-examination can be crucial. Since this is a situation where the witness's sincerity is accepted and the evidence itself is often reasonable, it is helpful in the trial to demonstrate how the errors may have arisen.

To expose the sources of mistakes or unreliability in evidence, a cross-examiner who is truly a professional should have a mastery of this subject. It is clearly one of vital importance, and the material is capable of systematic exposition and instruction.

Until recently, however, this type of practical psychology, which is essential for conducting criminal trials, has been omitted from professional legal training. It is not to be found in texts on the law of evidence.

Even more surprising is the fact that it is not to be found in any usable or practical form in texts on psychology, although psychologists have been investigating testimony experimentally for almost a century. Their research has been almost entirely confined to laboratories or artificial situations, so that they lack insight into the probative meaning of errors in real life situations, and in the courts. This subject has been dealt with fully elsewhere (Stone *Proof of Fact in Criminal Trials* (1984), Green)).

Advocates have had to rely on their common sense, in the hope that they will pick up this essential knowledge with experience. But this takes time, and may be incomplete when it is needed. An advocate may be faced at any time with evidence of a kind which he must challenge, and he would be handicapped if he had to do so on grounds of which he has no previous experience.

To meet this obvious gap in the advocate's training, the following account is given of how errors arise in evidence. This is an objective approach, concerned with what can actually occur in a witness's experience. It represents a fact-finder's guide to exploration and testing of evidence.

But this is not enough. Familiarity with this material, and testing evidence in this way, does not exhaust the advocate's skill. An advocate is not a fact-finder. His or her duty is to present a case as effectively as possible.

The defence may do this negatively, by sowing doubt in Crown evidence, so that the tribunal of fact finds it unsafe and is not prepared to rely on it for a conviction. This could be a proper conclusion even though it is not shown that the evidence is indeed mistaken. The Crown have the burden of proof beyond reasonable doubt.

Accordingly, advocates may use the material in this chapter to show that evidence is unsafe even if they cannot show that it is mistaken or incomplete. For the defence, this would be enough. The Crown would then have failed to discharge its burden of proof and acquittal would follow.

In addition, the defence usually lead evidence supporting a version of the facts which contradicts the Crown version. The use of material of the kind contained in this chapter, may cast doubt on Crown evidence and lead to a preference for the defence account.

This presentational aspect of advocacy, should be kept in mind constantly. It will be discussed more fully in section IV.

II ERRORS IN EVIDENCE

The subject of how errors in evidence are caused should really be a branch of applied psychology. While some use may be made of academic findings, they are generally inadequate for the task. Theoretical psychology has little to offer to advocates. The approach taken here is mainly a commonsense one, with a view to application in court.

Two types of error in evidence are considered: those arising in the course of observation, and those which developed in memory in the interval between the time when the observations were made and the trial.

The limitations of the subject, due to inaccessibility of the witness's mental processes, will immediately be obvious. Nevertheless, much can usefully be derived from analysing typical situations and patterns.

A Errors of observation

Errors of observation may arise in three ways, viz (1) from features of the event; (2) because of the conditions under which the event is observed; and (3) as a result of the state of the witness. Naturally, any of these factors may be combined.

Since the subject of discussion is how evidence may become inaccurate or incomplete, the focus is on various negative aspects of the situation which may give rise to errors of observation, eg poor lighting.

Equally, if these factors were favourable, eg good lighting, they would contribute to accuracy of observation.

1 *The event*

So far as features of the event are concerned, the discussion relates to the nature of what is observed, eg the vagueness of a driver's face in a car driven at high speed—not the circumstances in which it is seen, eg from a distance of 50 yards.

(a) *Degree of exposure.* The duration, repetition, or frequency of occurrence of an incident, fix the maximum time for watching it. How long this need last for accuracy varies with the kind of event and the attention given to it. The time and degree of attention need only be enough and no more, eg staring at skid marks adds nothing, but to grasp some facts needs time, eg suspicious conduct in a store. More time may increase the confidence of the witness, or the court, in his account.

Except where the facts fix the type and amount of exposure, eg the limited opportunities of seeing a runner's face as he looks back over his shoulder at those chasing him, estimates of time are notoriously subjective and unreliable. Time may seem longer when the observer is subject to stress.

Cross-examination can rarely show that accuracy is impossible because of the brevity of exposure; the lapse of time is usually undetermined and subjective, and witnesses who give positive evidence may be expected to insist that there was sufficient time for them to see what they claim to have seen. But there will usually be scope for casting doubt on unspecific evidence and for contending that it is too unreliable to be accepted. This could be so, for example, if too much detail is reported on the basis of a rapid glance, or the testimony is dogmatic, where some uncertainty would be expected.

Psychologists disagree on whether the time spent looking at a face affects later recognition. Probably, active attention to the face is a more favourable factor than seeing it for a long time. In daily life, the faces of many people, like waiters, bus conductors, counter customers or postmen, may be seen for long periods, or frequently, without registering sufficiently in memory for recall or recognition. On the other hand, the anxious scanning of the face of a radiologist who is looking at one's X-ray plates, may be more likely to fix his features in mind.

(b) *Movement.* The movement of objects or persons can create difficulties for observers. Other factors are often also involved, eg where one motor car obstructs the view of another. The degree of exposure is usually a part of the problem and much of what was said above on that subject is applicable here.

(c) *Number of persons.* To watch more than one person at a time is confusing for the observer, especially if the targets are separated or are moving in different directions, or if one blocks the view of another.

Cross-examiners often probe police evidence about offences committed by a disorderly group. In an unexpected and confusing situation, it is unlikely that one officer would have the visual and attention span to watch everyone, or that, by chance or design, each police officer would watch a different suspect, so that all the possible targets for observation are covered. The risk in such a situation is that rough and ready impression evidence may be given, e g 'They were all in it'.

Questions of criminal law may arise here. Mere presence without contributing to the crime, is no crime.

In these circumstances, it would be crucially important to know precisely what individuals actually did. Those who did nothing would be innocent.

In other situations, if the whole group were acting together with a common criminal aim, eg rioting and setting motor cars alight, exactly what individuals did might not matter as long as they did something to achieve the criminal purpose. But it would still be necessary to show that they were not innocent bystanders.

So, in observing a number of persons, accuracy of observation, and discrimination, is essential. In a prosecution based on such evidence it would be vital for the defence to scrutinise and test it carefully in cross-examination, to avoid possible implication of innocent persons in the criminal acts of others. There is usually a good deal of scope for doing this effectively.

(d) *Violence.* Eyewitnesses, as well as victims of violence, may experience stress. Cross-examiners may suggest that this hindered their observations by causing witnesses to become disorientated or distracted from what they were watching.

However, unless some substance for this type of challenge emerges in cross-examination, it may not have much success. People regularly report violent incidents with accuracy.

(e) *Ambiguity.* The facts which are observed may be ambiguous in themselves, or ambiguity may arise about what facts mean in relation to each other.

Evidence concerning some conduct-crimes may be open to ambiguity, eg whether touching a child in a swimming pool was accidental or indecent. Ambiguity about identification may arise if resemblance is confused with recognition. This could be a crucial defect. If evidence is admitted which contains an element of impression or interpretation based on observed facts, that basis should be probed. Another view may then be suggested, eg that a driver's slow speech was due to a defect, not drink.

(f) *Salient facts.* Commonplace facts may not be noticed, whereas novel, unusual, urgent or important facts may stand out, command attention, or even dominate the situation, eg a person may focus on the knife presented to him.

Salient facts may rob other facts of attention. This can be confirmed by universal experience. If there is a fire in the basement of a building which one is visiting, the wallpaper in the foyer will escape notice.

Some psychologists claim that facts on the periphery of attention may be absorbed, although the witness does not know this at the time or later, eg that despite the witness's concentration on a charging rhinoceros, details of the surrounding foliage may be registered. Such contentions are supported by reports of recall of details under hypnosis. But for the practical purposes of cross-examination, even if such unconscious retention of information occurs, it is inaccessible in court. For a cross-examiner, it will be more productive to show that there were pressing or salient facts to which a witness is more likely to have paid attention, to the exclusion of others.

This could devalue a witness's claim to have noticed secondary facts as fully and as precisely as he claims. In such a situation his evidence about peripheral facts would be vulnerable to suggestions that he had filled in the gaps by imagination or by discussion with other witnesses.

(g) *Sounds.* Sounds other than speech, eg bangs, breaking glass, screams, or screeching brakes, usually colour an event, but are not the main facts. Possible errors about the nature and location of sounds may be worth probing in cross-examination. The evidence about such facts is likely to be subjective and open to challenge.

(h) *Speech.* Evidence about spoken words raises questions of admissibility, for which reference should be made to texts on the rules of evidence. Various situations, where evidence is admitted, involve typical event factors related to the accuracy of hearing and memory of statements.

Evidence is admissible to prove that a statement was made, not that it is true, if the making of the statement, regardless of its truth, is relevant to the issue, eg as evidence of the state of mind or conduct of persons present.

Evidence of a statement led in order to prove its truth is inadmissible under the general exclusion of hearsay, subject to statutory exceptions concerning informal admissions and confessions made out of court.

A noteworthy common law exception covers statements which are part of the res gestae, eg which accompany and explain an act, reveal a person's physical condition or state of mind, or are spontaneous exclamations of a victim of an offence, or an observer.

Despite legal limitations therefore, a good deal of evidence refers to spoken words.

Attention to what is heard, and memory for what is attended to, are both selective. Much is ignored or rapidly forgotten. Months later, unless the words were noted at the time, or made a special impact, only the sense will probably be recalled, not the words verbatim. Generally, only police note spoken words, but in some situations, eg the locus of a crime, perhaps they cannot do this, and must await return to the police station, or other opportunity. In uncontrolled situations, as at the locus of a crime, it is quite easy for a witness to mishear what is said, because of various factors, e g poor articulation, background noise, people speaking or shouting at the same time, or distraction by what is happening. Evidence about speech, given from memory can seldom claim successfully, to repeat the exact words, and would be vulnerable to challenge.

A cross-examiner can easily cast doubt on such evidence. He has an opening for making a variety of suggestions, in accordance with the information given to him for the conduct of the case.

Apart from the lack of a verbatim account, what the words were intended to convey would involve facts such as tone, volume or emphasis, all in the context of what was said to or by the speaker earlier or later.

Where only the gist of what was said is reported from memory, it may be challenged on the ground that the words spoken were different, that the witess has misunderstood them, or that they meant something else in the context.

Such evidence may involve interpretation or some element of impression, but may be admissible if it is the only way in which the witness can inform the court of what he heard. At a certain level, admissible impression evidence about the gist of what a person said may shade into an inadmissible inference by a witness. Inferences are for the court alone to draw. At this stage, arguments, but not cross-examination, on the point would be allowed.

Untruthful evidence about speech is considered in the next chapter.

Statements taken by police officers include admissions and confessions by suspects, and statements from witnesses which may be admitted if they testify differently and deny previous inconsistent statements irrespective of their truth.

Where police witness are challenged about statements written in their notebooks, the circumstances usually exclude mistake, although lying may be possible.

Such statements are usually noted in controlled settings, commonly in police stations, where there would be no background noise or distractions. This reduces the chance of mishearing.

If the statement was read over to the person making it, and he signed it, the possibility of mishearing should be eliminated altogether.

Two or more police officers may speak to the making of a statement in identical terms. If it was incorrect, each must have made the same mistake.

In such situations, it is absurd for a cross-examiner to suggest that no statement of any kind was made, and to attribute the entry in the notebook and the testimony to mistake; but such inept cross-examination is not unknown.

In these circumstances, if no statement was made, the attack on the witness can only be that he is lying.

If the cross-examiner accepts that a statement was made, but claims that it was in different terms from those noted and spoken to, the position, while less extreme than outright denial, is close to it. Unless the suggested divergence from accuracy refers to only a word or two, with an ambiguous sound, which might have been misheard by one or more officers, mistake is usually out of the question, and the allegation again should be one of lying.

If the advocate accepts the terms of the statement, but contends that they have a particular meaning, cross-examination about that is likely to be excluded, although it may be allowed about the context and related circumstances. Here, the court has an exact record of the words spoken on which it can place its own interpretation.

Voice identification evidence is admissible but unusual. There are special identity parade rules for it. Such evidence may be weak. Tests which may be applied are familiarity with the voice, the circumstances in which it was heard, and the possibility of suggestive influence.

(i) *Touch, smell, taste.*   Evidence of touch, smell or taste is not common. It is subjective, and its reliability may be uncertain.

Witnesses may speak to sensations of touch to supplement visual evidence of the same facts, eg in indecency charges, or where blows left no injury. Evidence of touch may be given on secondary points, eg the heat of a car engine.

Evidence of odours is rare, apart from smelling alcohol from a driver's breath, or prohibited drugs.

Evidence of tracking suspects, by police dog handlers, depends on smell, but as the dogs are not available for cross-examination, it may have more value for narrative than for proof.

Evidence of taste arises sometimes, eg in charges of poisoning or contraventions of the Food and Drug Acts.

When evidence of touch, smell or taste is given, it is impossible, in cross-examination, to test the accuracy of the actual sensations which witnesses report, but the surrounding circumstances may be probed as a guide to reliability.

It may be hard to verify or contradict the evidence of a specially-trained police officer about the odour of cannabis resin in a room. However, other objective considerations might weaken such evidence, eg if perfumed room sprays had been used in the house.

The reliability of the witness might also be attacked with the result of discrediting his evidence. For example, the alleged odour may be regarded as an unsafe basis for conviction, if cross-examination suggests that the witness is unduly dogmatic, and possibly biased in an area of evidence where this is inappropriate because of its subjectivity. The court's view of such evidence is likely to depend on the extent to which the witness is trusted.

(j) *Abstract qualities.* Even the most concrete physical situations have abstract qualities, which may give rise to disputes.

Questions often arise about distances, eg in road traffic offences. Dates, times or intervals may be in issue in any kind of trial. The order of events may be crucial in many incidents. Physical layout, dimensions, and the relationship of things to each other, are often important. Features such as weights, quantities, colours, or speed may be of significance.

Accuracy can rarely be expected in evidence of such facts, even from conscientious witnesses.

Witnesses who speak to abstract facts will usually offer subjective estimates which, notoriously, are likely to support the general tenor of their evidence. This is only to be expected. If courts require such facts to be decided with precision, they should do so with caution. This area, again, offers excellent opportunities for a cross-examiner. The subjectivity of the evidence is highly vulnerable. It is often a good tactic to encourage the dogmatism of such a witness to highlight the extent to which he is biased.

But it can also be very effective to attack such evidence on an objective basis, where the necessary material is available.

Where possible, a witness who gives evidence of this kind should be confronted with something tangible, which is contained in the evidence of the cross-examiner's own witnesses, or real or documentary evidence, which the court is likely to accept.

Visual aids, eg maps, plans or photographs, are often available, but little effort is made to obtain them. By establishing something precise, the cross-examiner may avoid the inconclusive process of assertion and counter-assertion.

2 Conditions of observation

The surrounding circumstances in which a witness sees an event, differ from the event itself, and may encourage or interfere with the completeness or accuracy of observations.

Often, such facts, not being those in issue, are brought out for the first time in cross-examination.

It is generally to be expected that witnesses will support any positive evidence which they give, by claiming that the conditions of observation were adequate for this purpose. Such evidence may be subjective and difficult to challenge. A cross-examiner may have to rely on contrary evidence about the conditions of observation which he leads himself.

(a) *Lighting*. Offences often happen, and wrongdoers are often seen, in relative darkness. The quality of the light may then become vital. Apart from moonlight, issues often arise about artificial lighting.

Objective evidence about lighting, its strength, location, shadows, or how street lighting affects colours, is a rarity, despite its importance.

Few witnesses will admit in cross-examination that the light was too poor for them to see what they assert. Contrary evidence may be needed to support such a criticism.

Where the Crown case is based on visual identification in bad lighting, the defence should emphasise this barrier to good observation, in relation to the *Turnbull Guidelines*, which will be discussed later.

(b) *Distance*. If the witness was not close enough for clear observation, he may have filled in the gaps and completed his evidence by discussion or imagination.

Frequently, evidence about distance as an aspect of the conditions of observation, is inadequate. It only tends to be satisfactory when it is part of the issues, as in road traffic offences, where measurements are provided.

In giving estimates of how far they were from what they saw, adjacent witnesses usually differ significantly. Sometimes distances may be calculated from other facts, eg a number of car lengths.

Without objective evidence, the question of the viewing distance may not be settled.

Witnesses will again insist that they were near enough to see what they claim to have seen. The reliability of their evidence is unlikely to be decided by the matter of viewing distance alone unless some objective basis for comparison emerges.

A cross-examiner may depend on discrediting the witness if he can show dogmatism or bias.

(c) *Weather*. Visibility may be reduced by weather conditions of various kinds, eg rain or snow as obstacles in themselves, or by obscuring windows, windscreens or spectacles. Difficulty may also be caused by mist, fog, or dazzling sunshine. Witnesses who give affirmative evidence are unlikely to accept any suggestion in cross-examination that the weather created difficulties of observation.

(d) *Obstructions.* Natural or artificial obstacles, people or vehicles, may block observation of an incident, totally or in part.

If this is to be the basis of cross-examination, it is desirable to fortify it by objective evidence of the layout and the location of any obstructions, as shown by plans or photographs, or by leading evidence in support.

Otherwise, if something was not seen properly because of obstructions, evidence which depends on filling in the gaps by speculation, or which is the result of discussion, may escape exposure.

(e) *Distractions.* Observation may be impeded by something which diverts a witness's attention away from what is important. This might be something on which he is concentrating when an incident occurs unexpectedly, eg if he is driving a car or serving a customer. If something happens in front of him, he may be distracted by trying to find a way to escape from the situation. If he is under threat, or being attacked, the witness will not be watching another person who is being threatened or attacked. If the main facts are observed, peripheral facts may not be noticed. A cross-examiner should use his imagination to project himself into the situation.

3 State of witness

The completeness and accuracy of observation may be affected to some extent by the state of the witness. This consists of both his permanent eyewitness abilities, and any temporary physical or psychological condition.

(a) *Permanent features.* People vary in permanent eyewitness abilities, eg acuteness or deficiency of vision or hearing, or good or poor memory for faces, words or numbers, and so on. But psychological research has not provided any usable data for use in court in this respect. A witess cannot be said to be more or less trustworthy as an observer, by virtue of membership of any class, eg age, sex, or occupation.

There is no universal agreement about the abilities of children as witnesses, nor has it been proved that police are any better than lay observers, or that training improves ability to identify. A cross-examiner can only exploit any defects which come to his notice, eg whether the witness was wearing his hearing aid when the conversation took place.

Personal tendencies are difficult to pin down or to demonstrate, in an unknown witness, eg a tendency to exaggerate.

Generally, permanent eyewitness qualities offer few openings for cross-examination.

(b) *Physical condition.* Common physical conditions of a temporary kind which can impair observation include drink, drugs, illness or fatigue, and injury. Alcohol interferes with perception, but to what extent cannot be decided precisely, so far as witnesses are concerned. The degree of impairment depends on too many factors, eg amount and type of drink, when taken, food, physique, individual metabolism, and sometimes the sobering effect of what occurred.

Unless there is ground for suggesting that a witness was almost in a stupor, a cross-examiner cannot destroy, although he may weaken, his evidence, because he had been drinking.

The higher mental functions, eg understanding or memory, are those most affected, rather than the senses of vision or hearing. Since there is an element of interpretation in all perception, drink may produce some errors in reporting a complicated incident. But witnesses who give firm evidence will not accept that they were too drunk to observe what they claim to have seen. Usually it is only reluctant witnesses who agree that they were too drunk to report anything.

In cross-examination, to elicit that a witness had been drinking is worthwhile as it can weaken confidence in his evidence. But often, this line of enquiry is overdone to no effect, by probing every detail of what he drank, as if this were conclusive.

How particular medical or prohibited drugs may affect observation is a technical matter beyond the present enquiry. A cross-examiner who intends to challenge evidence on this basis, should take steps to acquire the necessary information, preferably with the assistance of his own expert witness.

In daily life, illness or fatigue may reduce alertness to what is going on. Some specific effect of the condition would have to be shown as a ground for a significant attack on evidence.

Injuries of various kinds could interfere with observation, either directly or by distracting the witness. If evidence is to be attacked on this ground, medical advice may be desirable. But often, the question is one of common sense. An injury, and accompanying pain and anxiety, could absorb attention to the exclusion of other matters. Again, perception could be affected directly, by blows to the eyes.

Unpredictable consequences may follow from heavy bleeding which diminishes cerebral blood flow, or traumatic head injuries.

Victims of serious attacks or traffic accidents may be intermittently unconscious or dazed. The kind of injury, where it was sustained, and how it was caused, may suggest limited observation. An attacker may have been unseen, if the wound is on the back of the head. If a victim who was kicked on the ground has multiple bruises, he would probably be protecting his face and head, and might be challenged about his identification of the assailants. Injuries may show that a witness was attacked severely, so that he would not be watching a similar attack on his friend at the same time.

(c) *Psychological state.* Some errors in evidence have psychological causes. Currently, psychologists have little to offer for practical use in court. Their claims about the selectivity of attention, the effect of expectations or stress, and other factors, are not unknown to common sense. This subject will be treated briefly. There is doubt about the extent to which the interfering processes exist, and in any event they are inaccessible in court.

Witnesses may not know that they are affected in such ways, and if they did know this, they would probably be reluctant to reveal it.

An acquaintance with controversial psychological processes of a subtle kind, which are unknown to the witness, or in any event private, cannot really help a cross-examiner. Interfering elements may sometimes be shown by inference from objective circumstances.

Attention is certainly selective, but psychology cannot specify what will or will not receive attention, nor is there agreement about whether or not peripheral facts are registered.

Common experience shows that attention has a limited span, is not continuous, and moves from one thing to another, in a voluntary or involuntary sequence. We cannot focus on every element in a situation at the same moment; something may be missed. An urgent fact, eg a burst pipe, may dominate a whole complex situation.

Attention to salient facts may rob other facts of attention. If so, it may be natural that some facts are recalled vaguely. As a result, dogmatic evidence may be given which is an unreliable blend of observation, imagination, and inference.

Witnesses who testify firmly about some fact will not normally concede that their attention was elsewhere at the time. However, it is not impossible for this to be shown in cross-examination, although it is difficult. The key is to approach the matter from the point of view of the objective circumstances. In many cases, they make it obvious what received the witnesses' exclusive attention, eg if youths are showering police with bricks, their identification of 10 assailants from observation at that very time may be reasonably challenged as doubtful.

When we perceive something, our higher mental functions weave sensations of sight or sound into meaningful patterns, which are partly based on experience, and our expectations may then colour our observations. Thus, psychologists say that we may sometimes tend to see what we expect to see. Hunters in America have been known to shoot each other, thinking that they are shooting deer.

While the influence of expectations on observation may be accepted, it is to be supposed that they would operate where the facts are inherently obscure or ambiguous. Advocates should not try to show that a witness suffered from a hallucination or optical illusion.

Inherently ambiguous facts include some conduct-crimes, in which the absence of physical results contributes to uncertainty about the action, e g young girls conditioned to expect indecency may see it in an innocent contact. Expectations may colour acts charged as attempted crimes, e g store detectives may see a shoplifter in every customer who takes an article from the counter.

Perhaps visual identification evidence is the most vulnerable to the influence of expectations, e g identification of a suspect who only resembles the offender, because he is expected to be in the identity parade.

In suitable circumstances, a cross-examiner may usefully explore the possibility that evidence in some way reflects what a witness expected to see, as well as what he did actually see. This could take the form of colouring the evidence in one direction or another, even to the extent of creating total misinterpretation of the situation, or misidentifying an innocent person. As a foundation for this, emphasis should be placed on the ambiguity, obscurity and doubtful nature of the facts, or the difficult conditions of observation. It is often possible to show how expectations or preconceived ideas played a part in the testimony.

The psychologist's view that stress sometimes enhances and sometimes impedes observation is of no help in cross-examination. A commonsense view would be that incompleteness of evidence might depend on the extent to which the witness was distracted from his observations, by features which created the stress. If he was disorientated, this could weaken his testimony, though he might still recall the central incident. Again, some special stressful element, eg a revolver pointing at him, might have dominated his attention, to the exclusion of other facts. Beyond that it would be hard to show any specific effect of stress on evidence.

B Errors of memory

Oral evidence is given from memory although it may sometimes be aided by writings, plans or photographs. Although memory is fallible, it is reasonably reliable for essential facts, and courts rely on the memories of honest witnesses for this.

If the witness's recollection is imperfect, his report may be incomplete or inaccurate; also he may testify less confidently, which may create doubt.

1 Forgetting

Memory fades with time, even if the original observation was strong. Inevitably, long periods elapse between the dates of most crimes and trials, while suspects are traced and caught, and cases prepared. The increasing volume of court business also causes delays.

Psychologists, in their classical curve of forgetting, say that it occurs more rapidly soon after the event, and then slows down. But whether this applies to recall of a face is controversial.

It cannot be said who will forget what after which interval. Not only the period of time, but also the degree of attention given to the facts, their significance for the witness, and his individual ability to remember, all enter into it.

The extent of forgetting may range from a mild dimming of a recalled image, and reduced confidence in it, to complete amnesia for a fact, event or face. It has been shown that secondary details are more quickly and more easily forgotten than the central facts of an incident. Recall of the nature and meaning of a crime as a whole, is likely to endure.

The essential facts, which are the subject of direct eyewitness testimony, are resistant to forgetting. Details, which have no significance for the witness, are the facts which tend to slip away. They may, of course, form part of circumstantial or indirect evidence, and their loss could be important. Minor discrepancies between witnesses to the same facts, which arise from universal fallibility of observation or memory, are commonplace.

Inexperienced advocates, on the basis of a list of such discrepancies, contend that the evidence which these witnesses gave about the main facts, must be held to be unreliable. This is usually an exaggerated and unimpressive argument.

The most critical danger of mistaken recollection after a long delay is that of misidentifying a person with whom the witness was not familiar. But if, on the other hand, he did know the suspect, the risk of mistake is less, even after a delay; what he recalls then is personal identity with its associations, rather than a face. What weight to give to a gap between the event and the trial is always a matter for the court's practical judgment in the circumstances.

Cross-examination on this would generally be based on probabilities, ie the aim would be to weaken the evidence. The hope that a firm report by the witness will be destroyed because of the passage of time alone is not realistic.

After a long delay, if too much detail is put forward, or if the witness is dogmatic about some facts, and unsure about collateral facts, his evidence may be suspect.

A jury will not be impressed by an unfair attack on a witness of obvious sincerity, who claims to remember something.

It may be best to suggest, without undue elaboration, and in a moderate and reasonable way, that he may be mistaken because of faded memory. This would be a foundation for establishing contrary facts by other evidence.

2   Suggestion

Suggestion occurs when an idea is accepted simply because it is presented, regardless of other reasons. The weaker the memory, the more vulnerable it will be to distortion by suggestion. Such errors are likely to increase with the extension of the interval after the crime.

If another person merely says something or conveys information to a witness, he may still influence him, without intending this. Media comment is restricted by law. The most likely suggestive influences are those of discussion between witnesses, and the effect of pre-trial enquiries and taking statements. There is considerable scope for evidence to be so affected. Suggestion can alter the recollection of the event in various ways which may be difficult or impossible to expose.

In the witness's recollection it can add facts which did not exist or exclude those which did, to the extent of changing the meaning of the incident. An image of the event may be formed which is a compromise between the true memory and the additional material. The witness, unaware of this, may believe that his memory is authentic and unimpaired. He would give his evidence persuasively with the same assurance as if it were unaffected. As occurs in forgetting, the essential facts are the most resistant to such distortion.

(a)   *Discussion of evidence.*   Discussion of an unusual event which they observed is natural for witnesses connected with each other.

Thus it is to be expected from members of a family, friends, neighbours, or fellow employees, that they will talk about what they saw and the evidence which they will give.

Such discussion is usually undetectable and is forbidden only if it is done in order to give false testimony. However, there is a real risk that evidence will be affected by discussion and it should be discouraged by those involved in conducting a trial.

Witnesses obviously feel guilty about discussing their evidence and they admit it only reluctantly or they deny its influence.

A denial of discussion is sometimes so unlikely as to be absurd, e g between members of a family who were involved in a dramatic event. At times, one witness admits that he discussed his evidence with another, who denies it. Such an improbable denial, or such inconsistency between witnesses, may be adverse to trust in these witnesses, and can give a cross-examiner the opening he seeks. It is surprising how often witnesses who appear to be otherwise honest, can be faulted in this respect.

It is the duty of police to discuss cases in making enquiries and preparing for trial. In good faith, and unintentionally, they may influence each other by exchanging information. In practice, cross-examiners do not seem to make use of this opportunity as much as they could. One reason may be defence concern lest an accused's previous convictions were to be disclosed.

Police knowledge of a defendant's previous convictions, communicated by one officer to another may tend to reinforce identifications.

Some police communications may be confidential.

(b) *Taking statements.* Initial police enquiries in order to trace and apprehend suspects are often made in informal settings even if notes were taken. Verbal exchanges at this stage, perhaps enhanced by the authority attaching to police officers, may, by unintended suggestion, introduce new elements to witnesses' eventual evidence. Police know that they should interview eyewitnesses separately, and should not ask leading questions, but realistically, these precautions may not always be observed if the matter is urgent. Hearsay, opinions and guesses, communicated between police and witnesses, may all be useful initially.

This may occur both in the course of making enquiries at the outset, in order to detect and apprehend a suspect, as well as in taking statements from witnesses, in preparing for trial. The risk of influencing evidence by suggestion here would be difficult to eliminate. But this can be a fertile area for probing by a well-prepared cross-examiner.

Pre-trial enquiries by, and statements given to, solicitors involve similar risks of unintended suggestion. Cross-examination on the matter would be defeated by the objection of confidentiality. Professional integrity would be put forward here, as the protection.

(c) *Self-induced errors.* It is a matter of common experience, confirmed by psychology, that over a period internal processes alone may affect a witness's memory of an event.

On a conscious and intellectual level, a witness may plan, streamline and rehearse his evidence, picturing and pondering on the event, completing gaps by speculation, settling inconsistencies and doubts by inference, and adjusting and modifying his evidence in various ways. He would be quite conscious of the fact that he is doing this.

However, he would be unaware of the working of emotional influences on his memory at an unconscious level. His motives, fears and wishes, could incline his memory in some direction. He might forget unpleasant aspects of the event, or prefer one verdict or another, or want to please the police, or play a worthwhile role as a citizen. Vanity, embarrassment or bias may enter into it.

Much testimony given by truthful witnesses is probably tainted by such common processes, but probably not to the extent of affecting the outcome. The commonsense view is that if the essential facts were clear initially, they are less likely to be affected by autosuggestion than minor facts.

Such psychological processes are inaccessible in court, even if they are accessible to the witness. Witnesses would deny a cross-examiner's contentions that they had consciously tailored their evidence, or that it was modified by autosuggestion. With no objective basis to put forward, making such suggestions in cross-examination is unlikely to have an impact.

However, insight into such psychological patterns is useful guidance for a cross-examiner in handling witnesses.

III   EVIDENCE OF IDENTITY

Whether or not the accused was the offender is perhaps the most common question in criminal trials. In exposing errors in visual or circumstantial evidence of identity, cross-examination can play a crucial role.

The sources of error described in section II apply to evidence of identity as well as to evidence of the crime. But there are additional or specific causes of error in evidence of identity, which require further discussion. In particular, the fallibility of eyewitness identification is generally accepted; special care is always needed, to avoid a possible miscarriage of justice. Convictions have been quashed and Royal Pardons have been granted for this reason.

Public concern about possible miscarriages of justice arising from visual misidentification, led to the appointment of the Devlin Committee. After conducting a thorough investigation, including interviews of many persons actively involved in the administration of justice, and psychologists, the committee reported in 1976. [Report on Evidence of Identification in Criminal Cases (HC, 26 April 1976) para 338]

Summing up their views, the committee stated the following.

> We are satisfied that in cases which depend wholly or mainly on eyewitness evidence of identification there is a special risk of wrong conviction. It arises because the value of such evidence is exceptionally difficult to assess; the witness who has sincerely convinced himself and whose sincerity carries conviction is not infrequently mistaken.

Lord Devlin was disappointed. The Report had little practical effect on the administration of justice. However it did contribute to the formulation of guidelines by the courts. These, which were laid down in *Turnbull* ([1977] QB 224), advocates must know.

They cover cases which depend wholly or substantially on the accuracy of visual identification, which the defence claim is mistaken. To meet special risks of error, listed there, of the kind considered in section II, various warnings and explanations are required about the circumstances of the identification

The guidelines apply to both trials on indictment and to summary trials. A conviction may be quashed if they are not followed where they should be.

On a submission of no case to answer, if the quality of identification is good, even if there is no supporting evidence, the decision should be left to the jury. But if the quality of the identifying evidence is poor, and there is no other evidence to support it, the judge should withdraw the case from the jury.

This leading judgment extends the application of law to dubious identification in cases to which *Turnbull* applies. These are primarily cases involving 'fleeting encounters'; it does not apply to every issue of visual identification. However, where *Turnbull* does apply, questions of law as well as questions of fact arise for consideration.

Reference should be made to appropriate texts for a fuller account. As the law is not the direct subject of this book, issues of identification will be treated as questions of fact in the rest of this section.

A   Visual identification

The Devlin Report distinguished three forms of visual identification: recognition; resemblance; and distinctive characteristics. The face usually dominates discussions of the subject. However a witness's general impression may include other aspects of appearance also, eg physique, posture, or ways of moving. Thus recognition or resemblance, may be combined with recalling distinctive characteristics.

1 Recognition

Recognition is the strongest form of visual identification. When a witness recognises a suspect, he recalls the offender's face and matches it with the suspect's face. This is accompanied by a subjective feeling of familiarity. If recognition is accepted by the court, identity is proved.

As objects of perception, many human faces are similar, unlike the difference between the face of a dog and that of a cat. Mistakes of recognition are not surprising. Psychologists continue to study the question intensively, but nothing significant for application in court has yet emerged.

Cases have occurred where a genuine feeling of familiarity with the suspect's face arose from seeing him previously in a context other than that of the crime, eg if he is the counter clerk at the local railway station. To suggest such possibilities in cross-examination may have value where the witness's sincerity is accepted and scope for previous contact can be shown, eg if the witness and the accused live near each other. Even if the suggestion is denied, the possibility would at least be conveyed to a jury.

A witness can only convey his feeling of familiarity with a face in terms of degrees of confidence. This is difficult for a cross-examiner to test or destroy, or for a court to assess.

The identification may be strongest if the suspect was already familiar to the witness before the crime. But even here, as well as in cases where the offender was unknown to the witness, the circumstances of the identification may have been liable to the difficulties discussed in the previous section and be open to challenge.

These include not only difficulties of observation, but also those involving the witness's memory.

These may all be subjects for cross-examination, eg forgetting a face in relation to the lapse of time, or the suggestive influence of witnesses' discussions about identity. In any case, where a defence advocate cannot destroy evidence of recognition, he may so weaken it that it will be defeated if he leads acceptable contradictory evidence. Even if he cannot achieve this, he may still succeed by raising a reasonable doubt about the evidence.

2 Resemblance

Evidence of resemblance is only evidence that the suspect's appearance is similar to that of the offender. This may be true although the suspect had nothing to do with the crime. Such evidence may support proof of identity, but it cannot prove it per se. Its weight would depend on the circumstances of observation and the context of all the evidence.

A cross-examiner should pay the closest attention to the actual words and nuances, and be ready to expose any ambiguity between recognition and resemblance, and to object to any leading.

Such evidence is inherently uncertain; it has a built-in element of doubt. The witness saw the offender but cannot say that the suspect is the same person. He only looks like him. This favours the defence as well as the Crown.

A defence advocate should not neglect the gain which may arise from highlighting the witness's inability to identify the defendant by the more incriminating test of recognition. This failure, by inversion, becomes positive evidence favouring the defence.

Evidence of resemblance involves similar risks to evidence of recognition. Although there is a perceptual similarity between the face of the offender and the face of the defendant, the witness's feeling of familiarity with the latter may arise from seeing him in an innocent context. Moreover, like any type of testimony, evidence of resemblance is subject to typical sources of error arising from the circumstances of observation, or the vulnerable processes of memory.

A defence advocate need not attack the sincerity of a witness who gives evidence about resemblance. He may probe the alleged resemblance for details to shake it, or he may even accept it.

He may intensify uncertainties, so that a reasonable doubt arises, or so that contrary defence evidence is accepted. Where suitable witnesses are available eg brothers who look alike, a demonstration may be held in court.

3 Distinctive characteristics

A witness may identify some special characteristic of the suspect which he also saw on the offender, eg a scar or tattoo.

Whether the characteristic was unusual or distinctive, or whether it was common, would be likely to determine the weight of such evidence.

Ordinary features like blue eyes or brown hair might have little value. On the other hand a unique birthmark might be convincing. In between, there may be a range of frequency of such features. To show that it is not uncommon might be a line of defence evidence, or cross-examination, in suitable cases.

In this type of evidence, what the witness perceives in the defendant's appearance is normally there for the court to see as well, and to that extent his evidence is beyond challenge. But, in suitable circumstances, the accuracy of his observation of the feature on the offender at the time of the offence may be open to the usual objections.

4 Descriptions

Witnesses may describe offenders to the police. This is often indispensable in the early stages of police enquiries and such descriptions are often circulated widely. They may include details like sex, age, height, build, hair, eyes, complexion, physical defects, facial blemishes, clothing, mode of speech, gait and so on.

Helpful though they may be for practical purposes in detecting and apprehending suspects, such descriptions are generally regarded as poor forms of identification.

Witnesses who are not on oath may describe an offender in informal but urgent circumstances, eg massive enquiries into abduction of a child, where thousands of people are interviewed. One witness might be questioned in another's presence, although this is not approved practice. They co-operate. Even a guess may help to trace the offender. Police may ask leading or suggestive questions to which helpful witnesses reply by stretching their image of the offender beyond the bounds of accuracy.

The danger is that unsound or incorrect verbal descriptions given in such circumstances, may persist into later procedure, and the trial. Studies have shown that verbal labels in a description may affect later identifications.

Also, a witness may feel that he is committed to an identification which is consistent with his original verbal description.

All this is valuable material for a cross-examiner who understands such processes and how they may lead to mistaken identifications or at least weaken their reliability. If material discrepancies between verbal descriptions and visual identifications come to the notice of the prosecution, or in any event if this is requested by the defence, they should supply them with copies of the initial descriptions which were given to the police. These can then be compared with the defendant's appearance in the dock.

5 Facial likeness systems

Other initial forms of identification are artists' impressions, or facial likeness systems, eg Identikit or Photofit, where a witness directs the creation of an offender's image for circulation.

This type of technology is likely to develop, with the use of computers and holography to produce coloured three-dimensional images. Images can already be distributed by telephone line.

These images are not normally produced as exhibits in the trial, as they are superseded by physical identification in a parade, or in the dock. Also, questions of admissibility, as yet not clarified, may arise. These questions depend partly on which party wishes to produce the evidence, and for what reason.

If these initial images were consistent with physical identifications, there would seem to be no reason for the Crown to produce them.

But the defence may seek their production, or comment on their absence, if they challenge the reliability of physical identification, eg on the ground of a material discrepancy between the image and the defendant, or because creating the image, with another person, may have influenced the accuracy of identification.

6 *Photographs*

To identify a suspect at an early stage, eg to trace an offender at large, police may have to ask witnesses to select the offender's photograph from those of persons with criminal records. But photographs should not be shown to witnesses after a suspect has been arrested, and identification in a parade is possible.

It is generally accepted that showing photographs is inherently suggestive, and that where it is necessary it must be done fairly. Risks can arise from the inferior quality of reproduction compared with the reality, physical identification always being better, or when the situation itself, or something said by a police officer, might influence the witness by suggesting that the offender's photograph is among those shown.

The procedure is governed by a code of practice and a judge has a discretion to exclude evidence of identification if there has been non-compliance with it, or irregularity in showing photographs to witnesses.

Essential rules are that photographs should not be shown if an identification parade is possible; that they should be shown in a series; and that they should not be shown to witnesses before a parade.

Perhaps the greatest danger is that a witness may identify a suspect physically because he is comparing him with a photograph, and not with the offender. Even if initial use of photographs cannot be shown to have caused mistaken physical identification later, it may reduce its reliability.

These matters could provide plenty of opportunities for destructive cross-examination, if it were not for a defence dilemma.

The prosecution should not produce the photographs or refer to their use for identification purposes, as this would inform the jury that the defendant had a criminal record. The prosecution should advise the defence of the existence and use of the photgraphs, and the defence should always ensure that they are told about this.

The defence dilemma then is whether or not to raise the question of the photographs in court. They would have to weigh up the advantages and disadvantages of such disclosure. In this situation, due weight should be given to the occurrence of any gross irregularity or any other significant basis for destructive cross-examination, which would have the effect of vitiating any identification.

7 Identification out of court

Identification of a suspect out of court may occur informally; in a confrontation with a single suspect; in a group identification; or in an identification parade.

In urgent and informal circumstances, a witness, accompanied by police, may identify a suspect, eg by going round an area in a police car soon after an assault on her, or by watching the door of a pub to which the suspect is likely to go.

Confrontations between a witness and a single suspect, perhaps in a police station, are discouraged by codes of practice. An identification parade is the preferred method. If it cannot be held, then the suspect should be identified in a group of people, in a non-suggestive setting, eg a railway station, and no leading questions should be asked. If this is impracticable, confrontation with a single suspect should be seen as a last resort, and the suspect's solicitor should normally be there.

Out of court identifications may be essential for police purposes, but they can create problems for proof, since the informal, uncontrolled, situation lacks desirable precautions. The witness may be influenced by things said or done, or unintended hints from police, or other witnesses if they are not excluded. One advantage, however, is that an identification out of court is often made at an early stage before memory has a chance to dim.

It is also a basis for, and reinforces, dock identification which may follow it.

In any event, in preparing the defence case, close enquiry should be made into the circumstances of any identification out of court, as a ground for possible cross-examination.

The danger is that of suggestion. Any suggestive elements in the situation which could have influenced the identification should be probed. Much may depend on the integrity and fairness of individual police officers at the time of the identification and in giving evidence. A mistaken identification out of court may persist, without correction, to the stage of dock identification.

The defence are assisted here by the Crown's obligation to prove guilt beyond reasonable doubt. It may be impossible to show conclusively, how subtle factors inclined the witness to make a wrong identification. It may even appear that possibly the identification is correct. But it could be enough, for the purpose of acquittal, to establish that, in the circumstances, the identification should be regarded as unreliable, thus creating a reasonable doubt about this crucial question.

8   *Identification parades*

The conduct of identification parades is covered by a code of practice.

Although the suspect is not compelled to take part, evidence of his refusal may be given in the trial and he would then become liable to identification in a confrontation or in the dock. He should be told about this.

The rules are designed to ensure that parades are conducted fairly, without any suggestive elements to influence the witness. The main rules include the following. Before a parade, no information about the suspect's identity or description may be given to a witness and no photograph should be shown to him. The composition of the parade should be fair. Witnesses at a parade must be separated. Proper instructions and warnings should be given to witnesses, including the fact that the offender may not be on the parade. Witnesses should be told not to make a positive identification if they cannot do so.

Cross-examiners must be familiar with the rules. Any breach may have consequences in law, as well as in judging the facts. Identifications may become inadmissible as a result. Naturally, however, such an exclusion of evidence would depend on the weight attached to the objection.

To prepare himself for challenging an identification at a parade, a cross-examiner should be in possession of all the relevant information. The defendant's solicitor should have attended the parade, to note, and to object to, any irregularities, whether adjustments were made at the time or not.

A cross-examiner would try to bring out any breach of the rules, including the omission of necessary warnings, or any unfairness. Anything would be objectionable which directed a witness's attention specially to the suspect, instead of to everyone on the parade equally.

Again, destructive cross-examination might succeed simply by showing that the identification has been rendered unreliable by irregularities, or words used by identifying witnesses which implied doubt, although it could not be proved that it was necessarily incorrect. To raise a reasonable doubt about this, would mean that the Crown had failed to discharge their burden of proof, and acquittal would follow.

9   Dock identification

The general rule is that a witness should not be asked to identify the accused for the first time in dock at the trial, unless in exceptional circumstances. The concern is that seeing the accused in the dock may influence a witness, so that he is more likely to identify him in error.

Dock identification is regarded as more reliable when it confirms an earlier identification. One exception is that a witness may make a dock identification for the first time where the defendant refused to take part in an identification parade.

The aim of defence cross-examination would be related to the crucial nature of visual identification, the real possibilities of mistake, and the burden on the Crown to prove guilt beyond reasonable doubt for conviction. Even if a defence cross-examiner cannot prove that the identification is inaccurate, he will try, at least, to show that it should not be relied upon.

Any out of court identification may be attacked on the grounds referred to above. If the cross-examiner has a mastery of what occurred, he should have abundant material.

The informality of the circumstances and the lack of safeguards, often provide openings for challenge. The fact that the witness was not on oath, and his possible motivations in the situation, may be highlighted so that doubt is cast on the identification.

Although a dock identification may be challenged on the ground that the witness has been influenced by the suggestive situation of the defendant, witnesses are unlikely to admit such irresponsibility in their evidence, expressly. Yet witnesses sometimes show that this has been an element in their testimony.

It may be better to persist in challenging the earlier identification, and to suggest that the witness may feel that he must conform to it, although it was dubious, and he is no longer sure of it.

Other opportunities for attack may arise if there are any inconsistencies between the earlier identification and the dock identification. Some witnesses may deny, or be unable to recall, the earlier identification, or they may say that they identified someone else, or they may even claim that the accused was not the offender. This can ruin the prosecution's case, even if the witness is distrusted.

In such circumstances, the Crown may try to repair the damage by calling other witnesses to establish the earlier identification by the defaulting witness. But this would raise questions of admissibility of evidence, for which reference should be made to the relevant cases.

B Circumstantial evidence

In any trial, visual identification evidence incriminating the accused may be supplemented by circumstantial evidence of identity, or the Crown evidence may be essentially circumstantial.

Circumstantial evidence of identity consists of evidence about circumstances from which the accused's identity as the offender may be inferred. Two factual questions arise, viz (1) what were the facts? and (2) what did the facts mean? It is the inferences from the facts which may incriminate the accused.

Each element in the Crown evidence may, in itself, be insufficient to implicate the defendant. Cumulatively, however, they may point with various degrees of probability or inevitably, to his guilt.

Single facts often seem to be trivial until they are linked together in a meaningful pattern.

Such evidence may consist of facts and circumstances of any kind. The accused may be implicated by evidence of his motives, conduct before and after the crime, personal traces which he left on a victim or at the locus of the offence, or traces of the victim or the locus which he carried away on his person, forensic evidence of many kinds, possession of incriminating articles, real evidence, or admissions made to the police.

Circumstantial evidence often includes fragmentary and neutral facts here and there, spoken to by honest and independent witnesses. Evidence of such facts may well be resistant to challenge in cross-examination. The more facts there are, and the more their variety, the less likely it may seem that a number of them are incorrect. However, they can still be questioned by methods already discussed.

The inference to be drawn from these facts may be the real issue, but this is not the function of Crown witnesses. It is a question for the court. The defence may therefore be prevented from attacking these inferences directly.

However the defence case may be put forward in other ways including direct evidence which contradicts the implication of the Crown circumstantial evidence. The most common example would be evidence from the acused denying his involvement, and this might be supported by eyewitnesses. Again, the defence may be one of alibi. The defence are also free to counter the adverse inference of guilt by argument in their final speech.

When police witnesses testify to admissions and confessions made to them by the accused, they are not giving direct evidence of the commission of the crime by him. Such police evidence is best regarded as a form of circumstantial evidence. The scope for exposure of error or unreliability in such police evidence, by cross-examination, has already been discussed.

IV TACTICS

A The role of advocacy

Any advice about, or training in, advocacy, should be given with a warning. Advocacy is not an exact science. It is impossible to guarantee that any particular approach will have a specific result in a given trial. There are too many variables, including the issues, the type of evidence, the psychology of individual witnesses, the composition of the tribunal of fact, and the psychology of its members.

Dogmatism about techniques of advocacy, by writers and trainers is therefore misplaced. But sound analysis and advice based on personal and collective experience can give useful guidance to practitioners at any stage.

Advocacy is a presentational art, like advertising or rhetoric. Advocates have to present a case as effectively as they can in an adversarial contest.

An advocate's personal beliefs about the facts, if he allows himself to form any, are irrelevant. Bluntly, within the limits imposed by the law, professional ethics, and his instructions, an advocate puts on a show, designed to persuade.

The truth, of course, plays a role somewhere, but not as the direct and immediate objective of advocacy. The truth is the concern of the court.

B Categories of honest evidence

The criminal justice system depends on the evidence of honest witnesses. As was shown previously in this chapter, such evidence may fall into several categories, either in fact, or in a court's judgment which is, in any event, the determinant:

- the evidence may be accurate and complete;
- the evidence may be mistaken;
- the evidence may be incomplete;
- the evidence may be unreliable.

This analysis was applied to the processes of observation and memory, and sources of error, in various practical situations; the issues arising from identification evidence were considered separately.

In that discussion, the guidance given to advocates, was related to the specific problems under consideration. But having regard to the advocate's overall objective, the tactical presentation of this aspect of his case can now be developed further, in more general terms.

C   The advocate's aim

The defence advocate's aim is an acquittal. To achieve this he does not need to show that Crown evidence about crucial facts is mistaken or incomplete. He need merely persuade the court to take the view that this Crown evidence is too unreliable to be a safe basis for convicting the defendant. If so, the Crown would fail to discharge its burden of proving guilt beyond reasonable doubt. Crown evidence may fail to pass this minimal test, through its inherent weakness, the Crown level of presentation, or effective defence cross-examination. An acquittal would then follow.

Although the unreliability of essential Crown evidence would be sufficient for the defence purpose, it may be difficult to predict whether the court will actually take that view. So, naturally, defence advocates will go beyond the minimal criterion. They try to show that the evidence is not only unreliable, but that it is in fact mistaken, or that it has significant gaps.

Moreover, although, by law, the defence need not prove anything, they will usually lead evidence from the accused and others. The purpose is to put forward an alternative version of the facts which, if true, would exonerate the defendant. This will be more effective if it takes the form of a coherent and credible human story.

These objectives are supported by the advocates' presentational skills. The result is that criminal trials often develop into quasi-theatrical, persuasive, displays—especially before juries. These dramatic displays tend to take on lives of their own, and to become contests between two stories in which the essential Crown obligation may be obscured.

This may affect the court's view as to whether or not, it can rely on the essential Crown evidence and is persuaded to convict. But on the other hand, there is no need to overkill a gnat with a sledgehammer!

For defence advocates, an important tactical principle is to have realistic expectations of what they require to achieve and can achieve. Exaggerated expectations may make their presentations more adversarial than they need to be for maximum effect. A common expression of this is that advocates cross-examine where it would be better not to do so or they may go on for too long in trying to saw sawdust.

It is recommended that no matter how he prepares and conducts a defence in any other way, an advocate should never lose sight of his primary target, viz to show that Crown evidence is unreliable and he should not let the court forget this. It is, at least, an ultimate fall-back position.

In this contention, an able advocate may derive massive support from reality. It is beyond doubt that human powers of observation and memory are fallible. They do not have the efficiency of a video camera. For almost a century, psychologists have been attacking the validity of testimony and of court processes on this ground.

Although their views are exaggerated, there is sufficient substance in their criticisms to justify caution in the acceptance of testimony by courts. But the need for this must be pointed out to courts. For this, the advocate must be well-informed about the subject. The earlier material in this chapter, which contains the essentials, should be of value.

This emphasis on the Crown's burden of proof does not mean that other approaches should not be used also, if they are likely to support the defence case.

To expose Crown witnesses as liars, or to show that their evidence is mistaken or full of gaps, or to prove the defence account of the facts positively, would be achievements and should be tried, if there are prospects of success. It would be imprudent to count on this, but such approaches might be taken simply to weaken the court's trust in the Crown evidence.

A criminal trial is not a free enquiry into truth, although it is concerned with truth. The time for discovery is over. It leads to a more limited decision based on the evidence available, and how the cases are presented. In a non-legal sense, the outcome is a preference for one case over another. But this context should not obscure the basic defence task of showing that Crown evidence on crucial facts falls below the standard of proof beyond reasonable doubt, and that it would be unsafe to rely on it.

D   Testing evidence of observation and memory

The sources of error discussed here are not part of some inaccessible branch of psychology which is closed to common sense and beyond the experience of judges, magistrates or jurors. Courts know that testimony is fallible.

This common experience makes courts receptive to reasonable cross-examination aimed at exposing mistakes, incompletness, or unreliability in evidence. But whatever success this may have, it is rarely conclusive.

In conducting such cross-examination, the following flexible principles, distilled from the best professional practice, should be found helpful with honest witnesses. If they are applied, they will eliminate much of the faulty advocacy which is seen in courts every day. Biased witnesses are considered in the next chapter.

(1) Approach the witness in a friendly, courteous and tactful way. Show the witness that you accept his or her sincerity. You are seeking the witness's co-operation. Beware of arousing resistance by implied criticisms of the witness's faculties. Let the witness save face.

(2) Maintain professional detachment. Never state your own opinions or appear to be giving evidence. Do not comment on evidence, especially by misinterpreting it. Be consistently fair and reasonable. Show no concern if you receive an adverse answer. Never argue with the witness.

(3) Control the witness, albeit in a pleasant and unobtrusive way, by using leading questions except where you can confidently and safely expect the desired answer from non-leading questions, which would have more weight. Each question should have a single point to which you know the answer which will be given. It may be necessary to achieve that eventually, by a progressive series of questions. Avoid 'fishing' questions to which you do not know the answer.

A useful form of controlled questioning is to ask the witness to confirm a statement which you make.

Ordinary questions may be used for variety, where there is no risk of unwanted answers.

Example:

Q: 'You saw this through your windscreen in heavy rain. Is that not so, Mrs Russell?'
A: 'Yes.'
Q: 'Your windscreen wipers would be operating, were they not?'
A: 'Yes they were.'
Q: 'Was it dark at that time of night?'
A: 'Of course, it was nearly 11 o'clock.'

Here a picture of impediments to observation is building up, without provoking a denial so far.

Avoid open-ended questions, involving 'Why' or 'How' since the witness may elaborate in a harmful way.

(4) Frame your questions in simple, short, lay language, in an informal conversational style, and cross-examine only briefly. Ask only about one point at a time. Don't repeat questions which are ineffective or produce adverse answers. Approach the topic from another angle.

Do not try to bully a witness into giving an unqualified 'Yes' or 'No' answer. That would not impress the court. Try another approach.

(5) In cross-examining a witness who gave harmful evidence-in-chief, while not allowing him to repeat it, this order may be followed:

(a) probe the foundations of the evidence, ie how the witness was in a position to observe what he says;

(b) ascertain precisely what he did observe. The aim here is to strip away any element of interpretation, with a view to correcting it;

(c) probe the sources of error in observation or memory which have been discussed here;

(d) probe the collateral facts and circumstances of the incident, to expose vagueness or uncertainty in the witness's observation or memory concerning related facts.

This is aimed at sowing distrust in his evidence about the main facts.

(6) In cross-examining a witness, the analysis of belief set out in the next chapter, should be kept in mind. Briefly, for evidence to be believed, the following must apply:

(a) the witness is trusted;

(b) the evidence is reasonable, ie neither inconsistent nor improbable;

(c) the evidence must be assessed holistically. This involves a comparison with other evidence with regard to mutual support or contradiction.

This analysis can guide a cross-examiner to weak aspects of the evidence, which he can exploit.

(7) The end-game is of great importance. The cross-examination of each witness should end on a favourable note. As soon as the desired answer has been given, the cross-examination should stop at once.

If an obsessional advocate tries to gild the lily, by further questions, the witness may retract or qualify the helpful evidence. There is much to be said for stopping even before the favourable answer is received, and for leaving the conclusion to the final speech. This is less likely to alert the opponent to the need for re-examination or further evidence.

A favourable point for ending cross-examination, would be where some inconsistency is disclosed within the witness's own evidence, or between his evidence and other evidence. Here, it may be best not to ask him to explain the inconsistency, which he might do. The point may be left to the final speech.

It would be a favourable ending if some substantial source of unreliability were disclosed. Then, it might be unnecessary and unwise to continue in the hope of establishing positively that the evidence was mistaken.

Where it happens that a witness concedes that his evidence was mistaken or doubtful, that is a positive achievement. But if the witness denies such defects, dogmatically, faced with strong grounds for criticism, he will be exposed as unreasonable. This too, is a gain.

A cross-examiner must always put his case to each witness who knows the facts, and this is often done at the end. To avoid point by point denials, and elaboration of harmful evidence, the case may be put to the witness in some comprehensive form with which he is invited to agree or disagree.

CHAPTER 4

The credibility of evidence

I   Introduction
II Analysis of lying

I   INTRODUCTION

In courts generally, and in this book, the term 'credibility' means the extent to which evidence is accepted as truthful. This is a matter of judgment rather than of objective fact. Evidence may be assessed as true, whereas it is actually false. Equally, accurate evidence may be disbelieved.

The assessment of evidence as credible is not concerned with unintentional inaccuracy, ie errors which were the subject of the previous chapter. Credibility refers to lies, ie intentional and motivated attempts to deceive. A judgment about credibility may not fall into an all or nothing category. The assessment may be a matter of degree, although it is unquantifiable.

Credibility is treated here as a question of the court's view of evidence, rather than of witnesses, although they are related. Statements are the object of belief; witnesses are the objects of trust.

To impute credibility to a witness implies that the person has a specific quality, a fixed quantum of veracity, which settles the question. It stems from a bygone division of people into truthful and untruthful categories, so that some are credible persons and some are not, independently of the context.

Modern views are more complex and more discriminating. It would be generally accepted that whether or not the witness will tell the truth is not determined by a specific trait which inclines him in either direction. It depends rather on the whole individual, his motivations, his relationship with and his reaction to the particular situation.

Lying is rife in criminal trials. It is a more serious problem for courts than mistaken evidence, although some errors may be crucial. The prevalence of lying is seen every day in conflicts of testimony, where witnesses must know the truth.

The trial process depends on belief in the testimony of those witnesses who are trusted. Misjudgments about this involve a variety of risks. Believing lies or disbelieving or doubting the truth may lead to miscarriages of justice.

Cross-examination by each party, whether or not it succeeds, can contribute powerfully to a proper decision. The value of destroying an opponent's evidence is obvious; but intensive cross-examination which makes no impact on evidence may enhance its credibility, and is equally valuable to the court, although not to the cross-examiner. It is tactically better to refrain from cross-examination than to do it badly. But sometimes an advocate has no choice, where he is bound to put his case to an opponent's witnesses who know the relevant facts. It is best to do this by comprehensive leading questions which anticipate and weaken the adverse answers, without giving the witness an opening to develop them, eg 'Despite everything, I suppose that you still insist that my client was the driver of the car?'

Since an advocate assists the court whether he succeeds or fails, he can cross-examine as forcefully as he wishes, unrestrained by ethical doubts. However, he must only challenge the truthfulness of evidence responsibly, on the basis of his information, which it is not his duty to assess.

The law cannot eliminate lying evidence, but tries to discourage it in various ways.

To some extent, the adversarial system, in itself, diminishes lying or belief in lies. The rules of procedure, evidence, and penalties, provide a context in which evidence may be led, tested, contradicted, and evaluated.

But this has its limits. Daily conflicts of sworn testimony signify that, for many witnesses, the oath or affirmation are mere formalities. Except for a few who take them seriously, they are feeble as deterrents to lying, and of no help in cross-examination or assessing evidence. Some witnesses may tell the truth because of the religious sanction, and others from a sense of duty or fear of penalties. The oath is unlikely to deter witnesses with strong motives for lying.

Penalties for contempt of court or perjury may have an unintended effect in reinforcing falsehood. In the first instance, witnesses must have strong motives to risk committing perjury. If they have overcome their fear of the consequences and have lied in their evidence, their motives for lying may be reinforced by fear of the penalties which may follow from exposure. This double motivation could discourage retraction of lies, even under forceful cross-examination.

Open misconduct in testifying, eg evasiveness or fencing with questions, can be dealt with at once, by warnings or penalties, but most lying evidence is more covert. Perjury may only become apparent in a later trial. Some forms of false testimony do not constitute perjury in law, or else are undetectable, eg omitting material facts, or giving evidence a twist in a false direction. Perjury is hard to prove. Most trials would be duplicated by later trials for perjury. Only a small fraction of false evidence becomes the subject of prosecution.

The law also tries to deter interference with witnesses, but often in vain. Intimidation by threats to witnesses or their families or fear of reprisals even without threats is a substantial cause of lying. Threats may be verbal, and undetectable, even if witnesses are not too afraid to report them. Police resources are limited. The protection available to threatened persons is often inadequate. Some have been known to move to other homes.

Intimidated witnesses, who are usually called by the Crown, are common figures in criminal courts. Typically anxious and subdued, they give evasive, inconsistent or improbable evidence in barely audible tones, and in a dilemma between fear of threats and fear of the law.

Under pressure, depending on the persons and circumstances, such witnesses may persist in their falsehoods. These often include fabricated 'amnesia', or inability to identify. Such claims may be suspect, but they are very hard to demolish.

Intimidated witnesses often reverse their true evidence completely, although they may have told the truth to the police at an earlier stage. A useful provision allows a cross-examiner to refer the witness to any previous inconsistent statement which he made on a specified occasion. If he denies it, the statement may be proved by other witnesses. If he admits the statement, or it is proved, it can be compared with and used to discredit his present evidence. The previous statement is only admissible for this purpose, but not as evidence on the issues. It will not prove the contrary of his evidence in court nor will it prove that the statement itself is true.

The oath, penalties for testifying falsely, or for interfering with witnesses, and the admissibility of previous inconsistent statements have a direct bearing on credibility, but cross-examiners should be familiar with many other areas of the law which are also important in this connection.

These include regulation by statute and codes of practice of evidence of confessions and admissions in order to minimise possible lying by witnesses on either side. The various discretions conferred on judges to exclude evidence which was improperly obtained, or which is unfair or prejudicial, should be known. The rules relating to pre-trial identification procedures were discussed in the previous chapter.

The requirements for proof include safeguards against the acceptance of lies, in the form of judicial warnings to juries or magistrates' self-direction about the risks of convicting on the basis of some kind of evidence, and in a few cases the need for corroboration. Above all, placing the burden of proof on the prosecution and requiring a standard of proof beyond reasonable doubt for guilt is the overall protection against wrongly giving effect to lies, by conviction.

Lying and its exposure are psychological processes. But psychology as a formal academic subject offers no help to the cross-examiner at this time. Psychological research into testimony since early this century has focused on perception and memory.

The psychologists' claim that their findings can contribute to court processes has been shown to be unfounded. The methodology of psychological research is experimental and statistical, and is confined to the laboratory or to artificial situations. The findings obtained by these methods add nothing material to common sense, yet many are still controversial.

This methodology cannot cope with the motivational processes, the real-life events, and the court situation in which lying occurs; hence, psychologists have ignored lying. No current body of psychological knowledge has any practical value for application to the problem of credibility in courts. If it were otherwise, the legal profesion would have seized on it long ago.

There is no known psychological technique or test which can penetrate the mind of an individual in isolation, to ascertain if he is lying. This insight can certainly not be derived from so-called body language.

Moreover, even if lie-detection in this way were possible, it would not reveal the truth, which is not necessarily the contrary of a lie. By psychological criteria alone, it is not possible to detect lies or discover the truth.

For attaining the truth about events, the best method developed so far, although it is not infallible, is the holistic comparison of various reports about a common reality, after they have been tested or challenged adversarially: ie a criminal trial. This highlights the function and importance of the cross-examiner. On comparing the experience and insight of the two professions, it is clear that, at the present time, it is the psychologist who can learn about lying from the cross-examiner, and not the converse.

A decision to lie must, of course, be the outcome of a complex motivational process, but it is unnecessary, and impracticable, to go into that psychologically. An understanding of lying must be practical, based on common sense, experience of life and the courts, and free from psychological jargon or theorising.

II   ANALYSIS OF LYING

Practical questions, 'Who lies?', 'What do they lie about?', 'How do they lie?' and 'How can lying be detected?', divide the subject naturally into lying witnesses, subjects of lying, forms of lying and detection of lying.

A   Lying witnesses

The first question, 'Who lies?', cannot be answered by suggesting that any category of witness is more likely to lie than another. Witnesses cannot be classified in this way.

To expect any category of witness to be either wholly honest or deceitful, irrespective of the circumstances, would now be regarded as naive and simplistic. As a result of many factors, including cultural changes, the spread of popular psychology, the development of the media, and the experience of the courts, people are more aware of the variety and reality of human nature than they used to be.

It is now less surprising than it used to be when persons deemed to have integrity are found to have lied. They include presidents threatened with impeachment, millionaires who resort to prohibited company practices, sweet old ladies who smuggle, or clergymen, protesting innocence, who are convicted of unpleasant sexual offences.

It is a common experience in summary criminal courts to see 'respectable' persons trying to bend the truth, eg offending motorists, otherwise of good character, who will go to any lengths to retain their driving licences.

In the above examples, lying may be explained by the strong motivation of persons accused of some offence. But witnesses other than the defendant may also be highly motivated, eg relatives or friends of an accused, or prosecution witnesses such as accomplices diverting guilt away from themselves, or who are acting out of malice.

Every day, in courts throughout the land, police witnesses, from whom impeccable standards of conduct are demanded, face attacks on their truthfulness. Even where they are unfounded, such challenges raise live issues.

For practical purposes, courts and advocates must assume that any type of witness may lie in some circumstances. Whether or not that will happen will be determined by the interaction of the individual, his motives, and the situation.

Lying is always the result of a complex process of this kind. People of the highest character will lie if the situation requires it. In deciding to do so, they will give expression to their own values, whether or not they coincide with social values. Any other view is unrealistic.

The variety and complexity of individual responses to particular situations must be stressed.

A court should never entertain fixed views about the truthfulness of any class of witness. To do so would be a prejudgment or a prejudice. However it will be helpful to indicate some common patterns.

1   Prosecution witnesses

Police are the most common prosecution witnesses. They testify in most criminal trials, but without special status. Nowadays, police evidence is attacked constantly, but the attacks are usually directed against the veracity of the police witness as an individual, not the policy, traditions or integrity of police as a body.

The mildest charge may be that the witness, convinced of the accused's guilt, and misconceiving the public interest, has wilfully coloured the facts to secure a conviction. The defence may hope that this charge of perjury will derive support from the partiality implied by the police duty to trace and apprehend suspects, and assemble incriminating evidence although that is a radically different matter.

On the other hand, it may be suggested that false police evidence is given irresponsibly or maliciously. This could be the allegation where an accused is identified as one of a group of wrongdoers, although there is little or no basis for this, or it is said unfairly that he resisted arrest.

A common accusation is that a confession or admission has been falsely imputed to the defendant, perhaps by two officers, and entered in their notebooks. Such evidence, if accepted, though false, could overcome any weakness in the Crown case.

The worst allegation would be that of a criminal conspiracy by a number of officers to convict a person known to be innocent, perhaps aggravated by 'planting' false exhibits, or intimidating civilian witnesses.

A common weakness of such challenges is that the defence often cannot suggest, let alone prove, sufficient motivation for such illegal conduct, despite the risks of detection, loss of career and pension, and imprisonment which such police witnesses would incur.

Sometimes the ranks, numbers of officers, and activities involved, create such a danger of exposure, that falsehood seems unlikely.

Moreover, even if lying in court seems safe, police officers know that unforeseen evidence might emerge later. This could occur if a genuine confession were to be made by the real wrongdoer, or if a public inquiry were to be held, which would expose the perjury.

Obvious reluctance and outright perjury do not combine well. A perjurer will wish to be plausible, not hesitant.

Accusations of falsehood against the police may simply be the desperate inventions of an accused. But it has certainly been established that it does occur. Every case must be investigated on its merits.

It is a defence advocate's duty to take such a line only on the basis of responsible information and instructions. However, unless extreme attacks are supported by positive defence evidence, he may be liable to criticism.

The defence may contend that the evidence of accomplices who are Crown witnesses is untruthful. This may derive support from the admitted bad character of such witnesses, and their potential motives for lying. Accomplices may minimise their own blame and add to the blame of others, in the hope of gaining immunity or receiving a lighter sentence. The evidence of accomplices has always been regarded with caution and as requiring judicial warnings.

Complainants in sexual offences may be accused of lying. It may be suggested that a female who consented to sexual intercourse now denies it for personal reasons, or that the charge is the result of hysterical fantasy or malice. This sometimes occurs where a woman has been under an anaesthetic for medical or dental purposes.

In charges of sexual offences, a jury must be warned of the danger of convicting on the uncorroborated testimony of the complainant. Thus the issue of credibility is often acute.

The rules relating to the evidence of children, however they give it, and the requirements as to warnings and corroboration, apply to situations where truthfulness is a very live issue.

A crime of violence may have involved a struggle between several persons, and perhaps issues of self-defence. Complainants and their associates may continue this battle in the courtroom, implicating persons falsely out of animosity.

2   Defence witnesses

Defendants are generally treated as untruthful by the prosecutor who cross-examines them. Presumably, they know the truth of the prosecutor's assertion which they deny. It would be highly exceptional, although possible, for an accused to be mistaken when he denies guilt, eg if he was unaware that the car which killed the child was the one which he was driving.

Defendants are accused of lying more than any other class of witness and are probably the most motivated. However, a defendant would be seeking acquittal, whether or not he was guilty, so that motive alone cannot determine the truth or falsity of his evidence. The defendant's denials of guilt may be truthful.

Friends, relatives, workmates or other associates of an accused, who speak to the main facts, or to an alibi, are generally challenged as lying, for similar reasons. They too are likely to know the truth.

If the evidence of independent defence witnesses is challenged, the criticism will normally be that it is mistaken or unreliable. Alibi evidence may be of this kind, eg if the manager of a bar confirms that the defendant was there with other alibi witnesses, but cannot recall the exact date and time.

3   Independent witnesses

Irrespective of whether they are called by the prosecution or the defence, some witnesses may be described in court as independent. By this is meant that they are witnesses with no apparent interest in or connection with the case, or the parties, eg persons passing by when a bank was robbed.

Since such witnesses are believed to have no other motivation than to tell the truth, courts often accept that they are likely to have done so, although their evidence could, of course, be incomplete, mistaken or biased.

Deliberate lying by such witnesses is not usually expected, on the view that no normal person would wish to contribute to an unjust conviction or acquittal, and risk severe penalties, for no reason. But, of course, there is no guarantee that even a plausible witness is normal. He could be a psychopath, or his evidence may simply be malicious. Naturally, this is not a matter where rules can be applied, but apart from challenging the reliability of the evidence, it is usually difficult to attack it as untruthful without any foundation in other evidence.

Witnesses who may fall into the independent category include eyewitnesses to an incident in which they were not involved or persons speaking to separate items of circumstantial evidence.

Expert witnesses may sometimes be regarded as independent because of their professional status. But, on the other hand, experts are subject to stresses and strains which can interfere with their impartiality.

4   Specially-motivated witnesses

Any witness, including an independent witness, may have some unsuspected and special reason for lying.

Examples are a sense of loyalty to the party who called them, hidden partisanship in the form of hostility to criminals or to the police, inflating the list of stolen goods to exaggerate an insurance claim, avoiding adverse publicity, vanity, fear of embarrassment, or the belief that justice will only be done if it is assisted by lying.

But to lie in any serious way, for such reasons, especially in any way which might contribute to an unjust conviction, is not usually to be expected.

Of course, an apparently neutral witness may really be a pathological liar with the ability to conceal his falsehood.

Such tendencies may not be obvious but they may be perceived by a cross-examiner who is alert for them and who listens to the evidence-in-chief with some imagination.

B Subjects of lying

What witnesses may lie about are the real issues of fact, which were examined in chapter 2. The 'rule of alternative defences' explained there means that if lying occurs, it will normally relate to either the commission of the crime or the identity of the offender, but rarely to both issues.

Exceptions can occur, of course. A neat example is where a disqualified accused is charged with driving a motor car, and claims that it was his passenger who was driving, this being a lie. The issue is primarily one of identification, the two men having been seen by police to change their seats. However, if the passenger was driving, no offence was committed by that act alone, as he is a qualified driver. Here the issue of identity and of the commission of the crime are inextricably bound up with each other, but such situations are rare.

Where the commission of a result-crime is the issue, questions of credibility may be expected to refer to the intangible elements in the situation, eg whether the alleged victim of rape consented to sexual intercourse, or whether the accused's state of fear justified his attack in self-defence.

Similarly, lying is common in conduct-crimes, because proof rests solely on verbal assertions which are not supported by tangible, physical evidence. Examples of such possibilities exist in charges involving corruption or blackmail.

No general comment can be made about the frequency and incidence of lying in object-crimes, because of their variety.

Where it occurs, it is likely to involve intangible issues, eg whether the knife which the accused was carrying was intended to be an ornament which he was taking to a friend's house as a present, or whether he regarded it as a personal weapon. Lies would not be told about the object itself, since it should be in court for inspection.

Where identity is the real issue, any lies will refer either to the accused's presence at the locus or to his alibi defence, but they are unlikely to be found in circumstantial evidence or in expert evidence.

C Forms of lying

1 *Affirmative and negative lies*

To assert a fact which did not happen, or to deny one which did, is a stark form of lying. This is the the type of lying which could constitute perjury. To lie like this, a witness must be highly motivated. When he has lied, he has an additional motive for not admitting his falsehood and disclosing the truth, viz the risk of penalties in the trial, or in a later prosecution for perjury.

So, because of this double motivation, such a witness will rarely retract such false evidence and substitute the truth. However, destructive cross-examination may succeed in weakening lying evidence of this gross type, so that it succumbs to the more credible evidence led by the cross-examiner.

That would be a typical pattern. Cross-examination would have performed its valuable function in gnawing away at the supports, but the final blow would be given by contradictory evidence which was preferred.

Alternatively, the cross-examination, alone, may weaken the challenged evidence so that in the court's opinion, even without the benefit of contradiction, its honesty cannot be relied on. For the defence, such an outcome would be sufficient for an acquittal. But generally, cases are decided on the basis of which of two alternative stories are accepted.

Such situations are closer to the daily reality of criminal courts than the image presented by popular mythology. For the cross-examiner to deliver a dramatic coup de grace by demolishing adverse evidence outright, without the assistance of other contradictory evidence, is a rare exception in criminal trials.

2   Reluctance and evasiveness

In witnesses who are not sufficiently motivated to commit outright perjury, unwillingness to tell the truth is often expressed as reluctance to testify rather than by specific lies.

Obvious reluctance to testify and outright perjury do not combine well. Such testimony would damage the impression which a perjurer would wish to make, viz that of a plausible story, told confidently.

Reluctant witnesses rarely fail to answer at all, as they would incur penalties. They are more likely to answer evasively. Their dilemma is that they want to hide the truth, but fear the consequences of being seen to do so.

This conflict may be aggravated if they made previous inconsistent statements, from which they fear to deviate too much. Typically, this occurs when Crown witnesses depart from the incriminating evidence expected from them, and give evidence which is harmful to the prosecutor's case. The prosecutor may then, with the court's leave, cross-examine his own witness.

The cause may be intimidation or spontaneous fear of reprisals, even where no threats have been made. Even if the accused is convicted and imprisoned, he could act through others and therefore he may still be a danger. The police, because of pressure on their resources, can only provide limited protection for witnesses of this type. Some witnesses ask if they can write their addresses, rather than state them in open court, and some even move to another area.

It is common for victims of domestic violence, or members of a family who have been in dispute, to give reluctant and evasive evidence, after a reconciliation has occurred. Wives who must have known about the abuse of their children by their husbands will often lie to protect him, because he is the breadwinner.

Faced with such evidence, a cross-examiner might exploit the witness's conflict by reinforcing his fear of the consequences of not complying with his oath.

If the witness has not yet gone beyond the point of no return, he may, by firmness, warnings, and perhaps by reference to previous inconsistent statements, be led into testifying properly. Otherwise the court may have to intervene. If the court imposes any penalty on a witness, this may have a persuasive effect on witnesses who have yet to be called.

Advocates should avoid extremes of pressure on reluctant witnesses for whom some jurors may feel sympathy, and with whom they may even identify.

3   Omissions

The question of omitting material information in evidence has some relationship to the oath and what it obliges a witness to do. The oath to tell 'the whole truth' imposes a duty on the witness to answer questions fully, not to volunteer relevant information and report all that he knows about the issue. So, in a sense, the advocate who omits questions is as responsible for omissions as the witness who omits facts in his answers.

Advocates prefer strictly controlled interrogation, which avoids the risks that unexpected and unwanted evidence may be given.

Since judges are impartial, they do not ask open-ended questions which might elicit evidence which is unfavourable to either party. After a witness has been questioned by advocates, it is not the practice for a judge to invite him to add anything which he thinks may be helpful. Nor do witnesses generally ask if they may do so.

At times, expert witnesses are aggrieved by this restriction. because they are dissatisfied with the curtailment and editing of their evidence which is typical of controlled interrogation.

As a result of the editing of answers to questions which are put, and failure to put other questions, vital facts may slip through the net. The omission of material facts may have a significant effect on the outcome of the trial.

This situation offers an opening for motivated witnesses who are willing to go so far to achieve a certain result, but who are unwilling to commit perjury by outright lying. Instead, they may omit important facts if they are allowed to do so.

Omitting facts is the easiest form of deception. It involves less guilt and anxiety than lying. It is simpler and needs no preparation or recollection. If it emerges that a witness has not disclosed something of significance, this could easily be excused as ignorance or forgetfulness.

The test of whether or not an omission is culpable, depends on the nature of the questions put to the witness. If a direct question about the facts is asked, and they are concealed, this would be non-compliance with the oath. If an indirect question is asked which brings the facts reasonably within its scope, concealment here may also be an offence.

The remedy is in the hands of the advocates. Cross-examination should be thorough so that every material fact is covered without giving the witness an escape route. Questions should be formulated carefully to eliminate possible omissions by preventing the witness from avoiding the real point. This can be done by combining specific leading questions such as 'Did the accused pick up a brick?' with general open questions like 'What was the accused doing?' Pairs of questions like these could cover the whole ground effectively.

The cross-examiner's objective in these circumstances is to make the witness disclose what he is concealing, as an alternative to committing perjury which this type of witness wishes to avoid.

If a witness has not already omitted any facts to which a direct question referred, he would not incur any risk by revealing them under this kind of interrogation. In that situation the prognosis for effective cross-examination is good.

It should be noted that not all omissions of evidence are due to culpability of the witness. The advocates are involved, and they may, for tactical reasons, ethical or otherwise, or owing to simple ineptitude, omit some area of relevant fact. This could not be described as deception on the part of the witness. It might or might not spring from acceptable conduct on the part of the advocate who calls the evidence. It might also be the result of the failure of a cross-examiner to explore a particular area.

However, from the court's point of view, the result is the same. The evidence is excluded, whoever is responsible for this.

The selection and omission of facts at the enquiry stage is outside the scope of this book.

4 False qualifications

In an effort to be objective, police testimony often lacks animation or colouring. Something may be lost thereby. Generally, witnesses, whether they are honest or not, do not testify like robots reporting laboratory results. Their accounts of facts contain many secondary elements, such as incidental perceptions, impressions and feelings, and they are expressed in personal and highly variable language which may convey implications. This is natural, everyday, human communication.

However, the danger in this is that it gives an opportunity to dishonest witnesses to twist and distort facts in subtle ways. They may state facts more or less truthfully while, at the same time, they give them an intentional bias in some way which can range from minor colouring to major distortion. There are many such subtle ways of deceiving the court. An appropriate generic term would be 'false qualifications'.

Some patterns are given below, but they are not exhaustive.

One way of qualifying evidence is to adjust the facts so that they will be interpreted in a desired direction, eg in reporting an admissible impression of a rather ambiguous incident. Examples would be a person's manner of driving, suspicious conduct in a shop, acting as look-out, or ambiguous contact which may or may not have been sexually motivated.

Another form of false qualification may be the way in which knowledge of facts is expressed. Truthful evidence may be given in a way which suggests that the witness is doubtful, when, really, he is sure. For support in this, they may refer to barriers to observation or memory, eg 'Everything was happening so fast' or 'It was a long time ago. I can't be expected to remember that.'

Conversely, witnesses may express certainty about facts of which they are unsure, eg if police witnesses after discussing the case make much firmer identification of the accused than their observations would justify.

If a cross-examiner thinks that evidence may have been tailored intentionally, to give a false impression, he should strip away secondary elements and should try to expose its factual foundations. This may have the effect of undermining the unwanted conclusion. Any unjustified gloss on the facts actually seen by the witness can be met by suggesting a contradictory alternative.

Cross-examiners should scrutinise the language used by witnesses, closely, when they describe their state of knowledge of the facts, to see if it may contain false innuendos or implications. But it is objectionable for an advocate to repeat an answer with a different gloss.

However, it is the falsity of the suggestions of doubt or certainty which is objectionable, not these features of the state of knowledge in themselves. Although definite evidence is preferable, the evidence of an honest witness may be quite acceptable, although it is less than definite.

Cross-examination often succeeds in moving false qualifications in a more favourable direction. The witness was insufficiently motivated to commit perjury, and may not have gone too far in a false direction, so that he is not at great risk if he is induced to rectify his earlier evidence.

Other innominate forms of deception exist which would be recognised when they are met, eg telling the truth in a humorous, sarcastic or exaggerated manner which induces disbelief.

However, it must be conceded that a good deal of dubious evidence of this type will escape exposure.

D   Detection of lying

A cross-examiner's ability to expose lying is aided by knowing how the court decides whether or not testimony is truthful, or why the court is unable to reach a decision. Primarily, this must be seen from the point of view of the court, not of the advocate. The desired judgment is the advocate's target. He can then apply this insight in cross-examination.

The evaluation of credibility can only be analysed in terms of practical courtroom psychology, based on general judicial and professional experience of what happens in criminal trials, and, ultimately, on common sense. No other basis exists. Psychology, as a formal discipline offers no explanation of lying and no help in its detection.

It is emphasised that the judgment of credibility is holistic. It depends on the assembly of all the evidence in the case. Single elements which enter into it may be unimpressive in themselves. However, when everything is compared and integrated, the conclusion may be compelling. During the discussion of the separate elements, it must be kept in mind that the whole is more than the sum of its parts.

The two main questions which arise for a court are 'Can the witness be trusted?' and 'Is the evidence itself acceptable?' For evidence to be believed, each of these questions must be answered affirmatively.

If a witness is trusted, but what he says appears to be unreasonable, his testimony is likely to be rejected on the view that he must be mistaken. On the other hand, even the most plausible story may be disbelieved, if the court has no confidence in the witness.

Within these extremes, various combinations may arise. However, the essential point is that belief depends on both the witness and the evidence, not on either one alone.

1 *The witness*

A witness begins as a cipher, a person unknown to the court. Trust has to be created. Whether or not the witness is to be regarded as truthful is still an open question. It has yet to emerge. However, it is very difficult to make a rapid assessment of a disputed quality in a total stranger, under restricted conditions, especially when the enquiry is conducted by other persons.

This judgment makes demands on the court's understanding of human nature, experience of life, intuition and common sense.

Four aspects of human nature enter into a court's evaluation of a witness, viz personality, character, motivation and demeanour.

Personality refers to the witness's individuality; character denotes the moral aspect of his personality; motivation refers to the directions in which he is impelled by specific feelings; and demeanour, here, means his non-verbal expression of feelings while testifying.

(a) *Personality*.   Personality refers to the distinctive features of a person which make him an individual. Questions which arise in the court situation are the following: 'What kind of person is this?' and `How does this help in deciding whether he is telling the truth or lying?'.

These are, of course, psychological questions. It might be expected that guidance would be forthcoming from academic psychology. However, modern psychology offers no guidance in this field.

The *Penguin Dictionary of Psychology* defines personality as:

> ... a term so resistant to definition and so broad in usage that no coherent simple statement about it can be made.
>   [Arthur S Reber (ed) *Penguin Dictionary of Psychology* (1987)]

Less wary psychologists have produced countless definitions of personality, and attempted classifications of people into types, which has only produced a mass of unhelpful controversy.

Therefore, courts must assess the relevance of a witness's personality on the basis of a commonsense view of human nature, although this too has its limitations, and the dangers of guessing and speculation must be avoided.

Obviously a court cannot be expected to attain deep insight into a witness's personality. For one thing the relevant information is not available. A trial is no place for autobiography or for a psychodynamic analysis of a witness, while he speaks of matters other than himself, ie the facts in issue. These limitations also apply to assessing a defendant as a witness, even where his personality may also be closely related to the issues of fact.

Despite these difficulties, it is inevitable that a court's impression of a witness as a person will contribute to its view of whether or not his evidence is truthful.

Snap judgments of the witness may be made, eg a courageous bystander who intervened and stopped the robbery, or else membership of a class of persons may dominate, eg the hospital surgeon who operated on the injured victim.

In practice, while the view taken of the witness's personality is usually part of the assessment of whether he is telling the truth or lying, it is impossible to state, explicitly, the nature of the relationship between personality and lying. In this field, the intuitions of the tribunal of fact play a large part.

Clearly, in this area, a court should exercise great caution. It has to be said that, per se, an impression of a witness's personality is unreliable as the sole basis for deciding on his veracity. At best, it has limited significance and, at worst, it can be misleading. Personality only acquires value as a guide to veracity in the context of the total equation, the holistic assessment of credibility. No single determinant of credibility can be relied upon by itself.

Cross-examiners are recommended simply to treat witnesses as individuals, not types, using their personal insight into human nature, and their experience of life. Whatever its limitations, this commonsense approach, is better than a theoretical classification which gives no practical guidance.

(b) *Character*. 'Character' as a general term, has many meanings. It is unnecessary, and would have no practical value, to discuss them or to try to define the word comprehensively. It is enough to say that, as applied to a witness, in the context of assessing evidence, character usually refers to the moral aspect of personality. Here, character is not regarded as a separate compartment of human nature with some special status; it simply denotes a number of personality traits which are normally valued, eg kindness, courage or sincerity.

It may be contended that a 'good' person is likely to tell the truth or, conversely, that a 'bad' person is likely to lie, or even that veracity depends on a specific disposition to be truthful or to lie. However, this simplistic contention is untenable. Veracity is not a fixed individual quality, regardless of other factors.

Some persons are, indeed, more trustworthy than others, but this is too imprecise for general application. In isolation, it omits the complexity of human nature and the reality of how a person is motivated in a particular situation. Character and truthfulness are abstractions. An abstract statement of their relationship has no practical value. The underlying human reality would be lost in generalisations.

Neither psychology nor common sense would divide witnesses into those of good character who are normally truthful, and those of bad character who are normally liars. No fixed quantum of veracity is inherent in anyone.

On a practical level, neutral facts, showing a witness's role in society, are normally elicited in evidence-in-chief, eg age, occupation, marital status, or children. Character may be assumed to be good unless it is attacked. But whether or not advocates try to set up good character or to attack it deliberately, a court is forming an impression about this in the course of the evidence.

Texts on the law of evidence should be consulted for the rules which regulate and restrict attacks on character.

With regard to a prosecutor's cross-examination of a defendant on character, the statutory rules are complex, although he can, of course, cross-examine other defence witnesses as to bad character and previous convictions. For this reason, it can be dangerous to the defence, to call witnesses with extensive criminal records.

Defence cross-examination of Crown witnesses as to character is also limited, not so much by direct regulation as by tactical risks.

If the defence cross-examination of a Crown witness makes an imputation against character, or if the accused puts his character in issue, or in certain other circumstances, the accused will be exposed to cross-examination as to his bad character and previous convictions. Thus, a defence advocate is likely to be cautious if the accused has a significant criminal record.

Where evidence of character designed to discredit a witness is admissible, it tends to be limited to his criminal record, although in certain circumstances evidence of other facts may be called to attack his credibility.

Applying the term 'credible' to witnesses, as lawyers do, wrongly suggests a general character trait. The witness's relationship to the whole situation will be much more significant.

The matter is really one of motivation, rather than general character. Good general character, alone, does not guarantee that a witness will be truthful. Even where it has some effect, it may be overcome by strong motives for lying in a particular situation. Following their own values, people of seemingly good character may take the risk of lying to help a friend or relative, eg in supporting a false alibi. Of what help is the concept of character in cases like the following?

Countless defendants of both good and bad character lie to avoid conviction. Reports in the media abound about the false protests of innocence of many persons who would commonly be regarded as respectable. Such cases include sexual abuse of children by schoolmasters, fraud or embezzlement by trusted executives or local government councillors, drink-driving offences by public figures, so-called 'sleaze' involving criminal offences of politicians, or shoplifting by mature ladies.

It is often represented, in excuse, that such offences when committed by such persons are 'out of character' and so they are. Frequently, a distinguished personal history is marred only by the event which is the subject of trial.

The required integrity of police witnesses does not exclude regular attacks on their veracity in practice. The allegation is that their normal good character is overcome by their specific motives in the particular situation, which lead them to lie. That is exactly the point.

Sometimes this allegation has been shown to be correct. The police witnesses might be motivated by malice, gain, or a distorted attempt to promote justice by securing the conviction of a suspect whom they believe to be guilty.

The conclusion must be that character counts, but that alone it is an inadequate guide to truthfulness. The view which a court is able to form of a witness's personality and character is of limited value in detecting lies.

Personality and character are hidden and complex; a court only gets a surface impression of them which is not clarified by psychological explanation. They are general qualities, without specific aims, not a response to his whole situation in the trial. A simpler and more practical notion of human nature is needed for court purposes. This is to be found in the concept of motivation.

(c) *Motives*. A motive is taken here to be a transient state of arousal which impels a person towards a definite goal. Some psychologists might disagree with this view, but it is a clear and practical working concept, which accords with common sense.

Above all, a motive is regarded here as directional, ie it has a specific aim. It is a witness's response to his situation, expressed in purposive action.

Naturally, a single motive cannot explain behaviour, which results from the interaction of many variables, including conflicting or unconscious tendencies—a mysterious and kaleidoscopic process best left to psychologists. Provided that one holds the directional quality of a motive firmly in mind, ie what the witness is trying to achieve, the psychological processes can be left unexplained.

'Motive' here means more than just wanting something to happen; that would just be a feeling. If a feeling is expressed in action, by doing something to achieve the desired end, that would be a motive. What a witness may do to achieve his end is to lie. Then his testimony is motivated, ie dictated by his aim, not his knowledge of the facts.

Emphasis has been placed on the difficulties of assessing personality and character. Do they not also apply to the detection of motives?

In fact, this presents few problems in practice. Whether a witness's feelings are involved in the trial situation and, if so, in what direction, is often clear to advocates and to the court. It can generally be inferred from personal links with and interest in the situation, and various objective circumstances. This does not depend on any deep insight into the witness's personality or character. It is a matter of common sense.

Feelings and preferences do not, of course, mean that the witness is prepared to lie to satisfy them. However, they are a precondition for motives which impel some witnesses to do so.

Apart from genuinely neutral witnesses, motives to falsify evidence may be classified on a simple directional basis, viz where the witness desires conviction or acquittal, or satisfaction of some personal purpose regardless of the verdict.

The distinction between feelings and motives to lie with a certain purpose may be illustrated by considering a mother's testimony to support her son's plea of alibi.

If she is normal, it will be obvious from her relationship to the accused that she hopes for his acquittal. Her feelings are consistent with either the truth or falsity of her evidence. Assuming the absence of any other information or guidance, what inference about the truthfulness of her evidence should be drawn from her feelings?

It would be unsound, illogical and unfair to conclude that the only explanation for her evidence is the motive to secure her son's acquittal, and that therefore she must be lying. The comment 'She would say that, wouldn't she' expresses this. But the mother may be telling the truth, although her feelings also impel her in the same direction.

Nevertheless, the mother's feelings are still relevant to the judgment of credibility, which would not be so with an independent witness. Although this does not settle the question, it may weaken her evidence and reduce the weight of the alibi. The relationship may cast some doubt on the credibility of her evidence. Yet if it succeeds in raising a reasonable doubt about the Crown identification evidence, it should lead to an acquittal nevertheless.

A prosecutor's cross-examination of the mother would not be confined to the matter of her motivation. Indeed, in a jury trial, it might be better tactics to ignore this altogether. The facts would be obvious, but jurors might sympathise with a parent in this situation, and might resent the distress which the prosecutor might cause.

The prosecutor could still test the mother's evidence objectively, showing that it was self-contradictory, or that it was in conflict with other alibi evidence, or was extremely improbable. In the context of such probative defects, her motive might become a dominant and sinister explanation for her evidence, so that it is rejected. But evidence should not be rejected simply because the witness might have a motive. That is only a factor to weigh among others.

To expose evidence as false due to motivation, a firm foundation should be laid by establishing the witnesses' personal interests in the issue. If this is obvious, eg close family relationship or business partnership, there is no need to belabour the point. But if the link is not apparent, it should be brought out clearly and specifically.

Animosity and malice towards a party, as well as favourable feelings, should be taken into account. Either could lead to lying.

If the witness admits his interest, the point is made. If he resists it unreasonably, his credit will suffer.

Any non-disclosure in evidence-in-chief, of material facts which link the witness to the issue or a party, is likely to be damaging to the opponent, and perhaps the image of his advocate. It may seem as if these facts were deliberately concealed. Such omissions should be exposed, stressed and exploited.

As was seen in the discussion of lying witnesses, some, who are indifferent to the verdict, may lie for personal reasons. Advocates should be alert to such possibilities, and they may need to probe the evidence imaginatively to reveal such motives.

If a possible motive for lying is clear, or emerges, a cross-examiner may suggest, expressly, that the witness is lying for that reason. Although this is denied, the cross-examiner has shown the court where he stands.

Feelings and possible motives which could lead witnesses to lie are factors to consider in assessing evidence, but alone they are inconclusive. Like other mental processes, extrinsic confirmation is needed to establish their presence and effect on testimony.

Again, it is stressed that any sound evaluation of evidence is holistic, and must take everything into account. Lie detection based on any single clue, however helpful, would be unsound and unsafe.

Realising this, a cross-examiner should try to expose objective probative defects in the evidence such as inconsistency, improbability and lack of realism. It may be tactically better to focus on this once the court has become aware of the witness's motives.

The combination of showing that the evidence is apparently defective, and the witness's motivation which may have brought this about, can be a very potent challenge to credibility.

Such attacks on evidence do not create a state of deductive inevitability so far as the verdict is concerned, but they will maximise the impact of cross-examination.

(d) *Demeanour*. The traditional view is that a witness's 'demeanour' gives some guidance to his veracity. The higher appeal courts, where evidence is not led, are reluctant to evaluate the accuracy of evidence, because they have not seen the demeanour of witnesses in the lower court.

Dictionary definitions of 'demeanour' are not informative, eg 'bearing or mien'; 'outward behaviour'; or 'the way a person behaves towards others'.

The subject of demeanour raises a question of human nature, ie a question of psychology, viz 'Can one tell, just by looking at a witness, whether he is speaking the truth or lying?' The psychologists' approach will be considered below.

A commonsense view of the nature of demeanour in court is that it consists of all the visible and audible facts about a witness, other than the content of his evidence. This includes both fixed and variable characteristics, and all forms of self-expression, whether simple or complex, voluntary or involuntary.

Fixed characteristics such as age, sex, physique, appearance, hairstyle, clothing or ornaments, do not change in court.

Variable and voluntary aspects of demeanour include posture, gestures, movements, or facial expressions which can be controlled; audible features include the rate, emphasis, pitch volume or fluency of speech.

Variable and involuntary signs include uncontrolled facial expressions, eg blushing, blanching, perspiring, tremors and the like.

Variable and complex conduct includes fainting, having to go to the toilet, crying, asking for water, loss of temper, hysteria, illness, or distress.

These examples are not exhaustive.

What help can psychology offer here? Is a witness's demeanour a reliable guide to whether or not he is lying? What signs of lying should a court look for?

The term 'demeanour' is absent from psychological dictionaries. But the divisions of psychology include the study of non-verbal communication (NVC), ie forms of communication other than language. The popular term is 'body language'.

Paralinguistics, another branch of psychology, studies forms of vocal communication other than semantic, viz how the voice is used, rather than what is said.

The adoption of physiology by psychology, to create the subject of physiological psychology, should also be noted.

These disciplines cover the whole field of demeanour, viz non-verbal and vocal signs, and physiological manifestations. If there is any merit in basing lie-detection on demeanour, it should have been supported by psychological research in these categories. Is this so? It is not.

Starting with the last topic, no psychologist or physiologist can either claim that any identifiable physiological processes occur in the brain during the complex cognitive act of lying, or that there are any specific physical or vocal signs of lying which express that process.

The physiological psychology of emotion, itself controversial, is another question. Emotions and lying are different processes.

There are no scientific findings about a physiological relationship between demeanour and lying.

Apart from this lack of a fundamental relationship, has any link between demeanour and lying emerged from pragmatic scientific research?

Typically, psychological research consists of experiments in controlled but artificial settings, combined with statistical analysis to extract correlations between the variables studied. Dominated by behaviourist views, until recently psychologists, with few exceptions, concentrated on experimental study of behaviour ignoring inner mental experience.

The problem of lying with its cognitive and motivational complexities, especially in real-life situations, was beyond the scope of this methodology. Not surprisingly, therefore, since a few psychologists did begin to study lying in this restricted way, the results to date have been negative. One researcher states this starkly, while implying an unscientific assumption that cues to deception exist:

> A major problem lies in the researcher's present inability to specify the cues that signal deception or prevarication on the part of the Witness.
> [Gerald R Miller & F Joseph Boster 'Three Images of the Trial: Their Implications for Psychological Research', in Bruce Dennis Sales (ed) *Psychology in the Legal Process* (1977) p 31]

The most impressive statement of the position is that of Professor Paul Ekman, in the USA, perhaps the world leader in the field, summarising his findings after 25 years of intensive psychological research into bodily signs of lying:

> People would lie less if they thought there was any such certain sign of lying, but there isn't. There is no sign of deceit itself—no gesture, facial expression or muscle twitch that in and of itself means that person is lying ... No clue to deceit, in face, body, voice, or words, is foolproof, not even the autonomic nervous system activity...
> [Paul Ekman *Telling Lies* (New York, 1986)]

Ekman's research counters claims by those who claim to be 'judges of men' who can tell whether or not someone is lying, just by looking at the person. Ekman finds that few persons achieve better than chance accuracy:

> Most people believe they can detect false expressions: our research has shown most cannot.

Ekman's overall conclusion is that most liars can deceive most people most of the time. Of course, his approach is concerned with deciding truthfulness on the basis of demeanour alone. Judgment of testimony by a court is not confined to assessing demeanour; it depends on many other factors.

Ekman found that bodily signs of anxiety sometimes accompany lying, but that they do not, in themselves, indicate lying. On the other hand, he agrees that the absence of signs of anxiety does not indicate truthfulness. Some liars show none.

Ekman's intensive research has made a valuable contribution in the form of negative findings. These are to the effect that while there are physical signs of emotion or anxiety, there are no specific signs of lying. Psychology offers no support for the view that from a witness's demeanour alone it is possible to know whether or not he is lying. Obviously, in court, no final conclusion, and certainly no conviction, should ever be based on physical signs alone.

The caution engendered by psychology, ought to be paralleled by commonsense views, but unfortunately mistaken popular myths persist.

It is very risky for jurors or magistrates to decide credibility in the conceit that they are 'judges of men' or to believe that signs like an averted gaze mean that a witness is lying.

In this connection, the views of Lord Devlin, a distinguished judge, are welcome. He questions the traditional view of the significance of demeanour in lie-detection:

> The great virtue of the English trial is usually said to be the opportunity it gives to the judge to tell from the demeanour of the witness whether or not he is telling the truth. I think that this is overrated.

Adopting the views of Mr Justice McKenna, Lord Devlin makes this refreshing statement:

> ... I doubt my own ability ... to discern from a witness's demeanour, or the tone of his voice whether he is telling the truth ... For my part I rely on these considerations as little as I can help ... It is the tableau that constitutes the big advantage, the text with illustrations, rather than the demeanour of a particular witness.
> [The Rt Hon Lord Patrick Devlin *The Judge* (1979) p 63]

Experience in court shows the limited value of a witness's demeanour in judgment. Mostly, witnesses show no significant signs at all. At times, obvious signs of anxiety are seen, but the anxiety could arise from many causes.

Individuals vary. The witness may just be an anxious person. How can a court know whether anxiety is not his normal state?

A witness may merely be anxious about the court situation. Many find it an ordeal to testify in public, or fear that they may be made to look foolish in cross-examination.

Some people may fear the responsibility for the consequences of their evidence, eg the verdict or the sentence, or other consequences. Intimidated witnesses may be caught between the fear of reprisals or penalties. Truthful witnesses may be concerned about the possible verdict.

Honest and conscientious witnesses may be worried about being disbelieved though they are telling the truth.

Other feelings, eg anger or surprise, may complicate the picture.

Whatever the witness's overall and anxious response to the situation may be, this could persist throughout the whole of his testimony. How can this unchanging state of mind be related to the truthfulness of particular statements?

On the other hand, many lying witnesses appear to be quite calm. They may show no signs of anxiety, for many reasons.

Perhaps they are not anxious at all. Some persons are relaxed by nature and they keep calm in situations which others would find stressful.

Some witnesses may be quite indifferent to the outcome in circumstances like the following.

An accused may already be serving a long sentence of imprisonment and be unconcerned even about the possibility of a consecutive sentence in the present trial.

The present charge may be minor or one where a severe penalty or imprisonment would be incompetent or improbable, eg for a first offender. A wealthy accused would not be worried about a possible fine. There may be mitigating grounds for expecting a lenient sentence.

An accused's associates may be willing to lie, although they are not as worried as the accused is, about the possible verdict.

On the other hand, even though a witness is, in fact, anxious, he may not be a person in whom this manifests itself physically.

Many people are natural or experienced liars with good self-control or acting ability. To some extent, the ability to act is universal.

A witness may be confident that his lie will either be believed or that, at least, it is undetectable.

The complexity of responses and individual variations are such that, in isolation, anything about a particular witness's demeanour may mean anything so far as veracity is concerned.

However, apart from this, there is a further major obstacle to be faced. Even if, contrary to psychological findings, signs of deceit did exist, who can be trusted to interpret them correctly, and on what basis could they do so?

Neither magistrates who conduct summary trials nor juries—the tribunals of fact in serious charges—are trained in this skill, if, indeed, there is any ground for describing it as such. Such powers would exceed those claimed by Lord Devlin. Readers may like to ask themselves if they could assess credibility from demeanour, on a jury and, if so, on what principles.

Does demeanour, then, have any value at all?

Notwithstanding court traditions and popular beliefs, it is submitted that scepticism must be maintained in the face of any claim that the credibility of evidence can be evaluated merely by observing a witness. Accordingly, at most, a witness's demeanour should only be allowed to play a minor role in lie-detection, and, by itself, it should never be the basis for conviction.

It is accepted that people do communicate meanings and feelings non-verbally. The display and interpretation of emotional signals is a matter of universal experience. But mostly this occurs below the level of consciousness, is very variable in forms of expression, or ability to detect, and it lacks precision. For practical reasons, and in the interests of justice, it is submitted that, in court, the role of non-verbal communication in assessing credibility should be limited to colouring evidence which is evaluated on some other reliable basis.

If this view is correct, what significance does demeanour have for the cross-examiner?

In the first place, a witness's demeanour is rarely a direct target for the cross-examiner. It would be unusual for an advocate to ask a witness, 'Why are you blushing now?' or 'Can you tell me why the pitch of your voice has just risen?' or 'Why do you seem to have become angry since I asked you if you had discussed your evidence with other witnesses?'

There are reasons for not questioning a witness about his demeanour. If some noticeable change in the witness has taken place, the court may be expected to observe this directly.

Such questions may seem to be irrelevant, meaningless or pointless.

Moreover, close questioning of a captive witness about his or her personal reactions may create distress, or may appear to be unnecessary, offensive, inhuman or unfair. This may be tactically unwise, and could antagonise a jury. A judge would, of course, disallow improper treatment or harassment.

But, above all, cross-examiners would do better to probe the evidence about the facts of the case. Lying is protected by an inpenetrable shield, and can only be exposed indirectly, by exploring the issues, followed by holistic judgment which compares all the evidence, and applies various tests, so that the enigma of lying is overcome in the only available way.

Earlier in this chapter it was said that two conditions of belief in evidence were (1) trust in the witness and (2) reasonableness of the evidence. The most effective type of challenge is one which attacks both conditions.

The sources of trust or distrust in witnesses arising from personality, character, motives and demeanour, have been discussed. In any trial, whatever the role played by these qualities of witnesses, the main indication that evidence is untruthful is derived from its defective features.

2   *The evidence*

An effective challenge to the credibility of evidence, is generally a three-stage process.

One stage is where the witness is cross-examined with the aim of showing both that he cannot be trusted, and that the evidence is defective per se. In theory, a defence cross-examiner might achieve this objective at the first stage alone, if he can, at least, create a reasonable doubt in the quality of essential Crown evidence; but it would be unrealistic to expect him to destroy it outright, there and then, as occurs in fiction.

However, in most trials, there is a competition between two versions of the facts in issue, and defence evidence is led in support of their account, although there is no obligation in law to do this.

Accordingly, the second stage of challenging the credibility of advocate Black's evidence, occurs where advocate White leads contradictory evidence-in-chief in support of the alternative story. If White's cross-examination of Black's witness had the desired effect of weakening that evidence sufficiently, White's hope is that his contradictory evidence will create doubt, at least, and preferably disbelief in his opponent's weakened evidence, and thus advance the destructive process started by cross-examination.

When the court finally comes to consider its verdict, this is the third stage at which a challenge to the credibility of evidence can become effective. The court would then consider, compare and weigh the whole of the evidence in the trial and it would evaluate the mutually supporting or conflicting bodies of evidence and their effect. It is only then that the process of destroying the credibility of Black's evidence can be completed if it is successful.

How does an advocate show that evidence is unreasonable?

Evidence will be regarded as unreasonable if on any material point, it is shown to be inconsistent, impossible, improbable, unrealistic, or contradicted by other accepted evidence.

If the witness who gives such evidence is one who must know the facts, the inference may be that he is lying. This could be put to the witness explicitly, perhaps at the end of cross-examination. Lying may be inferred by the court. Advocates should not expect witnesses to admit it, however forceful the challenge.

(a) *Inconsistency.* In this section, the term 'inconsistency' has a specific meaning. It refers to self-contradiction about material facts, by a single witness, or a conflict about material facts in the evidence of two or more of a party's witnesses who profess to tell the same story. This evidence would certainly be regarded as unreasonable.

As used here, the term 'contradiction' has a different meaning. It refers to the usual adversarial conflict between witnesses on opposite sides. Each story may be reasonable.

Inconsistency is a logical flaw, irrespective of the underlying facts. It means that two statements cannot both be true together, eg that the accused was, and was not, at home at midnight on 31 December 1995.

At least one statement must be, and sometimes both statements may be, untrue. Inconsistency shows that something is wrong with the evidence, but it does not determine what that is and it does not prove any facts.

What is the effect of inconsistency in showing that evidence is untruthful?

This depends on the type of inconsistency, where it is found, and how it is exploited in cross-examination.

Minor inconsistencies, wherever they are found, often mean little or nothing. They are common as a result of the normal fallibility of observation and memory. Eyewitnesses seldom give absolutely identical accounts of facts which they observed at the same time. Inexperienced advocates often exaggerate the importance of such discrepancies as a basis for the contention that a witness, or witnesses, are lying.

Details, of course, are sometimes important in questions of credibility and inconsistency about them may be significant.

Where evidence of collateral facts and circumstances is being elicited to test the truth of a central fact, eg an alibi, even small variations between a party's witnesses may cast doubt on their evidence about the main fact in issue.

Also, disagreement about details of circumstantial evidence, may have a crucial effect on the resulting inference. In either of these contexts, inconsistencies in evidence are far from being trifles, and they may point to lying.

Material inconsistencies require explanation and at least one alternative must be rejected. If they are found within the evidence of a single witness, who must know the facts, this may indicate that he is lying.

But if the inconsistencies only emerge on comparing the evidence of two or more witnesses for a given party, it may be difficult to say which witness or witnesses may be accurate, mistaken, or lying. Inconsistency alone, cannot settle this.

As the Crown must prove guilt beyond reasonable doubt for conviction, any material inconsistency in their evidence may imperil their case, especially about identification.

However, even material inconsistency in defence evidence may not be so crucial, since nothing need be proved and reasonable doubt about the Crown evidence is enough for acquittal.

Experienced advocates are constantly alert for evidence-in-chief which does not fit together, and for inconsistencies of any kind, which they can attack and exploit in cross-examination.

But even where inconsistency emerges, a cross-examiner should not suggest that a witness is lying, when a mistake is reasonably possible, or more likely. To do otherwise may offend the witness and antagonise a jury. On the other hand an advocate should not shrink from putting to a witness that he is lying, where that is appropriate. It is weak and unimpressive to suggest mistake, when only lying is possible.

The distinction between a mistake and a lie depends on whether or not the witness is bound to know the real facts.

The variety of techniques for challenging credibility on the ground of inconsistency will be explained in later chapters, but one or two possibilities are mentioned here.

One approach is to create inconsistency in the evidence of one or more witnesses by indirect tactics which lead them into invention.

If lying is suspected in part of one witness's evidence because of inconsistency, a cross-examiner should try to extend the taint to all his disputed evidence. To charge one such witness with lying is easier than imputing lies, mistakes or accuracy to two or more witnesses who disagree. Either one might be truthful.

As will be seen, when inconsistency is exposed, it is sometimes better to press an attack home, when the witness is in a trap from which he cannot possibly extricate himself.

At other times it is advisable to let inconsistency pass, so that the witness cannot correct it. Many experienced advocates take care never to allow a witness to explain any inconsistency.

Another gain from letting an inconsistency pass, is that the opponent is not alerted to the need for explaining it in re-examination, or for leading additional evidence about it.

An unclarified inconsistency can be very powerful material in a final speech.

Where two or more witnesses tell the same story, with inconsistent evidence about material facts, one can be confronted with what another said; this may produce unconvincing retractions, which discredit the evidence further.

Instead of clashing, the evidence of two or more witnesses may seem to be too uniform, so that collusion may be suspected. Here, the identity of wording or content should be brought out and highlighted. One way of doing this may be, as an exception to normal tactics, to ask the witnesses to repeat the whole or part of their evidence-in-chief. This comparison should expose collusion or coaching.

Similarity of evidence may arise from discussing it. It may be productive to ask witnesses if they have done so. Even reasonably honest witnesses often deny this, or else they deny that their evidence was influenced by the discussion. Such denials are often surprising where witnesses see each other frequently. If one witness admits and another denies such discussion, further inconsistency may arise.

(b) *Impossibility*.   Evidence-in-chief about alleged facts which could not exist is rare. Obvious nonsense should have been eliminated during preparation. Impossibility usually emerges from compared facts, eg recognising a suspect shown to have been round the corner. Here the cross-examiner's task should be simple.

(c) *Improbability*.   Improbable evidence is common. Improbability may be apparent in the evidence-in-chief, or it may only emerge under the pressure of cross-examination.

Individual facts, combinations of facts, or the whole story may exhibit improbability. Perhaps the most common issues of this kind are those which concern human nature and behaviour.

The test of improbability is ordinary experience of life. Probability is a matter of degree but it is only quantifiable in special contexts, eg in technical evidence like fingerprints or the frequency of blood groups.

For ordinary evidence, the attempt of some thinkers to create a mathematical model of probability is only of academic interest. It has no practical value in court.

Yet the degree of improbability does matter. Evidence of a rather unlikely fact may be believed, but evidence of an absurd fact may be rejected. Part of the art of the cross-examiner is to convert what seems to be unlikely into what seems to be quite absurd, by increasing the degree of improbability. This is done by expanding both the story and its context, so that it will be seen that they do not fit together.

By controlled questioning, a cross-examiner may intensify the improbability of evidence by drawing out its assumptions and consequences, and exploring its implications. The incongruity of what is asserted should become more and more obvious as the gaps between the evidence and reality are increased.

A witness, challenged about some initial improbability, may, in trying to justify it, add further unlikely details, to the point of absurdity. The same effect may be achieved by encouraging one who is over-talkative, either because of confidence or anxiety, to ramble on freely until he develops an improbable story to an unacceptable point.

The question arises as to when improbability will lead to rejection of evidence or not. Obviously, such a general question cannot be answered too specifically. No rules can be stated, but the following two approaches set out parameters within which a fair and sound decision may be reached.

A court must maintain an open mind, and apply some degree of imagination. Many strange facts are true. Odd and unlikely happenings are reported every day in criminal courts.

Some stories may only seem strange to jurors because of a cultural gulf, although they are commonplace in certain social groups. Evidence should not be rejected automatically just because it refers to unusual facts.

On the other hand, if the evidence is contrary to what happens in reality and suggests facts, ways of thinking and modes of conduct that are so unlikely as to be an affront to common sense, a court would be entitled to reject it.

For a court, there is no substitute for practical judgment based on experience of life, and applied to the particular circumstances. The proper decision cannot be worked out logically.

After wrestling with parts of the issue, it will, finally, be seen as a whole, one way or another. What usually helps in difficult questions is to consider other evidence, to use a variety of approaches, and to have more facts. As in all judgments, the improbability of evidence should not be the sole basis of decision. But if it is combined with other factors, increased grounds for confidence in the assessment develop, eg if improbable evidence is also inconsistent, and, after being weakened by cross-examination of motivated witnesses, it is contradicted by other acceptable evidence.

A decision whether improbable evidence which is rejected arose from mistake or lying, has consequences for trust or distrust of witnesses. Sometimes, error cannot be excluded as a possible reason for an isolated piece of unlikely but not unreasonable evidence, which only becomes absurd in relation to the whole picture, known to the court but not to the witness.

In such a situation, the nature of the event, conditions of observation, state of the witness, or passage of time may seem to explain an error in the honest evidence of an independent witness.

But where a strongly-motivated witness, who must know the reality, gives extensive evidence (the whole story or a major part of it), which is obviously improbable in itself, he may well be held to be lying.

(d)   *Lack of realism.*   The form of statements may seem sincere or false, ie as having or lacking the 'ring of truth'. This does not refer to their content, consistency or probability. It is a way of evaluating forms of expression, by analysis, intuition, and comparison with what is likely in a true account.

There are no rules for this impressionistic approach to evidence, but it can help. Typically unrealistic features of false stories are lack of factual detail and colouring, or of personal involvement, and a tendency to be all one way.

The lack of factual detail and colouring arises because false stories often focus anxiously on the central theme alone so that, unlike true stories, they may be bare and lack surrounding detail. Facts are always related to others, often causally. True accounts often mention related facts spontaneously, whereas lying stories omit them because they did not exist, and have not been invented.

For similar reasons, false stories may lack any element of personal involvement of the witness. People normally react to events; they are not video cameras. Many persons find it hard to sort out what they saw from their impressions and feelings. Normally, in describing an event, they would include their responses to it. The lack of any human vitality in an account may be suspect. It may be missing because the event never happened, and the natural feelings aroused by a real situation, and reflected in a true story, have not been invented.

Of course, some truthful evidence may be given in a dry, impersonal and objective way, without factual detail or personal involvement, for various reasons.

The subject of the evidence may be something neutral like skid marks or documents in a fraud, where elaboration is not to be expected.

The court situation, or the advocate, may be inhibiting, or the witness may be of a class from whom impersonal reports are expected, eg a police witness describing a traffic accident, or a pathologist giving a post-mortem report.

Details may have been forgotten, or repeating statements during enquiries or in preparing for trial may have blunted the witness's feelings about the event.

Despite these qualifications, when a lay witness gives a bare account of some dramatic event, a court may, intuitively, be put on its guard by the unconvincing form of testimony (although it may be quite consistent and probable). Obviously, on the basis of such a quality of evidence alone, a court should not conclude that the witness is lying. But a cross-examiner, alert to the possible significance of lack of realism in evidence, may probe it for lies, sometimes with useful results.

Lying may be suspected when a witness gives one way evidence, inappropriately.

Firm evidence, in a consistent direction, is often truthful and convincing, eg a report of a clear-cut event, observed and remembered accurately. But if all the evidence points dogmatically in one direction, where there is room for doubt, probing to see if it is untruthful may be prudent.

True accounts of uncertain facts do not always follow one consistent line; they may include doubts or elements which seem unnecessary, odd, irrelevant, unexpected, or inexplicable, just because they happened; they may omit important items to which the witness cannot speak, or spontaneously add to or correct previous testimony. Such points are seldom found in false accounts, as they would complicate them needlessly.

Such realistic imperfections and inconsistencies are usually missing in invented stories. They tend to cover the essentials, directionally and dogmatically, without deviating from the main theme, omitting what does not help the general thrust. The excessive purposiveness of the evidence is clear. Its form is explained by its intended effect.

For a court, lack of realism in the form of evidence, as discussed above, may suggest lying, but not in terms of rules, conscious formulation, nor as the sole basis for deciding credibility. Although this may not be an intentional approach, eg in the minds of first-time jurors, an intuitive response to lack of realism, that testimony seems unconvincing, may find its way into the final holistic evaluation of all the evidence.

This approach is part of the psychology of persuasion, and the art of advocacy. Cross-examiners should be alert for the openings suggested by such clues. If they then probe and challenge evidence as untruthful on such grounds, subtle though they may be, they may find the court receptive to it, because of its intuitive response.

Sometimes, if the opponent's witness is allowed to tell his story again in his own words, its lack of realism may be highlighted, and this can then be followed up by leading questions.

3   Holistic assessment

To leave the subject of lie-detection at this point would be misleading. It is not exhausted by the above separate accounts of the guidance given by a witness's personality, character, motives or demeanour, or the inconsistency, impossibility, improbability or lack of realism of evidence. As was said, no one approach is reliable by itself.

In practice, all this must be put together by advocates and by the court, to expose lying, and in order that evidence may be rejected on that ground.

A broad approach is required in detecting lies, even more than for mistakes, where the co-operation of honest witnesses sometimes makes a narrower focus possible.

To confront the problem of lie-detection, head-on, the stark and inescapable fact is that when honest communication stops, people cannot read each other's minds. There is no direct way of knowing if someone is lying or not. A liar's inner experience is private and impenetrable. Thus, the credibility of evidence is never self-evident. It is a conclusion derived indirectly from related facts, with variable confidence.

To do this confidently requires the total approach of a criminal court to all the witnesses and all their evidence. A holistic, integrated evaluation which surpasses the sum of its parts is how sound decisions are made about credibility.

Generally, the greater the number of witnesses, the easier it is to challenge or to decide credibility. The tasks for advocates and courts are more exacting in convictions based on the uncorroborated evidence of one Crown witness, or acquittals following a reasonable doubt raised by one defence witness.

A major factor in testing and deciding credibility is the normal adversarial conflict between prosecution and defence evidence. After each party has put his version to the opponent's witnesses in cross-examination, to accept one version is to reject the other.

This is of crucial importance for the outcome. It may often seem that nothing is wrong with evidence, looked at by itself; yet, it may be confidently rejected as false, if it is contradicted by other accepted evidence. Likewise, a witness may seem to be trustworthy, yet he is contradicted by an opponent's witness who seems even more trustworthy.

Then, to trust one means distrusting the other.

The conclusion may be that the rejected witness was lying. Without the guidance given by this conflict between evidence and witnesses, it might not have been possible to reach that conclusion with confidence.

For a cross-examiner to show, or for a court to decide, that a witness is lying, may be complicated and may involve hard work. There are no magic techniques whereby this can be avoided.

CHAPTER 5

Examination-in-chief

I INTRODUCTION

A Relationship to cross-examination

The function of cross-examination cannot be understood in isolation. It must be grasped in the context of the trial as a whole.

As a response to an opponent's examination-in-chief of his witnesses, a cross-examination may be effective in two ways.

In principle, defence cross-examination may weaken Crown evidence to the extent of raising a reasonable doubt about the essentials which the prosecution must prove for conviction. This would result in an acquittal.

But in practice the defence generally call evidence which supports an alternative version of the facts, and success is more likely to depend on the court's preference for one or other of two competing stories.

Here, the outcome would depend on the strength of one's evidence-in-chief, as well as the weaknesses in the opponent's evidence.

In this situation, which is the more common type, when a cross-examiner challenges testimony as mistaken or untruthful, a realistic aim would be to weaken it, so that it is overcome by his own contradictory evidence-in-chief. In the course of this cross-examination, it is, of course, necessary to put one's conflicting case to witnesses who know the relevant facts. This confrontation gives them an opportunity to admit, deny, or comment on the issues.

Since an advocate's evidence-in-chief will itself become a target for cross-examination, he should anticipate the attack which will be made on it, and should rob it of its effect so far as he can.

This chapter on examination-in-chief, covers both the presentation of a version of the facts, and how to reinforce it against challenge.

B Aims of examination-in-chief

Examination-in-chief is the stage of criminal procedure when an advocate questions his own witness, irrespective of the evidence given.

This procedural definition gives no guidance as to the aims of examination-in-chief. The testimony may be disputed, undisputed, favourable, unfavourable or pointless.

An advocate, whether for the prosecution or the defence, is expected to call witnesses who will support his case although an adverse witness may do the opposite.

In addition, a prosecutor would have a duty to call material witnesses even though their evidence might help the defence. For removal of doubt, the subject of examination-in-chief is discussed in this chapter from the point of view of the advocate who seeks supporting evidence from his witness. His aim would be to elicit all the admissible, relevant and material evidence which the witness can give in relation to the issues.

Admissibility depends on the rules of evidence. Relevancy is a matter of logic—usually inductive logic. Materiality is a question of weight.

Much evidence-in-chief is undisputed. But on disputed issues, to be effective, it should meet three requirements. It should support the party's theory of the case, it should be comprehensible and it should be persuasive.

C Theory of case

A party's theory of the case is his consistent and integrated view of all the undisputed facts, his version of the disputed facts, and his argument about what he must prove in law for the verdict which is his objective. It represents a party's fully thought-out position, rather than his assessment of the evidence.

Sometimes, depending on uncertainty about what will be proved, alternative theories of the case must be held; if so, each theory should be self-consistent.

An advocate's theory of the case creates a frame of reference, for a consistent and purposive presentation of his case. It is best to draft the theory of the case in the form of his proposed closing speech, which will shape the aims of his examination and cross-examination of witnesses.

To conduct any case, strong or weak, without a well-prepared theory, would be unprofessional. This deficiency would rapidly become obvious in various ways. A court, looking at the case as a whole, would see that the presentation was not serious, which would impair its prospects of success.

An advocate's insight into his opponent's theory of the case will help him to anticipate and, if possible, to frustrate damaging lines of cross-examination.

The theory of the case will vary according to circumstances. Chapter 2, 'The anatomy of a criminal trial' outlined the possible nature of the issues.

The prosecution theory will always be that the crime was committed by the acts of the defendant as set out in the indictment or information (sometimes including the possibility of commission of a lesser offence). For conviction, a prosecutor must prove his whole case, ie that the crime was committed, and that it was the accused who committed it.

Although one or other of these two issues is generally uncontested, this does not relieve the Crown of the obligation in law to prove all the essentials of their case, unless the defence admit the uncontested facts formally. These facts, whether or not they are disputed, must be established by evidence which is admissible, relevant, sufficient in law, and of enough weight, to prove guilt beyond reasonable doubt. This determines the content of the Crown examination-in-chief of each of their witnesses.

Commonly, eyewitness evidence is led about the crime, and eyewitness or circumstantial evidence is led to implicate the accused.

In foreseeing defence cross-examination, a prosecutor may be limited, before the trial, by how well he can predict the defence theory of the case. His pre-trial information about the defence may depend on procedural differences between a trial on indictment and a trial before magistrates, or on other factors. However, the line of defence will emerge early in the trial, in opening speeches or initial cross-examination.

There may, of course, be no defence evidence-in-chief. If a 'legal defence' is presented, it may simply consist of resisting the Crown proof by objecting to the competency of procedure, or to the admissibility of evidence, or by submitting that there is no case to answer, or by probing, testing or challenging evidence, without trying to prove anything positive.

It is probable, in most cases, however, that positive evidence-in-chief is led by the defence, with a view to establishing an alternative version of the facts, or at least presenting one which has the effect of creating a reasonable doubt about the Crown version.

If so, as was seen in chapter 2, any positive defence will normally consist of one of two alternative contentions, namely that either the crime was not committed, or else that it was not committed by the accused but not both. This contention, combined with the undisputed facts, and relevant legal provisions, would be the defence theory of the case.

Where the defence positively assert an alternative version of the facts, their examination-in-chief will usually include the accused, and perhaps other witnesses, who give direct evidence in which it is either denied that the crime was committed, or else that the accused was the offender. Circumstantial defence evidence is less common.

D Comprehension

Evidence must be clear if it is to be understood, remembered, and applied in reaching the verdict. It may be worse than useless if a harmful meaning is conveyed. Apart from leaving the facts in a hazy state, for tactical reasons a vague and general image of an incident is less effective than a sharp and detailed picture etched on the memory.

Some facts themselves are inherently complicated, confusing, and difficult to follow, eg technical information or a situation where several defendants are charged with multiple offences in various combinations. Here, the need for clarity is particularly strong. But even quite simple facts can often be obscured by poor presentation. To avoid this is the responsibility of the advocate, not his witness, who is, in effect, under his control.

A very common reason for failure to communicate facts clearly, is that advocates, through familiarity with the case, make unconscious assumptions about facts, and fail to grasp the effect of evidence when it is heard by persons who are not familiar with it. In this way, quite a simple fact, like the location of a stairway can confuse an account of what happened in a house.

A judge's questions may clarify isolated points, but this may not be what is puzzling jurors; nor does the judge have any responsibility for the clarity of the overall presentation by advocates.

Forgotten evidence has no value and might as well not have been given. Trials on indictment may be lengthy and jurors may take few notes.

Evidence which is clear is easier to recall. The following guidelines will contribute to a comprehensible presentation.

1 *Speech*

An advocate's first concern should be with the elementary basis of oral communication—an acceptable quality of speech from his witness. Common problems in courtrooms, many of which have no microphones, are marginal audibility, poor articulation, and speaking too quickly. Unfamiliar accents can also cause difficulty. Because of variable hearing ability, court layout, differences in location within the courtroom, or other factors, one person may grasp what is said though another does not. Unless clarification is sought, evidence may be misunderstood or missed altogether.

2   *Language*

Problems may be experienced if terms with which the court is unfamiliar are used in giving evidence. They could range from an expert's jargon to everyday slang. Also some questions contribute to obscurity of language.

Unusual terms should be explained at once in ordinary language. Vague, slipshod or roundabout statements should be probed and the exact meaning should be extracted. So far as facts are within a witness's knowledge, the advocate should insist on precise and definite answers and be satisfied with nothing less.

3   *Place*

The scene should be carefully set, from the start, as the basis for understanding the action which occurred in that location. The evidence should help the members of the tribunal of fact to form a clear visual image of the physical layout and, where that is important, it would be desirable to support the description by visual aids.

As has already been said, the advocate should ensure that he is not assuming knowledge of something because he is familiar with it. Nor, if he realises this belatedly, is it impressive then to introduce facts which should have been explained at the outset. There should be no possibility that, in a dramatic account of a fight, the advocate must say, 'Please tell the jury where this glass came from?'

4   *People*

After the stage has been set, the dramatis personae, the persons whose acts are to be described, should be placed in their respective positions, before describing acts of importance.

Again, visualisation should be assisted, wherever possible; this could be done by referring to small pictorial details to distinguish people, eg 'the man with the striped scarf' or the girl with the blue raincoat. This, of course, does not mean that more precise visual identifications of persons concerned should not be obtained if possible.

5   *Sequence*

A logical sequence, invariably the chronological one, should be followed in describing the incidents and actions in issue. If witnesses have a tendency to ramble, firmness may be necessary to achieve this.

Sometimes the order in which events occurred may be a crucial part of the issues, eg when questions arise about who struck the first blow and the order in which other persons entered into a fight between a number of people.

6 Visual aids

Where practicable, an advocate should help the court to visualise incidents exactly, by supporting oral evidence with visual aids, e g plans, maps, diagrams, sketches, charts, photographs, video films, models or samples. They can simplify evidence enormously, and can save much confusion, pointless dispute and waste of court time.

Although such visual aids would be admissible as evidence, they are not produced as often as they might be. Cost is seldom a major difficulty for such items. Often, the reason may be lack of imagination.

7 Repetition

Simple evidence need only be given once. In theory, this should apply to all evidence. But it assumes perfect hearing, attention and recall, which may not be the case. It is often prudent to repeat evidence of crucial or complex facts, to make sure that they were grasped and, in any event, for emphasis. Repetition has value in every form of oral communication, as advertisers and teachers know.

8 Variation

When evidence is repeated, its effect will be enhanced if some variation can introduced into the way in which it is given. This can be done by varying words, angles of approach, the form of evidence, eg direct, circumstantial, oral, real or documentary, or by calling several witnesses to one event. The advocate should, however, guard against allowing variation to create any element of inconsistency.

9 Expansion

The significance of facts always becomes clearer if they are seen in their context. Within reasonable bounds of relevancy and materiality, evidence about the main facts in issue may be expanded to include some explanation of causes, collateral circumstances, consequences, and conduct in relation to the situation.

If any impression evidence, opinion evidence or circumstantial evidence is given, the facts on which they are based should be made explicit, and perhaps amplified, as a test of the validity of their interpretation. Rules of admissibility should be kept in mind here.

E   Persuasion

To persuade is the objective of advocacy, which includes the presentation of evidence. The Crown seek to prove their whole case. The defence, if they lead evidence, have nothing to prove, but usually they will try to persuade the court to accept their alternative version of the facts, or at least to feel reasonable doubt about the Crown version.

Before evidence can be persuasive, it must be understood and absorbed into memory. This is the foundation, but not the edifice. Beyond this, techniques of good presentation should be employed. These include features which are found in other fields than advocacy, although they take a muted form in criminal trials.

The main qualities of persuasive evidence may be stated briefly. It should tell a consistent and probable story, with human interest, which is realistic in quality and strong in visual content. The main theme should recur, and be kept in the forefront, for emphasis. Criticisms should be forestalled.

In any trial, if both the Crown evidence and the defence evidence satisfy these requirements, the decision will be difficult.

1   *The story*

The most persuasive form of evidence is a story with the features mentioned above. It will integrate the evidence and facts meaningfully. Facts are most easily grasped and remembered when they are related. A mass of fragmentary elements would have no meaning or impact, especially in a long trial. If few, or none of the witnesses can tell the whole story, it should be built up by several, including those who give circumstantial evidence.

2   *Realism*

The story should seem vivid and real, and should not resemble a business or police report. An advocate cannot manufacture dialogue like a playwright, but he may guide a witness into contributing to the 'ring of truth', by including factual and human detail and colouring, personal involvement, animation and spontaneity. Within permissible limits, the advocate may let suitable witnesses tell their stories by means of free narrative, with minimal questioning while remaining ready to resume control at once if this becomes necessary.

3   Visualisation

The visual elements of a story are aspects of its realism. This is worthy of separate mention if only to emphasise the advantage of expressing things visually where possible. If a witness claims that he arrived at the locus by public transport, this is less vivid than saying that he took a blue bus.

When evidence becomes heavy, pompous and abstract, it will be sharpened if it is converted to simple, concrete images, like this.

4   Theme

Although a realistic and convincing story benefits by being clothed in some detail, this should not be overdone, so that the essentials are obscured by minutiae.

Knowing what to select or omit is one key to advocacy. Evidence-in-chief should cover all the material facts known to a witness, thoroughly, and in enough detail. Omitted facts of importance, which emerge later in cross-examination, may seem sinister.

The main theme of a party's case should dominate his presentation, and should recur constantly.

Cases usually turn on two or three crucial points, which should be kept in the forefront. They should be brought out as early as possible in the trial and expressed consistently in the most forceful way. The court should be reminded of them constantly in the evidence.

To avoid diluting a strong case, weaker points should stay in the background, and evidence with only a remote bearing on the issues should be omitted, even though it is admissible.

Most pre-trial witness statements contain too much, including background and inadmissible material, much of which should not be led. However, this is usually prepared for the information of the advocate.

5   Weaknesses

Even a persuasive story may have weaknesses. They will do more damage if they only emerge in cross-examination. It will seem as if there was a lack of candour in the examination-in-chief.

On the other hand, disclosing these points in examining one's own witness permits better handling of that evidence, prepares the witness for later challenge in cross-examination and may impress the court.

II WITNESSES

It is assumed that advocates are familiar with the rules governing the competency and compellability of witnesses.

A Selection of witnesses

The selection of witnesses is a matter for the tactical judgment of advocates.

A prosecutor should call at least those who are needed to avoid a 'no case to answer' submission, or, exceptionally, for corroboration. He is expected to call, or to have available, all his material witnesses, even if their evidence may be adverse to his case unless their veracity is suspect. As a matter of duty, he might call a witness only to allow him to be cross-examined.

The defence, of course, need not call any witnesses. However, if they make serious imputations against Crown witnesses, they may be criticised if they lead no supporting evidence.

It may seem best for either party to call all the good witnesses whom they have. But this is an over-simplification. It is unnecessary and may be inadvisable to do this.

The weight of evidence on disputed facts may depend more on the quality of evidence and its resistance to cross-examination than on the mere number of witnesses. If this were not so, anyone rightly accused of misbehaving at a football match on the evidence of two police officers could count on acquittal after calling his numerous friends who were there as fans for the same team.

Calling more than a few good witnesses on one issue should only be done after careful assessment.

There are no rules, nor is there any substitute for good judgment in a particular situation, about which witnesses to call. Flexibility is the keynote. In practice, many witnesses who attend at court are kept in reserve without ever testifying.

The following are relevant points for consideration. Too many witnesses may suggest lack of confidence in any; adding witnesses increases the risks of cross-examination and inconsistency; if one strong witness resists cross-examination without damage, another weaker witness giving the same evidence may lose the favourable effect; to overprove facts, especially minor ones, wastes court time.

Moreover an excessive amount of evidence dilutes other good evidence and may divert attention from what is more important.

These are all reasons for limiting the number of witnesses, but there is no reason for not calling a number which is sufficient for reinforcing a case, even though it is strong.

B Sequence of witnesses

Apart from the accused as the first defence witness to the facts, the best sequence of witnesses is a matter of tactical judgment. It should take into account the best sequence of evidence, which is a separate matter.

The various considerations which relate to the order of witnesses and the order of evidence, may differ and the best compromise must be reached. There is no one 'right' order, but any logical or natural order is better than none.

Calling witnesses or leading evidence to narrate the facts in the chronological order of their occurrence, is easiest to follow but may not always be the best tactics.

However this sequence should be chosen unless other reasons prevail. That is often so, as the following considerations show.

Generally, the first witness called should be a good one, who can, preferably, tell the whole story, and withstand cross-examination. The main contentions should be put to him as early as possible. The first impression, when attention is at its peak, may persist, and support later evidence which would build on this foundation.

What the opponent selects for cross-examination of a witness who speaks to the main facts will reveal any vulnerable areas, as a guide to the further evidence which will be led.

It is also desirable to call a good witness last. The final impression is likely to be persuasive. If it is favourable, this is likely to endure into the crucial consideration of the verdict.

It is best if the last witness, also, knows the whole story, so that he can draw the threads together, and can correct weaknesses which have emerged. To end with a weak witness, whose evidence is damaged in cross-examination, could be extremely harmful to the case.

Witnesses who are weak because of personal inadequacy, or difficulties in their evidence, should not be called first or last, unless this cannot be helped. Weak witnesses should be interposed between strong witnesses.

Within the evidence of any particular witness, each topic should be taken in turn, usually in a chronological order, and exhausted before proceeding to the next topic.

C Anxious witnesses

Even truthful witnesses may be tense if they are naturally anxious, or fear to give evidence. Although they are rarely tongue-tied, anxious witnesses may be inaudible or excited, or apt not to answer questions properly, or to have lapses of memory. This may worsen as the evidence proceeds.

An anxious demeanour may be mistaken for a sign of lying in an honest witness, and he may be more vulnerable to cross-examination.

There may be little that an advocate can do about anxiety which has some substantial cause, other than not to make it worse. But it will improve the evidence, if he can relax the witness by means of tact, his tone of voice and manner, and suitable questions.

Instead of leading in introductory questions, as he could do, the advocate might ask non-leading questions about the witness's personal details and connection with the facts.

Making positive statements, instead of just replying 'Yes' or 'No', accustoms the witness to answering questions and to the sound of his own voice.

Sensitive topics should be approached gradually, letting the witness see the objective and giving him plenty of time to answer. If a witness's memory is blocked, the topic should be left until later, when he is more relaxed. If it is then approached gradually, the material may be recalled naturally, by association of ideas.

D   Unfavourable witnesses

If advocates obtain incomplete, unexpected, unfavourable or even harmful evidence from their witnesses, they should show no reaction which could influence the court's judgment.

Incomplete evidence about known facts may simply be due to lapse of memory, and may be overcome in the way previously described. Surprising deviations from written statements may also arise from this cause. But they may create inconsistencies between witnesses and liability to cross-examination. To forestall this, an advocate may seek admissions of possible error from his own witnesses.

The lines of questioning might stress the agreement of these witnesses on essentials, rather than their differences on secondary matters.

If an advocate's witnesses do give the expected evidence, but they exaggerate it so it becomes vulnerable to cross-examination, the aim would be to moderate it and extract concessions in favour of the cross-examiner which he would be likely to obtain anyway. On the other hand, if the evidence has been unduly weakened, it should be reinforced.

Even when unexpected and unfavourable evidence is given, the general rule is that a party cannot cross-examine his own witness, or put previous inconsistent statements to him, although he may call contradictory evidence.

But if this unexpected deviation is shown to arise from animosity towards the party who called him, or reluctance to tell the truth or an intention to testify unfairly, the advocate may be allowed by the court to treat his witness as hostile.

If this is allowed, he could then cross-examine the witness, ask leading questions, and put previous inconsistent statements to him apart from calling contradictory evidence.

If there are any initial signs that the witness may be hostile, it is best to elicit this as soon as possible, so that such an application may be made to the court. Even if it is not granted, the witness may be discredited by disclosure of his motivation.

III   QUESTIONS

Knowledge of the rules of evidence concerning questions in examination-in-chief is assumed.

In this procedure, the focus of attention should be on the witness and his evidence, not on the advocate. In the interest of spontaneity, and smooth continuity, the advocate should, so far as he can, examine from his memory of the essentials and not from the witness's statement.

A   Leading questions

In examination-in-chief the general rule prohibits leading questions, namely those stated in a form which suggests the answer. Such questions may influence witnesses or appear to do so. Even if the answer might have been the same, in response to non-leading questions the advocate seems to be the source of the evidence.

Questions may, of course, be suggestive in a subtle way, without coming into the leading category. But if they overstep the boundary, objection should be taken.

Regardless of the form of question, suggestion is inherent in some court procedures, eg dock identification or the identification of exhibits in court.

It is not a leading question to direct a witness's attention to a disputed topic. To ask him to choose between one of two alternatives, may not be leading, if the context is neutral. For example, to ask a witness if he admits or denies the terms of an alleged conversation assumes that he heard it—which may or may not be disputed.

The exclusion of leading questions only applies to evidence about facts which are in dispute. Therefore, exceptions to the rule include the following: the witness's personal details; how he became involved as a witness; introductory and preliminary matters not directly connected with the issues; topics where advocates agree to, or at least, do not object to, leading; dealing with facts proved by other evidence. Another exception arises where an advocate is allowed to question his own witness as hostile.

In practice, leading can be efficient and can save a great deal of court time in evidence-in-chief, without unfairness or causing prejudice to either side. It goes on every day, as a matter of course, so that the disputed point can be reached as rapidly as possible. As the real issues emerge and become more specific, the scope for leading on undisputed matters usually increases.

Objection should be taken to improper leading at once; even if the question is excluded and is not answered, it may be harmful by suggesting the answer to a witness, and the desired facts to a jury. If, however, an answer is given before objection was taken and sustained, it may have less weight.

Advocates should not take objection to questions as leading, without justification, merely for tactical reasons, eg to interrrupt a harmful line of evidence, or to harass the witness. This would invite judicial reprimand.

It is common for an advocate to allow his opponent to lead his witness, even where he would be entitled to object. The reasons for this include the following. It may seem to be obvious that the desired answer is inevitable, however the question is framed.

He may hope that if the evidence is elicited by leading, it may seem as if the witness had been coached, and be weakened in effect.

He may wish to avoid giving the impression to the jury that the evidence is important, or that he has something to hide.

A typical motive is that advocates who wish to have freedom to lead themselves, may tolerate it in their opponents.

Apart from the rules of evidence, there may be tactical advantages in not asking leading questions even where they would be allowed.

Evidence which appears to be given freely may have more weight. If it is obtained by leading, doubt may arise about whether it would have been given otherwise.

Leading emphasises the partiality of evidence, since the advocate, not the witness, seems to be its source.

Leading may confine answers to a formal 'Yes' or 'No', or equivalent words of agreement or dissent. If so, this may strip the witness of spontaneity or character, and may deprive his evidence of substance. It would eliminate some of the material which is the basis for forming trust in the witness in questions of reliability or credibility. He may remain a cipher.

On the other hand, even if evidence is obtained by leading, the court may still form the impression that the witness is honest, and would not give that evidence if he thought it was inaccurate.

Leading questions suggest the desired answers by being too specific about them, like this:

Q: 'Did the accused come into the pub around 9 pm?'
A: 'Yes, he did.'

This can be avoided by taking a step back from the expected answer, and, omitting any reference to it, by putting the questions in a generalised and more open form. Inevitably this will take much more time, as the following example shows:

Q: 'Did anyone come into the pub after you got there?'
A: 'Yes, several people came in.'
Q: 'Did you notice anyone in particular?'
A: 'Yes, Mr Butler, the defendant, came in.'
Q: 'About what time was that?'
A: 'It was around 9 o'clock.'
Q: 'Are you sure that it was Mr Butler?'
A: 'It certainly was. I know him very well.'

B Controlled questioning

A witness may be examined under strict control, or allowed to tell his story freely, or else both methods could be combined.

In practice, the controlled method is employed in examination-in-chief, with few exceptions.

It should be noted that while controlled questioning does dictate the subject of enquiry and how it progresses, it does not involve leading. It does not suggest any answers, although the evidence is controlled by selection and editing.

The witness is taken through his evidence by tightly framed questions, in small steps, and in an orderly and deliberate way, to ensure that all material facts are covered, and to avoid inadmissible, irrelevant, harmful or prejudicial evidence.

There are ethical limits to this editing of evidence for persuasive reasons, by selection, omission, and subtle moulding. The Crown must disclose facts material to the defence. The defence must not knowingly mislead the court by giving an impression which is not based on, or contrary to, their information, eg by knowingly asserting non-existent facts, or denying real facts.

It should depend on the witness and the nature of the evidence expected from him whether controlled questioning will be best, but advocates invariably adopt this approach in examining their own witnesses.

They prefer it where the evidence is important, where caution is advisable, or where the witness might be unable to sustain an account of the facts without detailed prompting.

Experts generally dislike this mode of questioning. They see themselves as impartial witnesses, with expertise on which the court depends, and who can be trusted to give an objective view of facts which are not understood by lay persons. Hence, they do not welcome inhibition or control in any direction, and they may feel that they have not been allowed to express their opinions freely.

Experienced advocates may meet this problem by allowing more freedom to expert witnesses. This may be done where they expect their evidence to be favourable, on the basis of a written report, produced in evidence, to which the witness is likely to conform. Hence, the questions may be quite open:

Q: 'What were your findings, Doctor?'

Controlled questioning tends to make the evidence more complete because the witness stretches his memory, in compliance with the pressure on him. Studies suggest that, in marginal areas of recollection, this may reduce accuracy.

For reasons already stated in regard to leading questions, too much control in questioning may diminish a court's confidence in stark, impoverished, forms of testimony, which are devoid of realistic factual detail or personal involvement. Eliciting evidence in this way offers less material for evaluating the reliability or credibility of the testimony.

C   Free narrative

Evidence-in-chief may consist of a free narrative in which the witness tells all or part of his story in his own words, with few questions. The scope for this is usually limited by the typical caution of advocates It may begin with a simple request:

Q: 'Please tell the jury in your own words, what you saw when you looked out of the window.'

The aim is for the story to be told naturally, spontaneously and conversationally, so that the event which is reconstructed by animated evidence, can be imagined vividly, thus enhancing trust in the witness.

If evidence-in-chief is genuine, this is often the most convincing way to present it. It eliminates the impression of coaching given by stilted 'Yes', 'No' or other short answers to controlled questions.

Very few non-suggestive and preliminary questions are needed to guide the witness's attention to what is to be reported. After he has told his story, it could be very impressive to ask no further questions, but it is usually necessary to deal with omitted points or explain something. If so, the fewer the questions the better.

The advocate does not abandon control. It is always necessary that he should be alert and that he should take over if the witness strays from the desired path. He must be ready to intervene with a corrective question at once if something inadmissible, irrelevant, damaging, prejudicial or otherwise undesirable is said or may be said, or if the witness starts to ramble or become garrulous.

But the less this control appears to be exercised, the better.

Whether to elicit testimony freely partly depends on the witness. Those who seem to be honest, confident, intelligent, likely to be at home with the jury, and unlikely to stray into undesirable areas, would be suitable. Witnesses without such qualities may present risks.

However, allowing evidence to be given freely is seldom free of the danger of harmful disclosures, eg if a Crown witness revealed an accused's previous conviction or a defence witness gave away some incriminating fact. This is why it is relatively uncommon as a technique of questioning in criminal trials.

Sometimes, if an area of evidence and a witness are thought to be safe, and suitable for this, free narrative may be combined with controlled questioning. The witness may at first tell his story freely and then, by controlled questioning, gaps could be filled, obscure points could be explained, and apparent inconsistencies could be reconciled.

Studies suggest that where a witness is not controlled and pressed to or beyond the limits of his recollection, his evidence may be less complete but more accurate.

D Purpose of question

If the examination-in-chief has been properly prepared, there can be no reason for aimless enquiries. An advocate should not be in the position of asking his own witness any question without a clear purpose which is based on his preparation and furthers his theory of the case.

Naturally, an unforeseen but promising point may sometimes be followed up to see where it leads despite the standard advice in the next section.

E Answer known

A generally accepted maxim of advocacy is never to ask a question to which the answer cannot be reasonably foreseen. The concern is that some unexpected harmful evidence may emerge.

This is a sound rule. An advocate may sometimes have to depart from it in cross-examination, but normally, he should not have to do so in examining his own witness. He should be guided by his knowledge of what his witness will say, although he can never be absolutely sure of this unless the witness has memorised his statement.

Of course unpredictable developments may occur. A witness may depart from his previous statement because he has forgotten what it was. He may have turned against the party who called him, so that he gives adverse evidence, or even qualifies as a hostile witness. In such cases, the advocate, though intending to follow the above maxim, might at first receive unexpected answers.

Again, if the opponent raised some quite new topic in cross-examining an earlier witness, the advocate may feel bound to explore it with his later witness, although he is uncertain of the kind of evidence which he may give.

Generally, the maxim is good, but few rules apply in all the circumstances which an advocate may encounter.

F   Rate of questioning

In examination-in-chief, the questioning should generally be deliberate and unhurried. The pace may be varied for effect. It may be slowed down, so that the evidence is elicited by small steps, to facilitate the court's assimilation of complex facts, or accelerated to convey an impression of the swiftness of an incident.

G   One point

Questions should cover only one point at a time. In isolation, compound or double questions, such as the following one, assume certain facts, eg that the person shouted from the window:

Q: 'What did he shout from the window?'

This really involves other evidence like this.

Q: 'Did he do anything?'
A: 'He shouted from the window.'
Q: 'What did he shout?'

So double questions should not be asked unless the assumed fact has already been established.

H   Brevity

The whole examination-in-chief, lines of enquiry, and questions should be as brief as possible. Short open-ended questions have a role in examination-in-chief:

Q: 'What happened then?'

Archaic circumlocutions and useless verbiage as shown in this example, should be avoided.

> Q: 'Now, Mrs Lawrence would you please cast your mind back, if you will, to the night of the first of June?'

I Clarity

Questions should be clear, direct and precise. Major evils are circumlocution, verbosity and pomposity. If the witness only answers 'Yes' or 'No' to a confusing form of question, this confusion becomes part of his evidence.

The meaning of anything in doubt should be clarified at once.

J Simplicity

Simplicity is the aim, although some facts are complicated. Questions should be framed in plain language. Complex facts should be broken up into simple ones and approached by small steps. The main outlines should be prominent and unobscured by unnecessary detail. Often facts may be simplified by expressing them in visual or concrete ways, avoiding abstractions.

K Detail

Judgment is always needed about how much detail to include. Only the essentials of a case, so far as necessary, need be proved—not every fact. The evidence should give enough information for the main facts to be clear and convincing. Adding details may be unproductive and sometimes creates inconsistencies and openings for cross-examination.

L Comment on answers

Once an answer has been given, an advocate can only ask further questions. He should never comment on answers at the stage of questioning a witness. It is objectionable to repeat an answer in different words, or in a tone of voice, which insinuate a meaning unintended by the witness.

An answer should not be repeated without a good reason, eg to emphasise it.

An answer might reasonably repeated as an introduction to a new question:

> A: 'He said "Give me the car keys".'
> Q: 'When he said "Give me the car keys", what did you do?'

IV ANTICIPATING CROSS-EXAMINATION

Examination-in-chief has been discussed as a way of presenting a positive case. But since this case will be challenged in cross-examination, it should be protected against this in advance, by anticipating the criticisms and reinforcing the evidence where necessary. In this context, to 'anticipate' means both to foresee, and to forestall, lines of cross-examination.

A Disclosure of weaknesses

Most cases have some weaknesses. A common dilemma is whether to face up to, and deal with, them in evidence-in-chief, or to risk their being raised in cross-examination, with the hope of repairing any damage in re-examination.

This is a separate question from where and how to fortify the evidence against cross-examination. This can be done at vulnerable points, without necessarily disclosing the weaknesses by doing so.

It is assumed that advocates will comply with their legal and ethical duties. A prosecutor must disclose any material facts which may help the defence, and the defence must not knowingly mislead the court.

The subject of disclosure can therefore be discussed solely as a question of the best tactics.

Tactics obviously depend on the nature of the case and the evidence, which may be infinitely variable. But in general terms, the following are the arguments for and against confronting difficulties in examination-in-chief.

1 *Advantages of disclosure*

To raise difficulties in the evidence-in-chief has the following advantages.

(a) *Candour.* To have one's witness admit a point in favour of the opponent's case creates a helpful impression of candour which applies to both the witness and the advocate.

Dogmatic evidence, which goes in only one direction, may be counter-productive, especially if contrary facts are, or become, obvious.

If adverse facts are not admitted, or are denied without good reason, and emerge later, confidence in the witness and in the advocate may be lost.

If this occurs in one part of a case, it may taint other parts.

(b) *Emergence of difficulties.* It is unsafe to lead evidence on the assumption that a competent advocate on the other side will not see its difficulties.

(c) *Effective presentation.* A topic can be dealt with more fully and favourably in examination-in-chief than in re-examination which is limited to what arises directly from cross-examination.

(d) *Preparing witness.* Questioning one's own witness on a matter about which he will face a challenge can, in effect, prepare him for cross-examination on the subject. He can derive guidance from this, as well as the benefit of rehearsal.

(e) *Reducing impact.* To introduce a topic in evidence-in-chief can take the wind out of the cross-examiner's sails. He will be in the weakened position of repeating questions which have already been answered by evidence which is unfavourable to him. His cross-examination may lack force and may seem to be pointless.

The more thoroughly the topic is covered in examination-in-chief, the more this will be so.

2   Disadvantages of disclosure

Revealing problems in the evidence-in-chief has fewer disadvantages, but there may be some.

(a) *Forcefulness.* Where possible, evidence-in-chief should be positive and persuasive, leaving criticisms and negative aspects to the adversary.

(b) *Suggesting challenge.* It is imprudent to put ideas into the head of an opponent who may not see the difficulty. Informal discussions between advocates, which often take place in court, may give a clue about whether the weakness is seen.

(c) *Inadmissibility of challenge.* The opponent may attempt to cross-examine in some inadmissible way to which objection can be taken, unless that line of evidence has already been raised in examination-in-chief.

(d) *Adding weight to challenge.* To put an opponent's contention to one's witness may suggest that it is to be taken seriously, and may give credence to something unreasonable. It may be better to leave the cross-examiner with the embarrassment of introducing some improbable challenges, eg an absurd attack on police witnesses.

3 Conclusions

Successful examination-in-chief presents a case clearly and convincingly, and weakens or destroys the cross-examination in advance.

It is submitted that unless substantial disadvantages are foreseen, on balance it is generally better to disclose difficulties in examination-in-chief and to meet them head-on, before the witness is cross-examined.

But it is best not to raise the problems until a firm foundation for one's case has been laid.

Once this has been done, a suitable time for raising difficulties may be in the middle of the evidence of a strong witness, who can counteract any harmful impression.

However it would be poor tactics to omit the topic from the evidence of one witness who could have spoken to it, and then to raise it later in the evidence of another witness. This might seem like an afterthought rather than candour.

There is one type of situation where evidence might be withheld in examination-in-chief, not because it refers to a weakness, but because it involves a strength. This would be done in order to set a trap for a cross-examiner who is sure to raise the topic. When he does so, he will be confronted with unexpectedly adverse evidence and this may have a considerable impact. Moreover the first advocate will be able to re-examine his own witness on the topic, as it arose out of cross-examination.

However this device may be frustrated if the opponent does not cross-examine on the topic. Then the benefit of the strong evidence will be completely lost to the advocate who called the witness. These tactics, therefore, should only be used with care in situations which are suitable for them, and where cross-examination on the topic can be foreseen with certainty.

B   Reinforcing evidence

Whether or not weaknesses are disclosed in evidence-in-chief, it should be fortified, where possible, to frustrate both constructive cross-examination seeking positive evidence, and destructive cross-examination.

The kind of reinforcement against a challenge, which is required, will depend on whether the reliability or the credibility of the evidence of one's witness will be attacked.

This can often be known or predicted, arising from pre-trial procedure or earlier cross-examination. In either case, the aim is to deprive the cross-examination of any force. This reinforcement can be valuable.

Prosecution evidence-in-chief about the crime or the accused's implication in it may need to be strengthened against attacks on the reliability or credibility of Crown evidence. Defence evidence-in-chief, again, may require reinforcement in regard to the same issue, but usually against an attack on credibility alone. This would be the typical situation.

1 *Reliability*

As was seen, either external facts or mental processes can cause errors in observation or memory.

(a) *Observation.* If the accuracy of observation is going to be attacked, external facts offer better support than mental processes.

Both the advocate who leads evidence and the cross-examiner are likely to have similar difficulties with intangible factors, eg the effects of stress, distraction, or expectations.

Trust in the witness and his assertions will, of course, count as well, but inferences from objective circumstances count for a great deal.

In seeking to support the accuracy and reliability of evidence which will be challenged, an advocate should fortify it wherever possible, with objective and concrete evidence.

As an illustration, a cross-examiner may suggest to a witness that, as he was driving a car in lashing rain, and at high closing speed, he has wrongly identified the accused as the driver of an oncoming car. Such facts are easily visualised and are acceptable. Motorists in the jury will understand the situation.

However, in anticipation of this challenge, the identification might be supported by contradictory objective evidence. This might be to the effect that the rain had stopped, that the cars were going slowly, that powerful headlights shone on the driver's face, and that the witness had known the accused since they were at school together.

To support the accuracy of observation in such ways, preparation of evidence should assemble any helpful objective data, eg lighting, distances, times, weather, amount drunk and so on.

Where practicable, the accuracy of observation should be supported by such evidence as visual aids or exhibits, plans, diagrams, measurements of distances, precise oral testimony, documents, evidence of the location or absence of obstructions, photographs of layouts, the number and location of street lamps, weather reports, or medical reports on injured witnesses.

In practice, the value of providing such supporting evidence is not sufficiently realised, as occurs in so many trials, where assertions and counter-assertions compete for approval.

Notwithstanding the desirability of supporting accuracy of observation by objective data, the warning may be repeated that witnesses should not be asked in examination-in-chief for exact figures or details, unless they can state them correctly and consistently; otherwise this simply exposes them to cross-examination as inconsistent.

(b) *Memory.* Challenges to the accuracy or reliability of evidence about adverse facts may frequently be foreseen, on the ground that the witness had forgotten facts or that his recollection had been influenced in some way. To counteract this, in advance, that evidence might be supported by any objective material which is available.

Although time plays a part in forgetting, accuracy of memory cannot be proved or disproved merely by the duration of any given period of delay. But it may help if a witness can specify any important time intervals precisely, eg when he was first asked to point out the suspect or direct his attention to the facts, when this was repeated, and when he gave the police a statement.

Notes which police officers made at the time of, or shortly after, an event may offer strong support for the accuracy of recall unless they are attacked as invented.

How external suggestion, or a witness's internal mental processes, may have affected his memory, are beyond direct enquiry, but related facts and circumstances may generate inferences which confirm that facts have been properly recalled.

An advocate might have his witness admit that he discussed his evidence with other witnesses, where this was inevitable, in order to overcome the usual reluctance to admit this, which the opponent might exploit in cross-examination.

(c) *Trust in witnesses.* Despite the emphasis, so far, on supporting the accuracy or reliability of evidence liable to challenge with objective material, it is not always available. Often, it is a question of accepting or rejecting a witness's assurances about the accuracy of his evidence. In effect, he assesses the quality of the evidence himself and, if the court decides to trust him, it relies on that self-assessment. If so, this would supersede any doubts caused by various impediments to observation and recall. It is therefore essential to create and maintain the court's trust in the witness, as a bulwark against possible attacks in cross-examination.

To do this, the advocate should try to show that the witness is fair, reasonable, and unbiased. This should be kept in mind in eliciting evidence which is likely to be challenged. It should be taken firmly, but reasonably. Obvious points which favour the opponent should be freely conceded.

2   Credibility

In areas where evidence is susceptible to attack in cross-examination as untruthful, steps should be taken to strengthen it. The factors on which credibility depends were discussed in the previous chapter. A few salient points have been selected here for emphasis.

(a)   *Previous convictions.*   It was seen that the scope of attacks on character is limited by law and by the court situation. Where such attacks are allowed, and made, it is usually on the ground of the witness's previous convictions. If they are known to the opponent, who is likely to bring them out, the tactical problem is how to reduce their impact—especially if they are substantial.

Leaving it to the cross-examiner to bring out the previous convictions involves risks that the examination-in-chief may seem deceptive, and that the convictions will be revealed in a way which worsens their effect.

An advocate normally tenders his witness as creditworthy. Failure to disclose his previous convictions may seem like a damaging lack of candour.

A witness may be unsure about the cross-examiner's knowledge of his criminal record or be embarrassed about it. He may disclose his convictions reluctantly and evasively. There are ways of cross-examining skilfully which could convert this into a transparent attempt to deceive the court in the current trial. This could be more destructive of the witness's credibility than the previous convictions themselves.

But if an advocate brings out the previous convictions of his own witness, he eliminates these dangers. The advocate has been frank, and a good impression of the witness may have been formed.

But in addition the advocate can present these convictions in the most favourable light, which the cross-examiner would not have done, eg as youthful folly which did no great harm, and which happened a long time ago, since when the witness has married, started a family, obtained employment, and has become a model citizen.

If an advocate discloses the previous convictions of his witness, and handles the matter properly, the cross-examiner may be left with little basis for attacking that witness's character and his persistence in this may be counter-productive.

Cross-examination on the matter of previous convictions may then seem to be unnecessary and unfair, and to be a mere attempt to create prejudice against the witness, by insisting on questions which had already been asked and answered.

(b)   *Motivation.*   A witness who is not independent may be exposed to challenge in cross-examination on the ground that his motivation has led him to lie.

The advocate who called him may anticipate this by disclosing the witness's interest, by eliciting his evidence in a convincing way and, sometimes, by asking him to confirm that he is telling the truth.

It is better to disclose the witness's interest in examination-in-chief, if it is not obvious, but is likely to be raised by the cross-examiner. However, it should be done incidentally, and as a matter of course, without creating an impression that his interest has any sinister significance.

The witness should be encouraged to give his evidence in such a way that it does not seem to be motivated. It should be seen to be realistic, in the sense discussed in the previous chapter.

Excesses and exaggerations should be toned down and balance and moderation should be maintained in the evidence to eliminate any impression that it is motivated.

Sometimes an advocate will ask his own witness if, despite his interest in the case, he is telling the truth, in the hope that the sincerity of the reply will be persuasive.

To have this effect, the question should relate to the present trial. The witness should not be invited to claim permanent veracity.

It is doubtful, in any event, whether such assertions count for a great deal.

(c) *Demeanour.* In the previous chapter, a critical view of demeanour as a method of lie-detection was stated but this view might not be accepted universally. Any court is free to attach what weight it thinks fit to a witness's demeanour in a particular trial. Advocates should therefore do what they can so that their witnesses' demeanour will be convincing if the cross-examiner accuses them of lying.

An advocate cannot control his witness's demeanour but he can try to make him relax so that his bearing suggests sincerity to a tribunal who may regard this as significant.

An advocate can help a tense witness to relax by a reassuring manner and tone of voice, and by the content of his questions.

If a sincere but tense witness can be induced to relax, spontaneous and natural forms of expression and realistic elements, as discussed in the previous chapter, may emerge and have some weight.

This may help but of course there can be no guarantee that anxiety may not, after all, persist and create a bad impression of the testimony. An advocate should, of course, be ready to object to any lack of consideration by a cross-examiner, or if his witness becomes unduly distressed.

(d) *Inconsistency.* It is to be expected that a witness will be cross-examined about any inconsistency in his own evidence-in-chief, or any inconstency which arises on comparing the evidence of more than one witness called by the same party.

This should certainly be corrected so far as it can be. The consequences of not doing so could be serious; inconsistency which suggests lying could taint the whole of a witness's evidence about disputed matters.

The best remedy, where this is possible, is to reconcile the two alternatives, by some explanation which shows that they were not really inconsistent at all.

If this cannot be done, the witness would have to elect between one alternative and the other. However, it would still be necessary to explain how the inconsistency arose, eg as the result of misunderstanding, uncertainty or mistake.

Whether the inconsistency has already done any damage or not may depend on the extent to which explanations are accepted. Some harmful effect may remain, but this is at least better than leaving the raw inconsistency for the cross-examiner to exploit. It is certainly better to face up to the problem in the examination-in chief.

Where inconsistency arises on comparing the evidence of two or more witnesses for a party, it may range from minor discrepancies to conflicts about material points.

Minor discrepancies arising from the common fallibility of observation and memory mean little or nothing as signs of lying, although their importance is often exaggerated in cross-examination and in speeches by inexperienced advocates.

Typically, one advocate's argument that the differences between witnesses indicate lying is met by the argument that they mean the opposite, since lying witnesses would have made up a uniform story. Assessment would depend on the circumstances—not on either proposition alone.

If an advocate notes that his witness differs from one of his earlier witnesses, on a point which he regards as minor, he may either ignore the variation or else seek a concession that the current witness may be mistaken, if that might be so.

It would be more serious if the differences between two or more witnesses on the same side were material; this might create a risk that any of them may be taken to be lying, or that none of them will be trusted. Important variations in the evidence of Crown witnesses about essentials, may result in an acquittal because of the standard of proof required for conviction.

To forestall the inevitable cross-examination where witnesses for a party give conflicting evidence can be difficult, since the earlier witnesses have already testified and been cross-examined. They are out of reach. Such defects should have been dealt with at the time.

With current witnesses, who differ from his earlier witnesses, the advocate's options are limited.

He cannot lead his witness in the desired direction. He can only ask him about facts, and should not give him information about what his earlier witnesses said.

Even if he manages to extract a concession from his current witness that he may be mistaken, or if he can bring him to alter his evidence to conform to what his earlier witnesses said, this would be adverse to credibility, and would itself invite cross-examination on the ground of self-contradiction.

Once serious inconsistency emerges from the comparison of the evidence of several witnesses for a party, the final argument may offer the only hope of meeting it effectively.

The position would be rather different if, with the court's permission, the current witness could be treated as hostile, so that leading questions could be put to him, and he could be challenged about the inconsistency directly, or about previous inconsistent statements. This, of course, would become the cross-examination of that witness, rather than an anticipation of cross-examination.

(e) *Improbability.*   If evidence-in-chief contains something which is so improbable as to be virtually impossible, it may be treated like self-contradiction, ie by guiding the witness to the topic and giving him a chance to explain or modify his evidence spontaneously.

If he is cross-examined about this later, he will, at least, be prepared for it. If such a difficulty is not tackled beforehand, in the examination-in-chief, a cross-examiner might exploit it in a damaging way.

An advocate can usually foresee which parts of his evidence-in-chief will be challenged as improbable, and which should therefore be reinforced against cross-examination.

Since improbability is a matter of degree, he will try to reduce it, whereas the cross examiner will try to increase it. In either case, the story wiil be probed, and expanded by adding circumstantial details and surrounding facts, in order to colour it in the direction of being more or less likely.

This is what an advocate should do with his own witness, by foreseeing the directions which cross-examination will take.

The advocate should build up the story, providing explanation of any odd points, until it seems reasonable and likely to be true.

(f) *Realism.*   As was seen, the realism and 'ring of truth' of evidence are related to its richness of factual detail, and inclusion of the witness's personal reactions to events. Lack of these realistic qualities is not so much a specific danger which may expose the evidence to cross-examination and which must be dealt with in advance. It is rather a matter of poor presentation, viz the evidence will be less persuasive than it might be.

However, as a measure to be taken to strengthen his case generally, an advocate should be aware of these factors in the evaluation of evidence, and should allow them to permeate his examination-in-chief.

By allowing honest witnesses to testify freely with minimal control, where practicable, factual detail and the witnesses' personal involvement are more likely to be included spontaneously, thus adding to the persuasive effect of the evidence.

Evidence which is dogmatic, over-purposive, and over-directional, may seem to be false.

This is particularly so, in a situation where some deviations or elements of uncertainty might have been expected.

This situation should be distinguished from another, where the evidence consists of a firm report of a definite incident seen under good conditions of observation,

Such good evidence does not fall into the unrealistic, over-purposive category, for which the explanation is falsehood and invention. In the latter type, such evidence should be toned down and the one sidedness and exaggeration should be corrected. It is better to do this than to leave to a skilful cross-examiner the opportunity of exposing evidence as being unrealistic and unreasonable.

(g) *Contradiction.* One party's main witnesses normally contradict the other party's main witnesses on the essential issues. This takes the form of different versions of a connected story, although some may only be able to speak to parts of it.

In examining his principal witnesses, an advocate should anticipate that his opponent, in cross-examination, will put his case to them on facts which they know.

The advocate can offset this, to some extent, by putting his opponent's case to his own witnesses. He should do this in some way which tends to weaken the challenge.

He also has the opportunity of developing whatever answers they may give, which he would lose if he did not anticipate the cross-examination. This is a valuable way of forestalling the opponent.

CHAPTER 6

Cross-examination: foundations

I PREPARATION

A   Time required

At the earliest stage of preparing for the trial, an advocate should formulate his overall theory of the case and plan the strategy by which he will present it. These are separate but related processes.

Ample time should be allowed for this. Everyone involved in creative activities knows that once the essentials have been grasped and worked on consciously and intensively, unconscious cerebration over a period of time can make a very real contribution to a task.

This occurs during sleep, leisure or while attention is given to other tasks. This mental work is part of the brain's integrative function, and is indispensable for simplifying and organising complex material.

A period of time is necessary to allow an overview of a case to mature. It provides opportunities for revision, as new aspects develop. It also promotes assimilation and mastery of unfamiliar material.

Although sufficient time is required for all this, in practice it is often limited by the nature of an advocate's profession. Advocates may have excessive workloads, or they may receive late or even last-minute instructions which they must accept. If they try to accelerate the above processes, their efficiency may suffer. Fortunately, this may be offset by an experienced advocate's familiarity with patterns which recur in many trials.

B Theory of case

An advocate's theory of the case is his total and integrated view of all the facts, and the law which applies to them, in conformity with his objective.

Undisputed facts present no problem, whether or not they are agreed expressly or formally or lack of opposition is simply foreseen. If the defence contend that the accused was not the offender, the commission of the crime is unlikely to be an issue. But if the crime is contested, identity is unlikely to be disputed.

This follows from the analysis in chapter 2, 'The anatomy of a criminal trial'.

The disputed facts for consideration at this stage consist of the parties' respective contentions based on their supporting evidence.

This may have been disclosed by opponents, formally or informally, or obtained directly from the advocate's own enquiries. It is in this area that cross-examination will be planned.

The theory of the case will also cover any disputed points of law which may arise, such as the admissibility of evidence, a submission of no case to answer, or the application of the law to the facts proved.

Although an advocate's theory of his case has an adversarial aim, it should not be an exercise in one-sided propaganda. Its prospects of acceptance will depend on the extent to which it has a sound basis in fact, evidence and law, even where alternative views are possible.

C Outline of strategy

The theory of the case is an analysis, but strategy is a plan for presenting that analysis, convincingly, so that the court accepts it.

An advocate's closing speech is the final stage of a trial, at which he sums up and presents his whole case. It is therefore recommended that the strategy should be focused by means of drafting a provisional closing speech. This has two advantages.

The speech is ready for presentation whenever the trial reaches the appropriate stage. It is difficult to predict when this will be. Having the speech ready will eliminate hasty improvisation.

This speech will also be a blueprint for the advocate's conduct of the case and it will integrate all the relevant law and the facts on which his final argument will rest.

Those parts of the draft which deal with contested evidence should contain outlines of the proposed cross-examination. Summaries of the evidence elicited in this way are what will be presented to the court.

This may be illustrated in a disputed visual identification of a suspect by a police witness. Police officers receive a radio message in their van to look out for a stolen white Ford Sierra, of a specified registration number, which is suspected of having knocked down and killed a child. They see and chase the vehicle. It stops, and the driver runs off across a stubbled field in darkness, chased by an officer who fails to catch him, but who claims that he recognised the driver as the accused.

The defence advocate, in challenging the visual identification, may note such points as these:

- location of suspect at point where recognised
- lighting at that spot
- distance of witness from suspect then
- extent to which field was stubbled and needed care in running by suspect and witness
- number of times suspect looked over shoulder
- distance from suspect increasing or decreasing
- why suspect was lost unless far away
- previous familiarity with suspect, but omitting prejudicial material, eg convictions.

Each of these eight points could be a focus for cross-examination in which the identification is challenged as mistaken or untruthful. Allowing for individual variations in note-taking, each point would only require one or two words to call it to mind.

This outline of strategy would include a list of the witnesses to be cross-examined, the proposed topics and tactics, and related matters.

Naturally, this will be subject to variation in the trial, according to what witnesses actually say, how they say it, and the context at the time. In the above illustration, the cross-examiner would have to decide whether to treat the police identification as an honest mistake, or a deliberate lie and he would modify his tactics accordingly. He would decide this in the light of the officer's testimony, which might suggest one or other alternative.

The outline would be in the form of bold headings, sub-headings, and any crucial details. It should cover all important points, but must be flexible to allow for suitable questions to be improvised, in response to the unpredictable form and content of the evidence which will actually be given.

The draft should certainly not contain verbatim lists of intended questions or detailed notes. Instead of being a help, preoccupation with notes could be a real handicap by interfering with the necessary alertness to the witness, and to the evidence and its nuances as it emerges.

This could impede the ability to make swift tactical decisions, and may suggest inexperience and lack of confidence. In advocacy, thinking on one's feet is essential. The plan for cross-examination is only an overall guide. It is a map, but not the territory. To omit such preparation would be less than professional. But even thorough preparation cannot replace good practical judgment in the actual trial. They should be combined for maximum effect.

II STRATEGY

A Deciding to cross-examine: objectives

Like surgery, cross-examination is often of crucial importance, but neither technique should be used indiscriminately.

It is a fundamental principle never to cross-examine without a clear and definite purpose. Skilful advocates only cross-examine when they must. When they do rise to their feet, the effect of their cross-examinations is enhanced by the expectancy that they will be significant.

Inexperienced advocates often ignore this principle with resulting damage to their cases.

Much of an advocate's skill consists of knowing when not to do something, where inaction is the more effective option. This negative form of skill is really an expression of purpose and control. It should pervade everything in cross-examination, eg keeping it as brief as possible, and stopping whenever the aim is attained.

Aimless cross-examination wastes time, gains nothing, invites criticism, suggests the absence of a real case, emphasises challenged evidence, elicits harmful testimony, dilutes any gain achieved, or creates new rights to re-examine.

Such effects, by themselves, or in combination, may be seriously damaging or fatal.

The commonest type of futile cross-examination consists of going over the evidence-in-chief aimlessly or, perhaps, with a vague hope that some defect will emerge or that it will be changed somehow in going over it again. An aggravation is to delve into pointless detail.

This is not cross-examination in any meaningful sense; it only qualifies as such in the procedural sense of questioning another party's witness.

The probable effect of doing this is to emphasise the harmful aspects of the evidence-in-chief in various ways.

These include repetition giving the witness a second chance to assert the unhelpful evidence more firmly, and allowing him to add supporting detail.

This can convert even relatively harmless evidence into a real difficulty. It would be hard to imagine any greater fault in cross-examination than to achieve precisely the opposite effect to that which is intended.

Such aimless questioning is not converted into anything significant by suggesting finally that the witness is either lying or mistaken, where no foundation was laid for this. The witness will simply deny such suggestions of inaccuracy. Little more can be expected.

Confronted with such a feeble challenge, it would be a very shaky perjurer whose facade disintegrated, or a very timid witness who conceded that he was mistaken.

However, it is a quite different, and possibly worthwhile, technique for a cross-examiner to ask a witness to repeat his evidence-in-chief in the expectation that he will do so in nearly identical terms, which will show that it is memorised.

An advocate should not cross-examine if he cannot foresee any significant and helpful result.

It is not justified if, at best, it will achieve no more than a minor gain, eg if the evidence to be challenged is merely neutral, unhelpful, or only slightly or remotely unfavourable. It is often best to disregard trivial points, even if they are contested, in order to avoid diluting what counts.

To ignore evidence minimises its importance; cross-examining on it shows concern and emphasises it.

Cross-examination is not designed to discredit truthful evidence. If unfavourable evidence will obviously be accepted as true and accurate, it may be more effective to concede it with good grace than to challenge it or pretend that it does not exist.

Despite these reasons for not cross-examining, a party is expected to put his case to his opponent's witnesses who know the facts, partly as a legal duty and partly for tactical reasons.

Texts on the law of evidence should be consulted for the obligation in law, and the consequences of failure to comply. Sometimes an advocate who fails to challenge evidence at the time may be deemed to have accepted it, but in any event this failure may become an impediment to later forms of challenge.

The legal position may differ in trials on indictment and in summary trials.

Within the ambit of these requirements, a case may be put in ways which range from asking about one point after another, in full detail, to one global and comprehensive question, so framed as to elicit a 'Yes' or 'No' answer. Even though this answer is unwanted, it does minimal damage.

Where the rules of evidence leave the matter open, a tactical decision should be made. If the case is only put for formal purposes, the more briefly this can be done the better, viz by one comprehensive question, or as near to it as possible. This minimises the harm which an adverse witness can do. The danger of emphasising adverse evidence by cross-examining a resistant witness in detail should be avoided. It may be better for the cross-examiner to contradict him by relying on the evidence which he will lead himself.

Assuming that a decision to cross-examine has been made, what are its objectives?

The objectives of cross-examination are not laid down by law. They are tactical. Tactics may be divided into those which have a constructive purpose and those which have a destructive purpose.

The aim of constructive cross-examination is to build or strengthen one's case with positive and favourable evidence obtained from another party's witness, which supports one's evidence-in-chief.

Witnesses called by another party are not necessarily hostile, biased or unwilling to co-operate. If they are honest they may be expected to concede favourable facts where this is justified. Even if they are partisan or untruthful, the context may oblige them to admit some indisputable facts.

The techniques of constructive cross-examination are the subject of the next chapter, viz: emphasis; eliciting new meanings; eliciting new facts; and putting the alternative case.

The aim of destructive cross-examination is to weaken, and if possible to destroy, harmful evidence given by a witness (including one's own witness if the court allows this) in order to defeat the opponent's case.

To achieve the rejection of evidence led by the opponent, a cross-examiner usually has to rely on the support of evidence which he calls himself, to contradict and overcome the evidence which he is challenging.

But while cross-examination alone may not destroy the opponent's evidence, its contribution is indispensable. To confront one point of view with another in cross-examination is the heart of the adversarial process. It is an essential factor in persuasion. It is the most natural reaction to ask a witness, 'Well, what do you have to say to this?', and to evaluate the reply. Failure to challenge adverse and material evidence can be fatal. A court should not be left simply to adjudicate on competing versions of facts without putting the conflicts to appropriate witnesses.

The techniques of destructive cross-examination will be dealt with in chapter 8. The overall approaches are either to challenge the witness as a mistaken or untruthful source of evidence, or else to attack the evidence itself as inconsistent, improbable or unrealistic.

While these two main approaches of challenging the witness or the evidence are separable on analysis, this is somewhat unrealistic. In practice, one implies the other and they are normally combined, as in this illustration:

> Q: 'You agree now that there was a seven feet high wall in the yard, blocking your view. Were you not lying when you said that you saw the fight?'

B   Witnesses liable to cross-examination

The rules of evidence and procedure which govern rights of cross-examination should be known. Restrictions apply to one's own witnesses, co-defendants and their witnesses.

As a general principle, any witness called by an opponent is liable to cross-examination once he has been sworn.

This applies even if the witness does not undergo any examination-in-chief. Sometimes a Crown witness is called for the sole reason of giving the defence this opportunity.

Co-defendants may cross-examine each other and their respective witnesses, within certain limits.

As a general rule, an advocate may not cross examine or discredit his own witness although his evidence is unfavourable. He should end the process as quickly as possible, and meet the difficulty by leading other evidence to correct the unwanted evidence.

Exceptionally, on the application of an advocate, if his witness seems to be testifying unfairly and to have no intention of telling the truth, a judge may allow the advocate to treat the witness as hostile. If so, the advocate may cross-examine his own witness and may confront him with previous inconsistent statements.

C   Subjects of cross-examination

Within the bounds of the rules of evidence, a witness may be cross-examined on any subject which is relevant to the issues of fact or his credit, although it was not raised in examination-in-chief.

The issues of fact in criminal trials were analysed in chapter 2: almost always, the two main issues of whether the crime was committed or whether the defendant was the offender, are limited to the one which the defence choose to dispute, the other being proved formally.

Crimes were classified into result-crimes, conduct-crimes and object-crimes, and issues of identity were grouped into those in which the defence was that the accused was, or was not, at the locus and, if he was not, defences in which he pleaded alibi.

Cross-examination on the issues will refer to the facts involved in these forms of crime or, alternatively, in these questions of identification.

By asking about character, previous convictions, bias, previous inconsistent statements, on reasonable grounds, where imputations may materially affect credibility, cross-examination as to credit is intended to show that the witness should be disbelieved.

This differs from similar fact evidence tending to show a defendant's disposition to commit an offence of the type charged, and which is only admissible in exceptional circumstances.

The general rule excludes evidence in rebuttal of facts affecting a witness's credit which he denies in cross-examination, since this raises collateral issues. But exceptions exist. If bias, previous convictions or previous inconsistent statements are denied in cross-examination, evidence may be led to prove them.

Complex rules, which should be known, restrict rights of cross-examination as to character. A prosecutor can only attack the accused's character in the specific circumstances set out in the Criminal Evidence Act 1898.

These rules for protecting the accused, also discourage defence imputations against Crown witnesses, or attacks on co-defendants, lest an accused who has previous convictions may lose the shield provided by the Act.

To avoid this risk, cross-examination may simply suggest that testimony is mistaken or untruthful without attacking the character of the witness generally.

D   Sequence of cross-examination

Cross-examination should follow the best tactical sequence, although it ought to balance what is effective for extracting wanted evidence from witnesses and what is effective for convincing the court. No one type of sequence is always best; it depends on the context.

A chronological or logical order helps the comprehension and retention of evidence. This may be best where the advocate's approach is open and direct, eg if he is eliciting helpful and positive evidence from a co-operative witness, or is trying to have him concede that he may be mistaken. Here, the aim will be clear to the witness and to the court.

But a cross-examiner must often conceal his disbelief of a witness suspected of lying, and his intention to expose the deception. If so, he may follow an indirect tactical sequence which the court does not grasp, by asking questions whose point is not immediately obvious.

A cross-examiner should be prepared to justify his line of enquiry, if objection is taken, or the court intervenes either in the absence of the witness, or by assurances or circumlocutions which the court, but not the witness, understands, so that the purpose is not revealed and vitiated.

Where an indirect sequence is followed, in order to conceal the aim from the witness, this will be followed by a direct challenge, at the appropriate stage.

In such an indirect approach, the cross-examiner may follow an unpredictable order, perhaps with rapid questioning. He may switch unexpectedly from one topic to another, swing back and forward from crucial to secondary facts, or change the angle of approach. This can disrupt a memorised story, or interfere with attempts to improvise, leading a lying witness with no foundation of reality on which to rely into confusion and inconsistency.

A cross-examination may start boldly by attacking evidence as untruthful; the sequence is from strong to weak points. Early success may eliminate the need for later challenges. A good first impression may shake the witness and cast doubt on his later evidence.

The opening of cross-examination is significant. Often, it has maximum impact since interest is at its peak, and attention and expectancy are focused on the confrontation.

The sooner a cross-examiner puts forward an alternative version of the facts to those stated in the evidence-in-chief the better, especially if the witness is the first important one. Ideally, the first questions should state the whole issue and lay a foundation for the rest of the cross-examination.

It is therefore good to begin cross-examination as forcefully as possible, especially by challenging the evidence as untruthful on the strongest grounds available, eg manifest inconsistency or improbability, or confrontation with some strong material which contradicts it. If the witness can be taken by surprise, the impact may be even greater.

Sometimes where cross-examination must begin indirectly, in order to lead a lying witness into a trap, it may be necessary to conduct some preliminary probing in order to find the best approach. However, this should never be allowed to deteriorate into the kind of aimless repetition of the evidence-in-chief which has been described.

An obvious sequence may be followed in constructive cross-examination with the objective of eliciting helpful evidence. The cross-examiner should open his questioning reassuringly, showing trust in the witness and the appearance of simply asking for additional information.

To open tactfully is also desirable where it will be suggested that the witness is mistaken.

A neat way to open, which shows alertness, and exploits continuity, is to ask a first question which follows on directly from the last answer in evidence-in-chief, as in this example in a charge of indecency:

A: 'As I've told you, I was too afraid to tell my mother about what he did to me.'

(Evidence-in-chief ends)

(Cross-examination starts)

Q: 'Even if you were too afraid to tell your mother, why did you not tell your big sister?'

How cross-examination ends is also important. As soon as any specific objective has been attained, the cross-examination should stop altogether or an unrelated topic should be taken up at once. Cross-examination should never continue beyond the point at which everything material has been covered fully.

An advocate may be tempted to go further, in the pursuit of some perfectionist aim like improving the evidence by confirmation or emphasis or to develop a helpful theme. It is rarely beneficial to yield to this temptation. It could ruin the whole result. The risks of continuing usually outweigh the possible gains. It gives the witness a chance to qualify or retract what he said. For the opponent, it highlights the need for re-examination, leading further evidence and final argument, to meet his difficulty.

It is effective if the cross-examination of each witness can be finished by making a good and enduring impression, especially if the last answer sums up as much as possible of the cross-examiner's case in a favourable way.

A good ending would be an explicit victory over the witness such as a trap which exposes lying, inconsistency, statements contradicted by other credible evidence, or obvious improbability. If the trap is inescapable, the cross-examination may exploit it from as many angles as possible, but this may involve risks of the type which have been described.

The same caution about pressing cross-examination too far also applies to pursuing the same lines of enquiry with several witnesses.

Unless the effect of a valuable admission is reduced by re-examination or by further evidence led by the opponent, it may be unwise to endanger it by asking other witnesses the same question with a view to strengthening the favourable evidence. The possibility has to be faced that they may weaken or contradict it.

This is, of course, a different situation from the obligation to put one's case in cross-examination, to witnesses who know the relevant facts.

For obvious reasons, no sign of satisfaction should be shown when favourable evidence is obtained. This may highlight its signficance to the opponent who may then undertake remedial measures to counteract it. If the importance of the evidence can be concealed until the stage of closing speeches, it will be too late for any response based on further testimony.

One refinement of stopping with a triumph is to do so just before it occurs. Proof does not always need an explicit statement from a witness provided that the evidence is sufficient to support a desired conclusion. Not asking a witness to explain an inconsistency is an example. If given that chance, he may succeed in explaining or improving his position.

It is often better to leave the point, and to exploit the inconsistency in the closing speech. In any event, a jury might reach the desired conclusion by inference, with more force since it is the result of their own reasoning processes.

Possible disadvantages of not asking the final question are that the point may not be seen, or that it may be regarded as weaker because it was not conceded expressly. The opponent may argue that the witness was not given the opportunity to contradict or explain the evidence, since the matter was not put to him. This might reduce the weight of the evidence, but it would not invalidate an inference drawn by the court.

Whether or not to ask a final question is always a question for good judgment in the particular circumstances. Despite the benefits of restraint which have been listed, it is probable that most advocates would prefer favourable evidence to be express rather than leaving an important point to inference.

E   Brevity

Witnesses usually persist in the evidence which they give. Naturally, they wish their testimony to appear consistent. Under cross-examination, this is so whether the evidence is helpful, adverse, true and accurate, honestly mistaken, or false. This adherence to a line of evidence gives rise to the danger that a cross-examiner who wishes to change it, may go on too long, when an obstacle is insuperable, instead of desisting or turning to something else.

Whatever harm the evidence may have done to his case will be increased by prolonging the cross-examination. The longer it continues, the more this demonstrates the advocate's view that the evidence which he sees fit to attack is important, and the more it emphasises adverse evidence by repetition, often supported by added detail. Moreover, additional evidence, which may be even more harmful, could emerge.

Another drawback of unproductive persistence, is the disappearance of the initial expectancy that the cross-examination would be significant. This favourable attitude may be replaced by inattention and boredom.

A brief cross-examination, even if it is unsuccessful, tends to reduce the importance of the evidence. It also maintains attention.

The cross-examination of any witness, and on any topic, should be carried out as rapidly as possible. It should last no longer than is absolutely necessary to cover the material thoroughly.

The advocate should select and concentrate on the few essential points on which a case usually depends, presenting them as early as possible to put what follows in a favourable light, and keeping these points to the forefront, in order to attain his objective as quickly and as efficiently as he can.

Success on major points, if they are properly selected, should have the effect that the minor points will count for little. Enquiry into every disputed fact or detail is unnecessary.

Brevity is not only a matter of the extent to which topics are covered. It is helped by using short questions, excluding those which are unnecessary, and by eliminating needless repetition or elaboration.

If the only purpose is to show that evidence is not accepted, a question such as 'Is your story not completely untrue?' might suffice where it is unnecessary to be more specific. As soon as the desired answer is given, that line of cross-examination should cease.

F The story

Almost every criminal trial is essentially a conflict between two stories about a human event, not a legal debate. All the advocate's arts, including the techniques and devices of cross-examination, should converge to tell a party's story, in such a way as to persuade the court that it is true. Belief or disbelief in a story is the ultimate test for most practical purposes although, of course this is not the legal criterion, proof of guilt beyond reasonable doubt being required for conviction.

It is a story which integrates all the isolated facts into a coherent whole so that they are understood and remembered. It is a story which arouses interest and empathy, so that what is communicated as a real and living event is persuasive.

For an advocate, his witnesses are the principal medium by which he tells his story. But he should also seek confirmation and support from constructive forms of cross-examination or by destructive challenges to the competing story.

Cross-examiners should try to do more than just score isolated points. They should continually promote their stories.

With each witness, the relationship of the topic of cross-examination to this story should be introduced at the earliest stage, and kept to the forefront wherever possible. The main theme should recur, again and again. It is in cross-examination that one story confronts another, although only parts of each may come into contact.

G   Tactics: the alternatives

Janus-faced, a cross-examiner has to look in two directions—at the witness and at the court. He seeks to induce the witness to give certain testimony, and he wishes to persuade the court that a certain version of the facts is true. The most effective steps towards either objective may not always be identical.

To extract desired evidence from a witness may require challenge, and open distrust, eg in a direct attack on the alleged perjury of a police officer. But this may not impress the court. Not knowing of the ground for this attack, initially, the court may be critical, feeling that the police inspector should be treated with respect and courtesy. What helps the advocate to elicit the evidence may antagonise the court.

On the other hand, by concealing his suspicion and by misleading a witness, within the limits permitted by ethics, a cross-examiner may lead him into a trap by indirect methods. Here, the court may be mystified about the purpose of the line of enquiry; yet if open tactics were used for the benefit of the court's understanding, the witness would also understand them, and they would be frustrated.

Generally, getting the desired evidence, by any permissible means, is the primary and main consideration. If that evidence is obtained, eventually everything will be clear to the court. But during the process, the focus must be on the witness, and this is what mainly determines the tactics at this stage.

But there is no point in eliciting testimony on which the court is unwilling to rely because of the way in which it was obtained. To persuade the court to accept or reject what the witness was led to say is the essential and ultimate aim. For this, the focus must be on the court, and this must qualify the tactics used with the witness.

Consequently, a cross-examiner's strategy must maintain a balance between manipulating the witness and presenting the case to the court.

A major distinction in cross-examination is between constructive tactics, aimed at eliciting positive and favourable evidence, and destructive tactics, aimed at weakening or destroying adverse evidence. These tactics will be discussed in later chapters. Here, the question is that of electing between them, viz which tactics to use for particular witnesses.

Should they be combined in cross-examining one witness or, if not, which tactics should be chosen?

A constructive approach to a witness may sometimes be combined with a destructive approach which does not go too far.

If the challenge goes no further than to suggest some reason to regard the evidence as unreliable or honestly mistaken, this would leave the witness's credit intact. The door would then be open to the use of constructive tactics with a view to obtaining positive and favourable testimony.

However, since some people dislike even a suggestion that they are mistaken, considerable tact should be used in this situation. If possible, it would be better to obtain the positive evidence before criticising other evidence.

However, if the witness is accused of lying this will both alienate him, so that he will not co-operate, and may undermine the court's trust in favourable concessions which he makes. This would obviously be an unsound approach. Here, the prognosis for combining constructive and destructive tactics would be poor.

A choice between seeking helpful evidence or attacking the witness as untruthful depends of course on the relative value of either type of evidence in the particular circumstances.

Sometimes favourable and material evidence is preferable to attacking evidence. Helpful concessions from an opponent's witness usually have a strong impact. Cases are generally won by proving, not by disproving facts. Moreover, to weaken evidence is not necessarily to destroy it, and to destroy it is not necessarily to prove the contrary. But, despite this general comment, the actual situation must settle the matter.

In destructive cross-examination, either the witness may be challenged as an unsound source of the evidence, eg as lying because of his motivation, or the evidence may be attacked as intrinsically unsound, eg inconsistent and improbable.

These approaches complement and imply each other. If a witness is mistaken or is lying about something, that part of his evidence must be inaccurate because of a mistake or falsehood about the matter.

So challenging either the witness, or the evidence, are different modes of contending that evidence should be rejected. Generally, both forms of challenge are combined, although greater emphasis may be placed on one or the other according to the circumstances.

The dichotomy between mistaken and untruthful evidence is not always respected and made clear by cross-examiners. They are not averse to claiming that evidence is mistaken. The problem arises from reluctance to accuse a witness of lying. This may lead to confusing tactics.

From the defence point of view, they are entitled to an acquittal, simply by raising a reasonable doubt about the essentials of the Crown case. They need prove nothing. Everything need not be explained. It is unnecessary for the defence to clarify whether witnesses who gave inaccurate evidence were mistaken or were untruthful. Doubt about accuracy may be enough. This is the position in law, but it is not the most persuasive approach.

It is more convincing to explain how defects in evidence arose, by exposing the sources of inaccuracy. This is the most common objective.

Allegations of falsehood or error require different tactics and different processes of judgment. For example, where the question is whether the witness is lying, the focus may be on motivation, the witness's knowledge of the facts and the improbability of his testimony. But where the dispute is about whether the witness is honestly mistaken, quite different considerations arise, such as the conditions in which he observed the event, and forgetting.

Because of the exacting burden of proof on the prosecution, it would generally weaken the Crown case if the court was left in doubt about whether witnesses to essential facts may have been mistaken or untruthful.

Cross-examiners should therefore be clear and consistent about which source of inaccuracy they seek to expose. But in many trials they neither communicate their purpose nor achieve the desired result.

If a witness must know the facts which he reports wrongly, the inaccuracy of his evidence can only be intentional, ie he is lying.

But even where this is obvious, cross-examiners often refrain from charging witnesses expressly with lying. They may do so for various reasons, of which some are good and others bad.

A good reason for not disclosing the intention to treat the witness as untruthful is that the cross-examiner is using indirect tactics of the type to be discussed below. At the proper time, namely the stage of exposure, his real view of the witness as untruthful will become explicit.

In another situation, a cross-examiner may wish to lead an unintelligent witness into thinking that his deception has succeeded, which can help in cross-examining him on other topics. The inference that the witness is lying may be left to the jury at that stage, and can be argued in the closing speech.

But apart from such deliberate tactics where there may be some value in concealing the point of the challenge, there are also bad reasons for confusing mistakes and lies.

Some advocates may think that to accuse a witness of lying may make their performance seem less polished or may antagonise a jury. But neither need be the case. A cross-examiner can suggest lying without abuse, or he may insinuate it in a roundabout way.

In suitable circumstances, where lying becomes obvious, he might leave the topic without pressing the allegation home explicitly.

This deprives the witness of the chance of retracting or modifying his lie, and reduces its significance for the opponent, so that he may fail to correct it by remedial measures.

But apart from such calculated and deliberate tactics, leaving the court in doubt about whether the witness is regarded as mistaken or untruthful is weak advocacy.

Where a witness must know the truth, the common practice of suggesting that he may be 'mistaken' as a euphemism for lying is tainted with insincerity on the part of the advocate and is quite unconvincing.

Disbelief in one's own challenge seems to explain much reluctance to accuse witnesses of lying.

Although advocates should present their cases without judging them, it is understandable that they may be half-hearted about some unreasonable and improbable suggestions which their instructions oblige them to make. Formal ethics do not eliminate human nature. Common examples are some extreme defence attacks on police officers alleging seriously criminal conduct.

Often, the advocate appears to have no faith in what he is suggesting. Such accusations are true at times, but less commonly than the many occasions when they are made.

Whether the opponent's witnesses are alleged to be mistaken or untruthful should be made clear either during the cross-examination or in argument. Otherwise, no help is given to the court on the vital questions of how the witness is related to his evidence, and whether or not the advocate is asking that he should be trusted.

To challenge evidence as mistaken or untruthful is only meaningful after prior enquiry into the factors which were discussed earlier. A few casual questions, followed by 'I suggest that you are mistaken about this' or 'I put it to you that this is untrue' are inept and only indicate a cross-examiner's formal stance.

The standards of conduct expected from advocates allow considerable freedom in their manner towards witnesses, within a normal range.

Today, cross-examination is generally quiet and moderate without the histrionics of earlier times. The bench ensures that captive witnesses, are treated considerately without abuse, harassment or unnecessary offensiveness. This applies even where witnesses may be perjurers or rogues.

Advocates should try to achieve their goals objectively, by intellectual power, keeping control at all times. They should be professionally detached, on the court's level of thinking, and should not show excessive partiality or identification with their cases. They may be forceful and firm, but they should combine this with fairness, reasonableness and courtesy. These ideal qualities are not universal.

Within reasonable limits, advocates are free—as they see fit—to indulge in deliberate role-playing in cross-examination, by employing tactics which can be described as 'friendly' or 'hostile'. Friendly tactics give an impression of trust and belief. Hostile tactics suggest distrust and disbelief.

Friendly tactics are often the best way to start cross-examining any witness, even those who are seriously biased, partisan or untruthful. The tactics may change later.

Friendly tactics are suitable in seeking the co-operation of honest witnesses with a view to eliciting helpful evidence, or concessions that they may be mistaken.

Such tactics may disarm a defiant, but not necessarily dishonest, witness, making him less determined to do as much harm as possible. Friendly tactics, in their most calculating form, may also be employed to set a trap. They may be used to prevent a dishonest witness from realising that he is being led into this by an indirect approach. At the appropriate stage, the tactics would then become hostile.

If hostile tactics become necessary later, it should by then have become increasingly clear that the witness, not the advocate, is responsible for this. The need for open challenge and firmness should have emerged from the witness's evasiveness, partiality, inconsistencies or improbabilities. If this has been well done, in rapport with the court, hostile tactics will then be seen to be fully justified.

Starting cross-examination in a hostile way is usually advisable only if there is strong contradictory material with which to confront the witness. This would show the court at once that such hostile tactics are necessary.

Another way of classifying tactics is to divide them into those which are direct and those which are indirect.

In direct tactics, an advocate allows the witness to see the aim of his line of cross-examination, and in indirect tactics he conceals it. These tactics may be combined in various ways.

A combination of direct and friendly tactics would be appropriate in cross-examining honest witnesses, where, quite openly, helpful evidence or an admission of mistake, is sought.

Direct and hostile tactics would be chosen by a prosecutor for cross-examining defendants; indirect approaches are unlikely to work with them.

Direct and hostile tactics would also be employed with any lying witnesses where the cross-examiner was instantly able to put strong material to them, eg any self-contradiction or improbability in their evidence, previous inconsistent statements, the contradictory evidence of other witnesses on either side, exhibits, documents, or facts not in dispute.

Forceful leading questions, put in a challenging tone and manner, about one point after another, would be directed to making the witness commit himself firmly and precisely by admission or denial. This is a frontal attack in order to drive the witness into concessions.

Under such pressure, a dishonest witness may be unable to invent persuasive facts with circumstantial details, or recall what he said before quickly enough.

III QUESTIONS

A Purpose

It should hardly be necessary at this stage to emphasise that no question should be asked in cross-examination without a clear aim. It should have a specific point in the context of the strategy which was planned before the trial.

A special aspect of this is the generally accepted maxim that no crucial question should ever be put in cross-examination to which the answer is unknown and cannot be reasonably foreseen, lest this elicits damaging evidence.

Sometimes, if a cross-examiner thinks that he must disregard this maxim, he should approach important matters and essential issues cautiously by small steps, testing the ground. Any risk taken must be as calculated and under as much control as possible. Questions about unknown aspects of minor facts are common enough, and are often safe.

B Form

The law excludes some types of question whether in cross-examination or at any stage of a trial, eg those which would elicit inadmissible or irrelevant testimony. But this refers to the content of the question, not the form in which it is put.

The main permissive rule about the form of questions in cross-examination is that leading questions are allowed. Apart from this, the form of question is decided by common sense, tactics and the ordinary use of language.

There are no magic formulae or trick questions which guarantee success in cross-examination. Questions are framed spontaneously and intuitively as the advocate's personal response to the total situation, including his aims, the previous answer, the meaning of the question, and the context. Individuals may put equally effective questions in different ways. But it would be better to replace common phrases like these tired cliches which sound like testimony from the advocate, rather than questions:

Q: 'I suggest that ...'
Q: 'I put it to you that ...'
Q: 'My information is that ...'
Q: 'My client will say ...'

C Control

By its nature, destructive cross-examination tends to be highly controlled, allowing as little freedom as possible. To let an adverse witness tell his story freely might be damaging or disastrous. But in cross-examining a co-operative witness constructively, the credibility of testimony may be enhanced if control is relaxed so that it is given spontaneously and naturally. Free narrative by a witness may also be helpful where an over-confident lying witness is allowed to elaborate on his story as he wishes.

He may develop it to such a point of exaggeration and improbability that it can be easily discredited even without contradictory evidence. If several lying witnesses are encouraged to do this, literal similarities in their stories may suggest that they have been memorised in collusion, or inconsistencies may show that they are false.

D Leading questions

Leading questions—those which suggest the answer—are the normal form in cross-examination. In effect, the advocate asserts the facts, and the witness agrees or disagrees.

Typically, a cross-examiner will lead the witness forcefully on one point after another, keeping maximum control over him and his testimony with a view to excluding harmful statements. Any deviation from the point of the question, or evasiveness, may be countered by warnings, reminders, repetition of questions, and insistence on proper answers. Non-compliance exposes the witness's partiality or reluctance. Restricting the witness by narrow questions and small steps prevents him from dealing with the whole issue.

Open-ended questions like these would be avoided or used as little as possible:

Q: 'How?'
Q: 'Why?'
Q: 'What did you see then?'
Q: 'How did that happen?'

The purpose is to avoid general questions seeking explanations or reasons which would open the door to wide and perhaps harmful statements.

Alternatively, a comprehensive leading statement covering a whole incident may be put for acceptance or denial, which prevents the witness from disputing the details, one by one.

But forceful leading will be less effective if it gives the impression that the evidence is coming from the cross-examiner and not the witness. Thus, it is desirable to limit the extent of control and leading on secondary matters, while maintaining it where it is necessary. It is a matter of striking a balance.

E   Clarity

Since evidence obtained by destructive cross-examination consists mainly of accepting or denying leading questions, its comprehensibility as a whole will depend on the clarity of the questions. If they are not clear, the answers cannot be clear.

Evidence which is not clear will be neither remembered nor convincing. Moreover, a witness should not be given a chance to escape from a trap by claiming that a question was confusing, and that he did not really say or mean what is attributed to him.

Questions should be put briefly in simple and ordinary language, avoiding circumlocutions, pomposity, ambiguity, technical terms, or police jargon. If unusual or obscure terms must be used, they should be explained in the question.

Questions should be precise, and should cover only one point at a time (apart from comprehensive leading questions where a party puts his case, as has been explained).

Other impediments to clarity are questions which assume or imply facts which are themselves not clear or are unproved, including double questions.

F   Repeating answers

In principle, cross-examiners should only ask questions, and should not, for emphasis or other reasons, repeat answers. The mischief which can flow from non-compliance includes restating an answer in a slightly different form to insinuate a more favourable meaning, and comments or argument which should be left for speeches.

At times, repetition of answers is unobjectionable. The almost inaudible reply of a timid witness or a child may be repeated so that it can be properly heard, and put to the witness for confirmation.

The exact words, or the gist of a helpful answer may be incorporated in the next or a later question, eg 'When he said "Get out of here" did you leave the pub?'

A question may really amount to repeating an answer with a comment which conveys an advocate's personal reaction, explicitly or subtly. It may be an ostensibly interrogative statement, made in a sarcastic, scornful or incredulous tone of voice, eg 'Do you actually claim that you jumped out of an upstairs window?'

Such boundaries cannot be defined with complete precision. Cross-examination requires reasonable latitude. Reciprocally, advocates often tolerate minor or borderline impropriety in their opponents without objecting. If objection is taken, it is a question for the bench in the particular circumstances.

G   Misleading questions

Professional ethics take account of the interests of justice. They do not prevent a cross-examiner from misleading a dishonest witness within accepted limits, eg the advocate must not lie or misstate evidence already given, or make use of prejudicial or unfair material. But a degree of simulation is not only tolerated, but is often the only way in which the truth can be attained and justice done. The following are examples of such devices.

A cross-examiner, having mastered every detail, may, without saying so, by his tone, manner, or form of question, give the impression that he has only a vague acquaintance with the facts. Lulled into a false sense of security, an over-confident and dishonest witness may then invent or exaggerate evidence until his story can be easily exposed.

An advocate's tone, manner, or form of question may deliberately suggest that he seeks a certain answer, which in fact is the opposite of what he wants. A liar, to frustrate what he thinks is the advocate's purpose, may give the other desired answer.

The witness's attention may be distracted from the importance of a question, by asking it in a casual way, or by surrounding it with trivial questions asked in such a way as to appear crucial.

H Series of questions

A series of questions may have a powerful cumulative effect which they would lack singly, thus making a mountain out of a molehill. The questions may be put in random order.

A good point may be maximised if, instead of exhausting it rapidly with one or two questions, it is built up to a climax by a series of narrow questions, advancing by small steps, or with a slightly new element each time.

Again, a topic can be put in parts to different witnesses, so that none is asked the essential final question, or can answer it adversely, although the conclusion is clear to the court.

This can be done where the cross-examiner is not bound to put the question as a whole to any individual witness, as part of his case.

An answer may be made harmful or evasive by giving it in general terms. Generalisation is a common way of avoiding reality in any argument. If so, a series of questions may be put about the particular facts which lead up to the conclusion.

It will be more difficult for the witness to deny the truth, or to avoid the point of such specific and concrete questions.

A witness caught in a trap may be asked a series of questions from various angles, to exploit and intensify his defeat. To use these tactics an advocate must be sure, however, that the witness cannot escape.

I Rate of questioning

Varying the rate of questioning is useful in cross-examination. Note-taking should be minimised. It interrupts the flow of questions, reduces impact, and gives liars time to think. In jury trials, it should be left to an assistant, and in summary trials, without an assistant, only essential notes need be taken. Personal abbreviations can include initials, eg 'P' for police, 'c/c' for caution and charge, or symbols for verbs of motion, vision and hearing, etc which can speed up note-taking greatly.

The best rate of questioning for a co-operative witness, giving helpful and positive evidence, is that of normal conversation which creates no strain.

Rapid questioning, especially in an unpredictable order, may give a liar too little time to invent answers related to earlier evidence and the hidden truth. If he repeats a question to gain time, this may be obvious. Off balance, he may be led into inconsistencies, improbabilities, or testimony which can be contradicted by other evidence. But liars may also be questioned slowly and deliberately on crucial points, allowing ample time to reply.

This may demonstrate the falsity of the witness's answers, by highlighting his hesitations and difficulties.

To emphasise his pauses, questions may be repeated or, even better, they may be read back from the court record. This may unnerve the witness and it will certainly focus the court's attention on his answers.

CHAPTER 7

Cross-examination: constructive techniques

I   Introduction
II Emphasis
III New meanings
IV New facts
V   Alternative case

I   INTRODUCTION

Cross-examination with a constructive aim is important. A significant objective of cross-examination is to obtain favourable evidence by means of various constructive techniques. Cases are won by proving, as well as by disproving, facts, ie by the strength of one's case, as well as the weakness of the opponent's case. The importance of cross-examination is not limited to weakening or destroying the opponent's evidence, although this aspect is usually emphasised. Such opportunities should be grasped. Concessions by an opponent's witness may have a strong impact.

Two immediate questions arise for the cross-examiner, viz 'Does the witness know any helpful facts?' and 'Will the witness co-operate?'

It is commonly accepted that in principle, advocates should avoid questions to which they do not know the answer. They may have written statements of the evidence which a witness is able to give, including his knowledge of facts which would favour the cross-examiner's case. But in any event, the state of a witness's knowledge of favourable facts should usually be obvious from the evidence-in-chief. Eyewitness testimony about an incident which is in dispute places the witness at the locus as an observer who must have seen most of the facts, if not everything.

Witnesses to circumstantial evidence usually offer less scope for eliciting positive and helpful evidence.

In a strongly disputed issue, where some facts may be in doubt, it might be quite surprising if a witness's whole evidence pointed unequivocally in one direction, ie if it was either totally incriminating, or totally exculpatory, with nothing pointing the other way. If a cross-examiner does not know of any qualifying facts, which could help his case, he might probe the evidence for that purpose. If none emerge, they may not exist, or they may not be known to the witness, or the witness may be lying.

Dogmatism in an area where it would be reasonable to expect a certain degree of uncertainty is always open to question.

In theory, the witness's co-operation in responding to constructive cross-examination should not be a problem, but in practice it often is. However, the opponent's witnesses are expected to co-operate in the cross-examination as a legal obligation. Although the opponent called them to give evidence favourable to himself and unfavourable to his opponent, this does not define their duty.

The kind of difficulties encountered by a cross-examiner in seeking positive evidence, even from honest witnesses, may arise from two sources among others.

One is partisanship. There is a tendency for neutral witnesses called by a party to attach themselves to that party's view of the case, and to support it. This is more likely to be a matter of unconscious bias than deliberate falsehood.

Another source of difficulty arises from the tendency of evidence to crystallise and become fixed so that it resists alteration.

A witness's observations of an incident may be uncertain or incomplete. This is followed by conscious rumination about it or unconscious tendencies which influence it.

Discussion between witnesses may occur and, in any event, statements of their evidence will be given to solicitors or police. All this will tend to streamline the evidence, to fill in the gaps, and to make it coherent, continuous and meaningful. At later stages, witnesses may be recalling the last statement of their evidence rather than the original incident. Moreover, since memory always involves some reconstruction of the event which is recalled, witnesses come to accept their reconstructions as true images of what happened.

All this may be called the 'freezing effect' on testimony. It follows that a cross-examiner who attempts to disrupt this careful construction will be unwelcome. Even though the disruption may take the form of eliciting additional facts, it may be perceived that the aim is to disturb the comfortable image of the event which has now become a stable 'memory' of the witness. Accordingly, the cross-examiner may meet with resistance which could be either deliberate or unconscious.

Nevertheless, the position in law is quite clear. Witnesses must comply with their oaths wherever their evidence leads, not act as partisans for whoever called them. So while some difficulties of the type described can arise, they will be limited in witnesses who are honest and impartial.

Even biased, partisan or lying witnesses are under some constraint. To avoid the law's penalties, their evidence must fit into a context of other evidence, and a network of uncontested or obvious facts. Usually, even reluctant witnesses give relevant answers to such questions, whether or not they are accurate.

While, by definition, the aim of constructive techniques of cross-examination is to obtain positive and favourable evidence, as with so many distinctions the boundary between constructive and destructive techniques is not absolute. The classification is practical, not philosophical. Sometimes, an affirmative answer about one fact is also a negative statement—ie destructive—about another.

Also, in practice, constructive and destructive techniques may overlap or be combined, or there may be swift transitions from one approach to the other. Reference is made to the discussion in the previous chapter of the relationship between constructive and destructive techniques.

Generally, if favourable evidence is to be sought from a witness, co-operation is more likely if it is sought before challenging him. Depending on the results, it may then be better not to challenge the witness at all, or to do it only as a formality.

The main constructive techniques of cross-examination move away progressively from acceptance of evidence-in-chief to contradicting it. They consist of: emphasis; new meanings; new facts; and the alternative case.

II EMPHASIS

In the technique of emphasis, the cross-examiner notes something in the evidence-in-chief which favours his case. He accepts that evidence, and it is not his intention to try to change it in any way, although he may draw out some additional details. He makes the witness repeat that evidence for emphasis. Naturally he would do it in such a way as to highlight the favourable aspect, and to do this he might develop it in more detail. The evidence-in-chief on that topic is what the cross-examiner builds on. He simply focuses attention on it to make it more prominent and maximises its significance.

The application of this technique may be illustrated in a trial on a charge of robbery where masked men enter a shop, terrorise the staff with hammers, empty the till, and escape in a car. Later, suspects are apprehended, and the staff of the shop are asked to testify.

A sales assistant, claiming to have recognised one robber as a customer, by his build, hair colour, and typical way of walking and moving, remarks, in evidence-in-chief, 'It was all over so quickly.'

There is other physical evidence, and there are admissions to the police, supporting this dubious form of visual identification.

A cross-examiner may seize on the brevity of the event for emphasis, adding detail to build up a picture of how many things the witness seems to have attended to in a short time. These included the opening of the door, the entry of masked men, the shock of seeing them and the hammers which they carried, the vocal demands for money from the till, the act of opening it, the departure of the men with the money, and the sight of their motor car as it drove away. In addition, the witness admitted to experiencing the phenomenon known as 'weapon focus' which causes a potential victim of an assault to concentrate on the dangerous weapon. All this would leave her little time to study that particular robber who was one of three. The other two had to be watched as well. Here, the advocate accepts and focuses on one element of evidence of this witness, and perhaps other witnesses. To emphasise the brevity of the event supports his attack on the identification as unreliable or wrong.

It is usually easy to find at least some favourable aspect for emphasis, even in evidence which tends on the whole to be adverse.

One tactic for doing this is to use the principle of relativity, by comparing evidence actually given with more harmful evidence which might have been, but was not, given. The difference may then be emphasised to the effect of suggesting that the facts are less adverse than they might have been or seem to be.

A police witness may speak to finding the stolen goods in the living room of the accused's house. A defence cross-examiner may elicit, and emphasise the fact, that the accused invited the officer into the house.

He would highlight the facts that the officer had no search warrant, and that the goods were lying openly on a table in the hall. The cross-examiner would be emphasising the accused's lack of objection and the open display of the goods, as indicating an innocent state of mind. If the accused had objected to the officer's entry and the goods were hidden in the attic, this would have been more incriminating than the actual evidence. This comparison is favourable to the accused, and may be stressed.

There are frequent opportunities for using this technique. It is common enough for even adverse facts to be less than totally incriminating, so that a skilful cross-examiner may extract some advantage from emphasising this. This approach may be taken to any kind of evidence, eg the conditions of observation which are rarely perfect, but where the absence of even worse conditions may be stressed.

The logic behind this method of cross-examining is not impeccable, but as a persuasive device it has some merit, particularly as it does not involve any form of challenge to the witness, so that, as a result, he will be more likely to co-operate.

This is only one example of cross-examining for emphasis. It can apply to any favourable evidence. Some objections to the method may be considered.

In theory, it is enough for something said in evidence-in-chief to be heard once and understood. On the assumption that the tribunal of fact listen to the evidence with perfect hearing and attention, and that their recall is complete, the evidence which the cross-examiner wishes to emphasise has already been conveyed to them. Repetition should add nothing. Moreover it risks retraction or qualification by the witness.

Again, as was said previously, repeating the evidence-in-chief is one of the most common faults in cross-examination.

These objections may be answered as follows. With regard to the favourable evidence-in-chief, the assumption of perfect perception, attention, and recall, may be incorrect. The mind does not work with the efficiency and precision of a video recorder. If the evidence was important, its reception should not be left to chance.

Repetition of large amounts of evidence is not suggested here. Concise confirmation of the essential point could be enough. But even if the evidence and its favourable aspect had already been grasped by the court, there may still be some merit in a fleeting reminder. Such repetition figures in all forms of persuasive communication from advertising to teaching. Why exclude courts?

Moreover a cross-examiner can expand and develop the relevant part of the evidence-in-chief, and present it in an even more favourable light.

If there is any risk that the helpful evidence may be qualified or retracted by asking further questions, it may indeed be better not to cross-examine on the point. But if the evidence is likely to remain intact on repetition, and a worthwhile gain is foreseen, to emphasise it may help.

In the above example about the discovery of stolen goods in the hall by a police officer who had no search warrant, his evidence will not change to the effect that he did have a search warrant and that the goods were found in the attic. There is no apparent risk in raising the points mentioned.

Another gain from cross-examining for emphasis is that it may disarm a witness and make him easier to manage. Focusing on what is common to parties should lead to acceptance of the undisputed evidence by the court.

In this approach, part of the evidence-in-chief is accepted with approval and no attempt is made to change it.

This must be distinguished from the next technique to be considered, where the cross-examiner does try to to change the meaning of facts which he accepts.

III NEW MEANINGS

In cross-examination, new and favourable meanings may be given to facts stated in evidence-in-chief, which are accepted as accurate. Such meanings are also facts but they are derived from other facts and not perceived directly.

They range from a witness's impression or interpretation of what he observed to the inference drawn from circumstantial evidence.

Issues of admissibility can arise in this type of evidence. However, any issues of admissibility should have been settled in the course of the examination-in-chief. Whatever was admissible then, whether or not objected to, should be admissible in, and subject to, cross-examination.

Lay witnesses are supposed to speak to facts which they perceived directly. Texts on the law of evidence should be consulted for marginal exceptions to the general rule which excludes evidence of opinion from lay witnesses.

Identification evidence, or a witness's view of his own mental or physical condition, motives or feelings, may involve opinion, but it is still admissible. Some impression evidence is inseparable from the observations on which it is based and may be the only way to convey the facts to the court.

Some observations are too vague, obscure, subtle or ambiguous, to be otherwise described and communicated effectively.

In practice, it is difficult to apply rigid tests to this kind of impression evidence. Often, in summary courts particularly, the strict technical rules are not pressed to the point of absurdity. They are qualified by practical considerations, common sense, and necessity.

Impression evidence is often given about persons, their ages, condition, motives and conduct, eg that someone had been drinking, or was distressed, that a man was threatening others with a bottle, that youths were acting suspiciously in a car park, or that physical contact had a sexual intention.

Impression evidence may also be given about physical things, or situations, eg that there was a good deal of traffic about, or that a crowd of football fans were in a wrong area of the stadium seeking trouble.

These are examples of general statements of facts derived from observing other specific facts.

Expert opinion evidence also involves meanings derived from other facts, and is open to this technique of establishing new meanings.

The effect of circumstantial evidence depends on the inference drawn from it. It is for the court, and not for witnesses, to make such inferences.

In principle, therefore, drawing or altering such inferences is a matter for argument in the closing speech, not cross-examination, apart from tackling the facts on which the inferences may be based.

The technique is to give a new meaning to any adverse, material, impression in evidence-in-chief.

It should start with friendly and indirect tactics which proceed gradually, step by step. By careful leading questions, the witness is made to accept minor adjustments to the evidence here and there, stressing this and toning down that, so that the balance and pattern are altered subtly in the direction of the desired new meaning.

Little pressure is needed with reasonable and co-operative witnesses, but greater firmness, and perhaps confrontation with some contradictory material, may be required with those who are resistant. With both types, the objective should be concealed for as long as possible.

A general conclusion, which the witness might not accept at first, may be reached indirectly, by building it up from separate facts or points of view.

The important area of evidence should be approached with caution, while the cross-examiner decides whether to put the new meaning to the witness directly, or to leave the matter to his closing speech. This needs judgment.

The advantages and disadvantages of asking a final specific question, arise here. To stop just before that leaves the point to the court's inference; the result of its own judgment may be more impressive to the court than a witness's view.

The point can also be made in the final speech. Also, the witness has no chance to weaken or destroy the desired interpretation, by qualifying or withdrawing his earlier evidence. Moreover, the opponent may fail to meet the point by re-examination, calling other evidence, or final argument.

On the other hand, asking the final specific question also has advantages. The witness may accept the new interpretation as the correct one, conceding that what he said on the topic in evidence-in-chief was wrong. If so, the technique has been successful.

If the witness concedes only that the meaning put to him is equally consistent with the facts, or at least a possibility, this is also a worthwhile achievement. An alternative and favourable version of the evidence-in-chief will have been presented to the court out of the mouth of the opponent's witness. But if the witness dogmatically rejects a reasonable meaning put to him, his credit, and not the proposition, may suffer. He may be seen to be biased or untruthful.

Although the witness denies the proposed meaning, merely putting it is suggestive. By this technique, a story may be given a new orientation, without altering the basic facts.

The evidence-in-chief may be so weakened by this that it is rejected in favour of evidence led by the cross-examiner, or else a reasonable doubt may be created about a fact which is essential for conviction.

The technique is essentially constructive, since the aim is to build up one's case, but it combines this with weakening or destroying harmful evidence. Advantages are that it can be done without challenging the witness as mistaken or untruthful, thus gaining his co-operation, yet impressing the court, since the concession comes from a witness for the opponent.

IV   NEW FACTS

A common and important approach in cross-examination is to bring out new and material facts, which were omitted from the examination-in-chief. These facts differ from the secondary, collateral facts, elicited when a cross-examiner probes evidence in a search for flaws. Nor are they simple requests for further information such as the width of a road.

Opportunities to elicit new and material facts will depend on the thoroughness of the examination-in-chief discussed in chapter 5.

What should be disclosed by examination-in-chief involves questions of both duty and tactics. So far as duty is concerned, it differs in respect of the prosecution and the defence.

A prosecutor should conduct his examination-in-chief so that Crown witnesses disclose any material facts of which he knows, and which may be relevant to the defence. Obviously, there may be marginal points, where he omits something in good faith, because he did not think that it was significant. Moreover, the prosecutor is not expected to look for or to construct a defence.

The defence do not have as exacting a duty as the prosecution. They have no obligation to prove anything. They may deliberately omit material facts from their examination-in-chief. They are not obliged to disclose incriminating facts. But this freedom is nevertheless subject to the ethical limitation that the defence must not, knowingly, mislead the court. The defence must not assert what they know to be false or deny what they know to be true.

But apart from legal duties to disclose evidence, failure to do so will have tactical consequences, if cross-examination elicits new and material facts which were not disclosed in the evidence-in-chief of either party.

This may suggest bad faith and lack of candour which may put either party, their advocates and their witnesses in an adverse light. The effects of this will vary.

A cross-examiner should know that sometimes an omission may be a trap designed to damage his case if he raises the point unwarily.

In the pressing circumstances of a criminal trial, an advocate may miss out something important as a result of simple oversight. Advocates often ask their assistants if they have omitted anything.

So the evidence-in-chief of either party's witnesses may offer scope for bringing out new facts in cross-examination. The merits of doing this should be weighed up before embarking on it.

Sometimes it is better to leave something alone or in doubt. Advocates should avoid the lawyer's tendency to want everything to be express and stated in words.

New facts should only be sought if they are known, and expected to be helpful and material, but not simply because some area of evidence is incomplete because it has not been fully explored. The possible adverse effects of bringing out these new facts should be weighed.

This includes the opponent's right to re-examine on any point arising in cross-examination, although it emerged then for the first time.

If the cross-examiner ignores the maxim of never asking questions to which he cannot foresee the answer, and explores unknown territory, he will incur dangers. If he decides to take a calculated risk by doing this, he should proceed cautiously, while trying to anticipate the likely answers.

In cross-examination for new facts, although an advocate may lead his opponent's witness, the evidence will be more persuasive if it is given in response to non-leading questions. But if the witness resists, leading may be adopted.

New and material facts which emerge for the first time in cross-examination are likely to have a strong impact, as they come from an opponent's witness. If the new evidence is really helpful and important, the benefit gained from it may be negated by trying to discredit that witness in other respects.

V   ALTERNATIVE CASE

Whether or not he uses other constructive techniques, a cross-examiner should never fail to put his alternative version of the case to each of his opponent's witnesses who know the facts.

It is accepted practice that if a cross-examiner has led, or intends to lead, evidence to contradict a witness, he should give him a chance to accept, deny, or explain that contradiction.

Failure to put one's case in this way may have various damaging legal and tactical consequences. Legal restrictions, differing in summary or jury trials, may affect the further conduct of the case by cross-examination, leading evidence, or argument about the same facts. Tactical drawbacks include the adverse light thrown on untested contentions and obvious unfairness. Apart from this, there might be a battery of objections and recrimination from the bench. Failure to put the alternative case is not recommended.

How should it be done? If the case is put to the witness, point by point, a series of adverse answers, with continually increasing assertiveness and elaboration, may have a disastrous cumulative effect. Unless some specific gain is foreseen from putting the alternative case in this way, it should not be done.

One or two wide leading questions, provided that they are comprehensive enough, should cover both legal and tactical requirements completely. They should be framed in such a way as to call for a 'Yes' or 'No' answer.

This will minimise the harm which an adverse witness can do.

If, exceptionally, a witness accepts the cross-examiner's case, in whole, or in part, when it is put to him, success has been achieved to that extent.

If the witness only concedes the cross-examiner's contentions as a possibility, that too accomplishes something worthwhile, eg if a Crown eyewitness qualified his evidence about a crucial fact in response to defence cross-examination, it may be enough to raise a reasonable doubt and lead to acquittal.

Further, merely putting that alternative story to the witness has a suggestive effect in itself, which can add to the persuasiveness of the case.

CHAPTER 8

Cross-examination: destructive techniques

I   Introduction
II   Destruction of evidence
III   Belief and disbelief
IV   Contradiction
V   When to challenge
VI   When to stop
VII   Challenging the witness
VIII Challenging the evidence

I INTRODUCTION

The main aim of cross-examination is to weaken or destroy harmful evidence led by the opponent. Eliciting favourable evidence from an opponent's witness occurs less often.

It is emphasised throughout this book that an advocate should not normally expect to achieve his destructive aims by cross-examination alone particularly as a result of questioning a single witness. Attaining his objectives will usually require the support of his own evidence-in-chief to contradict and overcome the evidence which he is challenging. Such links between the testimonies of different witnesses demonstrate that skill in the art of cross-examination depends on insight into its role in the whole trial context, not on mastery of a set of tricks which are employed on one witness. In various situations cross-examiners must know what they can do, how they can do it, and the effect. They will then apply this insight in the particular situation. Without this kind of understanding, methods of cross-examination may simply consist of parotting the techniques of more experienced advocates or performing according to dogmatic forms of instruction. Some of the latter emanate from the USA.

Many training courses in advocacy make the mistake of developing the use of processes which the trainee does not understand. They seem to believe that it is enough to make him articulate when he is on his feet, and to have him follow traditional paths with little awareness of what is happening.

The development of a cross-examiner's natural ability by practice and experience should be based on an understanding of the processes of destructive cross-examination, which are described in this chapter. Enlightenment about the whole interplay of evidence is the key.

There are no rules or verbal formulae whereby anyone can acquire instant expertise or demolish any evidence automatically. There are, however, sound principles which can be applied flexibly as required. In planning and in conducting any cross-examination, nothing can replace the need for the advocate's good judgment in the particular circumstances.

II DESTRUCTION OF EVIDENCE

'Destruction' of evidence, here, simply means that the court rejects the evidence as the basis, or as part of the basis, for its verdict. This is what counts, whether it is due to the court's total or partial disbelief in the evidence, including acceptance of the opposite state of facts, or a reasonable doubt.

Although the effect of each step in destroying evidence may vary, the complete three-stage model of achieving this is to weaken the evidence by cross-examination, contradict it by other evidence, and attack it in the closing speech. But if no defence evidence is led, that and the Crown cross-examination are missing from the process. The prosecutor will simply direct his closing speech to the incriminating evidence which he has led.

If cross-examination is indeed so effective that the evidence which is challenged would be rejected even if it were not contradicted by other evidence, this cannot be known, or predicted with certainty, at that stage. It is a safer working rule that the whole trial process is needed to destroy evidence, and not to leave anything undone which could contribute to this.

Whether or not to lead evidence is a classic problem for the defence. Without it, they are unlikely to establish any version of the facts to compete with that offered by the prosecution. But the defence advocate may think that the evidence which he could call might be harmful or risky, or be unwilling to expose the accused to cross-examination; or again, the accused, for his own reasons, may decide that evidence should not be led.

If the defence rely on cross-examination and argument, they need only raise a reasonable doubt about the Crown case to succeed. Depending on the state and significance of the evidence to be challenged in the context of the Crown case generally, and the cross-examiner's skill, such a defence may succeed at times, but to omit helpful evidence which could be led, involves some risk.

Although the defence complete their cross-examination before deciding whether or not to lead evidence, they may be uncertain about whether the court will eventually reject the evidence which they attacked.

The defence advocate must calculate the risks in deciding whether or not to imperil his case on that cross-examination without leading evidence.

Realistically, a cross-examiner should not expect a lying witness to retract his story or to substitute the truth. His original strong motive for lying is reinforced by fear of penalties that may follow if he admits it. Moreover, lying witnesses seldom become incoherent or silent, to the extent of demolishing their testimony.

Mistaken evidence is sometimes retracted, or impartial witnesses may concede doubts about it although even honest witnesses, from bias, partisanship, vanity or other reasons may show resistance. But a cross-examiner should certainly try to get favourable concessions of this kind.

Destroying evidence only establishes the contrary if that follows logically, eg to destroy the accused's assertion that he was not driving the car makes him the driver. But in other cases, destruction of evidence about one assertion leaves other possibilities open, eg to destroy an accused's claim that he was in Leeds when the crime was committed does not place him in Watford or prove that he committed the robbery which occurred in that town. But despite this logical comment the psychological effect of such an exposure is another matter.

III   BELIEF AND DISBELIEF

Since the aim of destructive cross-examination is to produce disbelief, it is relevant to consider how belief in evidence develops. It depends on three elements—if any one is missing or deficient, evidence may be disbelieved. These essential elements are that:

A   the witness must be trusted;
B   his evidence must be reasonable;
C   his evidence must have weight.

A   Trust in witnesses

To trust or distrust witnesses is a daily reality in courts. It depends partly on direct and natural responses to them and partly on intellectual assessment. There can be degrees of trust, and it can be selective. The court may trust a witness as being truthful and sound, so that his self-assessment and confidence in his report may overcome any allegation of unreliability or mistake. Again, the court may trust a witness as truthful, but may doubt his capacity in some other way, eg memory for details. Trust in a witness's honesty is the crucial question when credibility is in issue.

In the context of the trial, acceptance of the witness's personal assurance as to what he saw, is one of the foundations of belief that the facts were indeed so. This belief depends on both feeling and thinking in a certain way about the witness in relation to the trial, eg 'That nice old lady, who has no personal connection of any kind with the case, has not come to court to commit perjury so that an innocent youth should be convicted'.

In court, as in daily life, a report about facts by a trusted person is well on the way to being believed. There is no absolute reason or compelling process of logic which dictates that any piece of evidence must be believed. It would not help to try to give some logical form to the reasoning process, like this:

> 'The witness says that X happened.
> I believe that the witness is truthful.
> Therefore, X happened.'

This is actually an illogical non sequitur. Even though the first and second sentences are true, the conclusion does not follow. The witness may be mistaken. This form would be better:

> 'The witness says that X happened.
> The witness's report is accurate.
> Therefore X happened.'

This is also flawed. It provides no validation for the second statement which assumes the conclusion.

The only valid way of stating the position is this:

> 'The witness says that X happened.
> I believe that the witness's report is truthful and accurate.
> Therefore I believe that X happened.'

This is logical, but it explains nothing. It does not show the ground of the belief that the witness's report is truthful and accurate. It is certainly not this process of reasoning. It must be something else.

However it is unproductive to discuss the matter in such terms.

Essentially, this trust in a witness is something which either happens or it does not. It is a perception which is formed, based on other perceptions of facts, and feelings.

B Reasonableness of evidence

However, despite the mysterious subjectivity of this process, for the trust to endure it must overcome difficulties and pass tests which are not subjective. Initial trust can be destroyed.

Trust alone is not enough for belief. Even a trusted person may talk nonsense. To lead to belief, what a persons says must be reasonable.

In daily life, if a trusted person reports something which seems to be reasonable, he is likely to be believed.

If the report seems to be rather unreasonable, while the reporter's good faith may be accepted, it may be thought that he is mistaken.

If the facts reported are unreasonable to a sufficient extent, trust in the witness may be lost and his report will be disbelieved.

Again in daily life, even statements from an unknown person, whom there is no reason either to trust or distrust, may be acceptable in themselves, because they are reasonable, ie they conform to existing knowledge. Their truth and accuracy may be self-evident, eg geometrical axioms, or highly probable statements, such as the report that there was no major earthquake in London this year.

But testimony in court refers to fortuitous facts which could be true or not, and about which the court knows nothing. Whether or not such evidence is reasonable must be approached in a different way. This cannot depend on its conformity to existing knowledge.

For the evidence of a single witness to be reasonable, ie acceptable in itself, irrespective of who gives it, it must not be self-contradictory, impossible or improbable to an extent which blocks belief. But even if such defects are absent, and these barriers to belief are removed, while this may be conducive to accepting the report, it is still insufficient. The lack of such obstacles does not necessarily make evidence true or accurate. It simply provides conditions where it could be true. For belief, something more is necessary.

C   Weight of evidence

The phrase 'weight of the evidence' is used in various senses in courts and in legal literature, mostly with reference to the effect of a whole body of evidence, or perhaps all the evidence in the case.

It is used here, as a familiar term, but with a specific and narrow meaning. It denotes the value or significance conferred on individual items of evidence as a result of comparing them with all the other evidence, for support and contradiction. These are the criteria for evaluating evidence in its context.

The model of belief which has been described requires trust in a witness whose evidence is reasonable, and fits into all the other evidence in a convincing way which gives it sufficient weight.

Evidence which is evaluated in the light of all the other evidence becomes more significant than it would have been alone as a result of comparing the testimony of one witness with another, and discovering that in essentials they are identical, or contradictory, or of noting how the evidence under consideration fits into a limited network of other testimony and facts. The weight attaching to a particular piece of evidence is enhanced or reduced by the context. Favourable factors of trust, reasonableness and weight, may then, combine to produce belief in the particular testimony.

IV   CONTRADICTION

The destructive function of the cross-examiner consists of interfering with this process of forming belief by undermining trust in the witnesses, showing that their evidence is unreasonable, attacking its weight in relation to other evidence, particularly evidence which is contradictory.

Destructive cross-examination is based on the concept of contradiction, the dialectical principle at the heart of the adversarial process. Starting from the self-evident truth that a thing cannot both be and not be at the same time, the aim of one advocate is to deny what the other asserts, or to assert what the other denies where this is based on his information and is relevant to the issues.

Applying this to the question of trust in a witness, a cross-examiner will try to contradict the factors which promote this. He may attack character, expose motives for lying, question sincerity, highlight bias or partisanship, or try to create doubt about the witness's competence in observation and remembering.

The attack on the reasonableness of the evidence will focus on self-contradiction or inconsistency in evidence, or improbability or lack of realism where the contradiction comes from the real world.

The weight of that witness's evidence will also be diminished by confronting him with facts which contradict his assertions, and which are spoken to by witnesses on either side.

All these lines of challenge usually proceed simultaneously, or in close juxtaposition, and one approach enhances another. For example, by exploring lies objectively on some point of improbability, the liar is revealed by his manner of answering.

The cross-examination of one witness after another should be orchestrated into a closing argument which is the ultimate contradiction of the opponent's case.

V   WHEN TO CHALLENGE

The aims of destructive cross-examination should be clear and should have reasonable prospects of being attained. An advocate should have a realistic understanding of what he can hope to achieve. Otherwise, he may cross-examine where he should not do so, or he may go on too long with increasing damage to his own case, when he should stop. The questions are whether to challenge a witness at all and, if so, on what parts of his evidence.

A   Negative indications

One obvious reason for not challenging evidence may be that it has caused only minor harm, and that it would be best to ignore it.

Another reason for not attacking evidence is that cross-examination is not the best way to counter any harm which it caused.

Yet another ground for restraint is that it may be preferable to seek favourable evidence and to sacrifice the possible gains from attacking.

Slightly unfavourable evidence may not merit challenge—trifling points, or those which are only remotely harmful, should be ignored. Minor discrepancies due to normal eyewitness fallibility rarely justify attack to support contentions that evidence of the main facts is unreliable, mistaken or untruthful. But sometimes small points of evidence can be important as clues in a question of whether an incident occurred at all, eg in the case of an alibi, slight differences in evidence could be sinister and might be probed by a prosecutor.

Facts which seem unimportant in themselves may be highly significant when linked together as circumstantial evidence and, if so, adverse evidence about details may have to be attacked.

With regard to other matters of no great moment, to ignore something is to treat it as having no importance. Then, the court may well disregard or forget it.

On the other hand, to cross-examine on the topic, especially at length, may emphasise its significance. This could turn a minor point into a real obstacle.

There are other ways in which an advocate can deal with unfavourable evidence sometimes, without challenging it directly, especially if it is weak.

Even strong evidence may be contradicted successfully by still stronger evidence. But in deciding not to challenge evidence, because he thinks that this will be ineffective anyway, an advocate must take any material risks into account.

A cross-examiner may let some evidence pass if he has successfully challenged similar evidence when it was given by an earlier witness. On the other hand, he might defer the challenge until he can make it with a weaker witness who is expected to give similar evidence.

Some evidence may be so strong that there is no hope of weakening or overcoming it by cross-examination. Also, apart from the strength of the evidence per se, its reiteration by a resistant witness might intensify the damage. Contradictory evidence or argument may offer the only prospect of meeting that adverse evidence.

This discussion of alternatives to challenge by cross-examination is not intended to mean that a party should not put his case to an opponent's witness so far as he knows the facts.

Even reluctant concessions by an opponent's witness are usually convincing. They should be sought before he is challenged in any way, when the witness is likely to be more co-operative and more likely to seem trustworthy.

If no helpful admissions are obtained, the advocate would then proceed to challenge the witness on other matters.

But if the cross-examiner elicits any helpful evidence, he should weigh the possible reduction of that benefit against the possible gain from going on to challenge other evidence. Sometimes, to abandon the challenge is worthwhile.

The benefit of favourable testimony may be impaired if it is followed by any challenge other than a suggestion of honest error.

B Positive indications

For reasons which are partly legal and partly tactical, a cross-examiner should put any material part of his case to an opponent's witnesses who know about those facts. He should also show, at least, that he disputes any adverse evidence about essential facts, even if he only does this briefly. This will avoid possible difficulties if he tries to challenge those facts later.

Often, a challenge need only be formal. At one extreme (as an exception to the the rule of keeping questions to one point at a time) the advocate may ask a single comprehensive question, which can only be answered by 'Yes' or 'No', or their equivalents, eg 'Is it not the case that your story about what happened in the lane is a complete invention?' This may satisfy the obligation to put one's case and, at times, may be the best tactic.

Apart from this, any evidence which is both harmful and material should be challenged. Whatever the strength of his case, an advocate should not refrain from cross-examination because of complacency. Even a good case may be vulnerable in some way.

Sometimes harmful evidence may be made worse by persistent cross-examination which only causes it to be repeated, and reinforced with emphasis and elaboration. If so, a single global question of the kind indicated above may be better.

But at other times, to put detailed and specific questions, point by point, may be the best tactic where progress is being made. Here, the repetition and its suggestive effect may work for the cross-examiner and not against him.

The category of adverse evidence which should not be allowed to pass unchallenged would include eyewitness evidence of the crime if it is disputed, evidence of visual identification of the defendant as the offender, if that is in issue, alibi evidence, evidence of confessions and admissions which implicate the accused, and any other material evidence.

Harmless evidence may be given by a weak witness who is in a position to know about matters on which other witnesses gave or may give damaging evidence. A cross-examiner might exploit this opportunity for attacking the other adverse evidence retrospectively or in anticipation, by questioning this witness about the same facts.

VI   WHEN TO STOP

For particular witnesses or topics, it is as important to know when to stop destructive cross-examination as when to undertake it.

To some extent, this can be planned, but unforeseen reasons for stopping may emerge. A planned point for stopping would, of course, be when a specific aim is attained. The value of ending with an explicit victory on some topic has been pointed out above. When some desired concession is obtained, the cross-examination on that topic should stop at once; the gain can be emphasised in the closing speech.

But encouraged by his success, a cross-examiner may be tempted to drive home what he has achieved, by further questions to make it even clearer or stronger. He may regret doing so. A witness, given a second chance, may withdraw or modify his answer, thus nullifying the gain.

For each witness, a cross-examiner should constantly bear in mind the question of whether he has sufficient material of value for his closing speech, where he can make the most of evidence which he has elicited. When he has enough of such material, he should not try to score additional points lest he lose what he has. He should stop to prevent retraction or qualification of the testmony by the witnesses, or alerting his opponent to the need for re-examination, further evidence or argument. Such decisions are crucial tests of the judgment and skill of an advocate.

Exceptionally, a cross-examiner might go on after getting a favourable admission, where the witness is trapped and cannot escape, so that his situation can be exploited from various angles, but the cross-examination should be ended if the witness could conceivably invent some way out.

A variation may be useful if the aim is attained to the extent that answers have reached the point where a final question would make the gain explicit. Instead of asking it, the cross-examiner leaves the point for the jury to infer, perhaps with more impact. Then it becomes less likely that either the witness or the opponent will try to meet the point.

Some objectives are unrealistic. Where this becomes clear, the cross-examination should not be prolonged unduly in the vain hope of achieving them. It is not the witness but rather the evidence which should be treated as the target for destruction.

Generally a cross-examiner should stop when he is satisfied that he has contributed significantly to the rejection of the evidence—and not go on unproductively in an effort to attain perfection.

Cross-examination which seemed necessary at first may turn out to be pointless, or even harmful. To go on may intensify the damage by repetition, emphasis and adding supporting detail. If so, the cross-examination should be ended at once perhaps by asking a global question which can only be accepted or denied. Prosecutors often do this.

Occasionally, in suitable circumstances, it may be worth going on, although the answers themselves are not those which are desired, eg, for the cumulative and suggestive value of repeatedly getting unreasonable denials of reasonable points, or to commit the witness firmly to statements which can be disproved later, so that he will be discredited.

But generally, where, for any reason, a witness is completely resistant to any modification of his evidence, the cross-examination should not go on beyond the point where it stops being productive and becomes harmful.

A cross-examination which is cut short may be replaced, eg by cross-examining a weaker witness, calling a contradictory witness or by argument.

Where a cross-examiner makes no progress at all, it should not be totally beyond his contemplation that the testimony may be truthful and accurate, and that he should not expect to overcome it.

VII CHALLENGING THE WITNESS

A Relationship to evidence

A complete attack on testimony would not only show why the account of facts cannot be accepted, ie challenging the evidence, but would also expose the mistaken or lying mental processes which explain the inaccuracy, ie challenging the witness.

These go together. Inaccuracy must be due to a mistake or a lie and a mistake or a lie must create inaccuracy.

Obviously, a cross-examiner who can do so should employ both forms of challenge. He must certainly challenge evidence which he does not accept. To show whether inaccuracy arose from mistake or lying may not be essential, but it can reinforce the attack on the evidence.

As was seen earlier, trust in the witness is the foundation of belief in evidence. To undermine that trust materially may lead to rejection of evidence which seems quite reasonable. But criticism of a witness per se, unrelated to anything in his evidence, would be an irrelevant personal attack and would be disallowed.

One or other approach tends to dominate at times, but most cross-examination is objective, ie it consists of challenging the evidence. This is the context in which the witness is also challenged. Challenging the witness is usually integrated with challenging his evidence so that personal criticisms are related to specific parts of his testimony. In the course of his main enquiry into the issues, a cross-examiner is likely to suggest that the witness's account of important disputed facts is mistaken or untruthful, and to enquire into circumstances which support such allegations, eg by showing that it was too dark to recognise the accused, or that the witness previously made an inconsistent statement.

Flaws in a witness may also emerge incidentally in his way of answering objective questions on the issues, eg the liar is revealed by enquiring into the lie rather than into the person.

B   Assessment of witness

During the evidence-in-chief, an advocate should assess a witness's mental state in relation to the parts of his testimony which are to be challenged as inaccurate. For this, no better guidance is available than his common sense, experience of life, and intuition. It is usually too difficult to discover much about the witness as a person; the more limited aim is to see where he stands in relation to his evidence, eg if he is lying or mistaken. He will be cross-examined on the basis of this assessment, unless it has to be modified.

In relation to a given item of disputed evidence, a witness may be truthful and accurate, truthful but mistaken, or untruthful. If he is biased and inaccurate, his testimony may fall anywhere between a mistake and a lie. It is difficult to be more specific without introducing unnecessary psychological complications. It is emphasised that this is not a classification of witnesses into types, for which there is neither a theoretical basis nor any need in practice. It merely groups forms of accuracy or inaccuracy in regard to a particular piece of evidence.

Even in the same trial, the relationship of a witness to his evidence may vary, eg from truthful to untruthful.

Evidence should not be assessed on the basis of general views about the accuracy of types of witnesses. There are no rules about the credibility or reliability of classes of witness—either in psychology or in law. A court's view of the accuracy of the evidence of any witness should be formed by what occurs in the courtroom. With that safeguard, it is harmless to say that independent witnesses are often truthful since they have no motives for lying, but could be mistaken. Witnesses involved in the situation in some way may have motives for lying, and may be suspected of this. On the other hand, they may be mistaken or truthful despite their involvement. Both independent and involved witnesses may also testify inaccurately as a result of bias.

Initially, the general treatment of a witness will correspond to his assessment. It may change later if the assessment has to be corrected, or as a result of the progress of the cross-examination.

C Mistaken witness

The aim in cross-examining a witness who is treated as truthful but mistaken is, ideally, that he should concede his mistake and accept the facts put to him by the cross-examiner.

This is not common. The next best objective is that the witness should concede some doubt which the cross-examiner can exploit, eg in visual identification of the defendant by a Crown witness. If no such concession can be obtained, the final option is for the cross-examination to sow doubt anyway, so that the evidence under challenge will be defeated by contradictory evidence.

If all truthful witnesses were as honest and impartial as their oaths oblige them to be, cross-examining them would become less of a contest and more an exercise in persuading witnesses to report the real state of the facts to the court.

But this is hardly the general picture. The basic intention of many witnesses to tell the truth need not necessarily exclude various forms of resistance.

To achieve his aims, the cross-examiner must try to overcome these.

If a cross-examiner has decided to treat a witness as honest but mistaken, he should establish a friendly rapport with him from the start and maintain it throughout. He does this to secure the witness's co-operation and to uphold his credit as the basis for any concessions which he may obtain. The tactics should be friendly. The advocate should make it obvious that he regards the witness as sincere and trusts him. He can do this at once by his tone of voice, manner and initial questions.

It reassures a witness to show that part of his testimony is accepted even if another part is not, eg 'Mr Wilson, when you noted the registration number, was it not getting dark?' This suggests that the fact of noting the number is accepted although the reported number itself is not.

Many people fear courts and especially cross-examination. They are afraid that they will be made to look foolish, or be accused of being unable to observe competently or of having a poor memory—or, worse, of lying. Short of telling the witness that he will not do this, the cross-examiner should convey that impression. By suitable leading questions he should show sympathy with the difficulties that may have led to incomplete or mistaken evidence, and he should allow the witness to save face.

Probing the accuracy of observation might be introduced by a question showing understanding: 'Mrs Davis, you were busy in the kitchen, and you had no special reason to watch these men through the window, had you?'

If the fading of the witness's memory is involved, the line could be commenced like this: 'Mrs Davis, it was well over a year ago when this happened, wasn't it?'

Everyone in the courtroom knows this, but Mrs Davis, like most witnesses, may be glad of any chance of saying that the incident happened a long time ago, to explain her forgetfulness, or as an excuse for her uncertainty.

Appreciation of the witness's human responses strengthens the bond: 'Was it really quite a shock for you to see what they were doing?'

Words of encouragement to help a witness over a hurdle should precede key questions of this kind: 'Could the man not just have resembled the defendant?' Here the witness may be anxious about departing from the firm evidence of recognition, and needs to be reassured.

In cross-examining an impartial witness to show that evidence is mistaken, the tactics are mostly direct and open. Usually, there is no need to conceal the aim of a line of enquiry.

It is unnecessary for the advocate to mislead or surprise the witness, or to lead him into a trap, as might be the case with an untruthful witness. The aim is often quite obvious, even from the first question: 'How far away were you from the fight?' This is clearly the basis of a challenge to the accuracy of observation.

But open tactics do not include pointless repetition of the evidence-in-chief, culminating, without any preparation or foundation, in this: 'I suggest that you are mistaken. Is that not so?'

This inept process simply wastes time and leads to denial, without any persuasive effect. It only shows that the advocate does not accuse the witness of lying. Such weak advocacy is not uncommon. A challenge to a witness, that he is mistaken must have some substance beyond the cross-examiner's mere assertion that it is so.

Having considered the cross-examiner's approach and tactics in relation to honest but mistaken witnesses, attention may now be given to how such a challenge may be built up by showing how the mistakes could have arisen. This is usually done quite openly since the cross-examiner hopes to persuade the witness to concede the contrary version of the facts. If he does this tactfully, there seems to be no reason for not seeking the witness's co-operation throughout the whole process.

Indirect tactics are unusual with an impartial and sincere, but mistaken, witness. The court may be puzzled if a challenge is approached by a devious route, and may think that it is unnecessary to treat an honest witness in this way. Moreover, the witness may resent such treatment, and become less co-operative.

Probably most challenges to evidence as mistaken concern visual identification of the accused by prosecution witnesses or intangible elements in result-crimes and conduct-crimes generally.

The various sources of interference with the accuracy of observation and memory were fully set out in chapter 3. In preparing for the trial, advocates should be alert for the presence of such factors which may provide a basis for cross-examination. In applying that material, it is helpful to keep certain general principles in mind.

As has been seen, if a court trusts a witness, his self-assessment can overcome objections to the accuracy of his evidence. He was there, and the court was not.

If the witness is confident about what he saw and remembered, and if his sincerity and judgment are trusted, then all the barriers to the accuracy of observation and memory suggested in cross-examination may be defeated.

This has practical importance in cross-examination. It should not be focused exclusively on the obstacles which the witness faced, such as poor lighting or distraction. The advocate should also note carefully how the witness is responding to the challenge. If there is any ground for casting doubt on the features in the witness which inspire trust, this may become the target. Questions may be adjusted with a view to undermining the witness's apparent sincerity and judgment, eg by exposing bias, or inappropriate dogmatism.

This must be qualified by the fact that if an advocate does this, he may lose the witness's co-operation. Extending the basis of the challenge in this way may remove the possibility of obtaining desirable concessions from him, and the attack on the accuracy of his evidence will have to succeed without his co-operation, or fail. Accordingly, which line to take is a matter for the advocate's judgment in the circumstances.

Another problem which a cross-examiner faces is that he can rarely show that any particular source of error leads inevitably to the conclusion that evidence must be inaccurate.

The relationship between barriers to observation or memory and inaccurate reports of an incident is not part of an exact science. Indeed, many of these impediments are just difficulties, not insuperable obstacles, eg the amount which the witness had drunk, a confusing target of one person moving among others, or lapse of time which may have caused some fading of memory. Certainly, these difficulties matter in their time and place, but it is not easy to show this in court long afterwards, by contradicting a witness who asserts that they gave him no trouble.

A cross-examiner should therefore maximise his criticisms where he can find reasonable grounds for doing so. If he can, he should not confine himself to only one obstacle. He should assemble a number of these difficulties, arising from the nature of the event, the conditions of observation, the state of the witness, delay, discussion of evidence and so on.

It is particularly difficult to probe a witness's private psychological processes.

A witness who is asserting that the evidence is accurate is unlikely to co-operate in any such challenge, eg an attempt to show that his recollection is imperfect as a result of such matters as these: that he missed certain vital aspects of the event because his attention was riveted on another compelling feature of the situation; that his expectations influenced his perceptions; that he is labouring under his self-induced errors; that the degree of confidence which he feels in his visual identification arises from what he was told by the police; and that, generally, his recollection is imperfect as a result of discussing the evidence with other witnesses.

To meet such difficulties, the cross-examiner should, wherever possible, elicit from witnesses, evidence of any objective facts from which these private psychological processes may be inferred.

For example, if a witness was being menaced with a knife in a bank, her attention would not be on the registration plate of the robbers' motor car outside. If a store detective stopped a customer almost at the moment when she took a scarf from the counter, his expectations might seem to have determined his perceptions.

If discussion of evidence is suggested as a source of distortion of evidence, it would help to know the exact details of time, place, persons present and subject.

In the light of the difficulties faced in this type of cross-examination, an advocate should concentrate on the really material points on which he wishes to show that the witness is mistaken. He may not succeed with the minor points and, if so, this may not matter.

While this section is concerned with challenging the witness rather than the evidence, it is relevant to note that a cross-examiner may be able to establish that a witness is mistaken because of probative defects in his evidence, ie self-contradiction, inconsistency with other witnesses on the same side, or manifest improbability.

An advocate cross-examines on the basis of his information about the accuracy of evidence. This is his working assumption; it is not a judgment which only the court can reach. On that basis, an advocate may think that a witness is resisting correction unreasonably because of bias. In fact, the witness may be impartial, honest, confident that his testimony is accurate, and is therefore simply being firm.

It is difficult to distinguish such justified firmness from the ordinary reluctance of witnesses to vary their testimony or from mild bias. Where bias is strong, however, a witness may or may not have some awareness of his partiality as a reason for resisting modification of his testimony. Although he still believes that he is telling the truth, he may be prepared to bend his evidence somewhat to support his view of the facts, or to promote justice as he sees it, eg by exaggeration or by becoming argumentative.

Bias may be shown by the exaggerated language, eg words or phrases like 'out of the question', 'absolutely', 'impossible', 'positive', 'never at any time', in contexts where milder or more qualified terms would be more appropriate to the situation. Such language may suggest subjective involvement and a lack of objectivity in the evidence.

Witnesses may become biased for a variety of reasons, only some of which may be detectable. Over a period of many months, what a witness recalls about the event and what he imagines about it may have fused into a rigid but wrong view of the facts, which he believes to be genuine.

If, between the incident and the trial, mistaken images were produced in a witness's mind, in any way, eg the suggestive effect of a discussion with other witnesses, these images would tend to become frozen in the witness's memory, and to persist into the trial.

A witness may feel committed to a view by what he said before the trial, eg to the police, or to solicitors, in statements which were taken from him. Witnesses, generally, are reluctant to appear irresponsible or inconsistent by changing their minds at the last minute.

Sources of bias may be the tendency to see things in black and white, or to take sides uncritically, or for witnesses to side with the party who called them, with some degree of partisanship.

Fixed attitudes or prejudices, or seeing people as stereotypes, and the indirect effects of the media generally, may also influence witnesses. Lay witnesses for the Crown may be hostile to types of criminal, eg drunken motorists, sexual offenders, or drug pushers. Defence witnesses may have preconceptions about police brutality. Some witnesses may be prejudiced against teenagers or wealthy people, and so on.

Such causes of bias and their effect on testimony are difficult or perhaps impossible to expose.

A cross-examiner must know of such possible causes for unreasonable resistance to his contention that evidence is mistaken. Bias itself can sometimes actually create inaccuracy, eg expectancy about the intentions of teenagers seen moving about a car park in darkness. But in other instances, the inaccuracy is caused by something else, eg poor conditions of observation, and bias affects the testimony, by making the witness reluctant to admit that the evidence is or may be mistaken.

The general tenor of the earlier discussion of suitable tactics for honest but mistaken witnesses, viz that they should be friendly, direct and open, must now be qualified for witnesses whose evidence is biased to a material extent.

A witness's mild bias or reluctance to alter his testimony is fairly common but often it may be ignored where it is not expected to affect the essentials of the evidence materially. Here, a cross-examiner may employ friendly, direct and open tactics, as he would with completely impartial witnesses.

Strong bias, however, may affect evidence significantly. In its most extreme form, the state of mind of witnesses may be as close to lying as to mistake because of the element of intention. While they think that, on the whole, they are being truthful, they may be partly aware of their resistance.

Where bias and resistance are material, the cross-examiner may treat the witness in a firm or even hostile way, keeping strict control by narrow leading questions, and using indirect tactics to manipulate the witness into making concessions.

It is, nevertheless, best to start the cross-examination of such witnesses in a friendly and open manner (albeit with reservations) and to continue in this vein until, from the unsatisfactory answers, the need for more forceful tactics becomes clear to the advocate and to the court.

Some sources of mild bias may be detected, and possibly removed, in the context of a friendly form of cross-examination, eg a witness's fear of departing from what he told the police or solicitors in written statements, by reassuring him that if honest doubts have emerged, they can be stated without repercussions.

But sources of strong bias require a different approach. Where facts can be brought out to support an inference that the witness is biased, eg some link with the defendant, whether or not previously revealed, these facts may be explored objectively, but it is important to do this at the right time.

If such enquiry is made at the outset, it may put the witness on his guard, and make him defensive and unco-operative. It would seem to be undesirable to do this until it becomes clear that there is no hope of obtaining any concessions from a strongly biased and mistaken witness, and that it is necessary to discredit him. If so, this should then be done as soon as possible, since the bias may colour the rest of his testimony unfavourably. The attack may be weaker if it is left until the end of his evidence.

One way to discredit a biased witness is to lead him into showing his bias fully by leading him to express it. This may be done by relaxing control of his testimony or by encouraging him to elaborate freely with apparent approval of the direction which he takes. The aim is that he will reveal his bias more and more until he discredits himself. Of course, if this goes wrong, by eliciting harmful statements which are persuasive because they are spontaneous, control should be exercised.

Again, a seriously biased witness may be drawn into displaying his bias by provocative or sarcastic leading questions.

Where a really partisan witness will say almost anything to support his side, a tactic already described may work. If the advocate wants an answer X but the form of question suggests that he seeks an alternative answer Y the witness may fall into the trap by giving the answer X which is really wanted.

Challenging a witness as mistaken can have a variety of results. The cross-examiner's overall intention, if the circumstances justify it, is to weaken or destroy trust in the witness's judgment (rather than his sincerity) as well as to attack part of his evidence. Unless both aspects of the evidence are challenged, the witness's self-assessment and confidence in his report may gain the day. Despite all the criticisms of the accuracy of an item of evidence, if a trusted witness assures the court that the facts were so, this might still be accepted. To attack this too is indispensable.

So far as the evidence itself is concerned, the best result would be if the witness conceded that he was completely mistaken and accepted the cross-examiner's version of the facts. This would be exceptional. The opponent is unlikely to call witnesses who will do this. If it did occur, it would have a highly persuasive effect on the court, although other evidence would have to be considered also.

The next best result for the cross-examiner would be that the witness concedes some doubt about his evidence, which the cross-examination created or intensified. This is a realistic objective in cross-examining an impartial witness. As was seen, challenging a witness as mistaken is aimed at persuading him, if he is impartial, as well as the court, of the mistake. This is unlikely to succeed with a biased witness.

Such a concession of doubt, if obtained, will be valuable. But even if the witness will not go so far as to admit to doubt, he may be persuaded to admit to the possibility of another view. The cross-examiner should strive, at least, to have him concede this. That an alternative is within the realms of possibility is a weakness in the opponent's evidence.

On the other hand, if the witness refuses to accept even the possibility that he may be mistaken, and this refusal can be shown to be unreasonable and dogmatic, it may, thereby, contribute to the cross-examiner's desired conclusion after all.

Concessions by the witness are helpful, but a challenge may succeed without them, if it satisfies the court that the evidence is mistaken or, at least, unreliable.

If essential Crown evidence is held to be unreliable, that is all that the defence need to show. Even if cross-examination alone does not establish that the evidence is mistaken or unreliable, it may be so weakened that it will be overcome by other contradictory evidence on comparison.

Generally, the more reasonable and moderate a cross-examiner's contentions are, the more impressive they will be. In particular, when attacking bias in evidence, it does not help to show it oneself by overstating the contention.

To show that evidence is mistaken does not per se establish the truth of contrary facts unless this follows as an inevitable logical conclusion, or where the court infers what the accurate evidence should be.

D   Lying witness

A cross-examiner must understand the personal aspects of false testimony, ie the characters and motives of lying witnesses.

The value of cross-examination as to credit, is limited by a narrow conception of the relationship of character to credibility. Its aim, typically, is to show that the witness should not be believed because of his character, ie because he is a bad person, with a disposition to lie.

This is derived from former divisions of people into either truthful or untruthful persons. It has some merit of course; a rogue is less likely to be deterred by the prospect of lying. However, this approach is too unrealistic and too simple for court purposes. Innumerable witnesses, of apparently good character, lie in criminal courts, because they are motivated to do so in the particular situation. It is likely that a person's motives in a particular situation creates false testimony much more often than a general disposition to lie.

Cross-examination of a lying witness should go beyond the eliciting of evidence which tends to discredit him because he is of poor character.

His motives in the situation should also be explored. In any event there are legal and tactical limitations on attacks on character.

Only some attacks on character are allowed by law. The defendant, if he testifies, is the witness whose character probably matters most. But he can only be cross-examined about bad character in circumstances defined by statute. The defence may refrain from making imputations against Crown witnesses in case the defendant loses that protection.

Where character is attacked, it cannot be blackened without restriction. Some criticisms, even if true, would not be allowed. The cross-examination must be relevant to the witness's standing with the court, and not be merely vexatious.

The general rule is that answers concerning credit and other collateral matters are final. This prevents a cross-examiner from calling contradictory evidence, except where a witness denies previous convictions or previous inconsistent statements, or to show that he is biased. Questions might arise of the admissibility of some contradictory evidence concerned with the witness's motives as being collateral matters or as being too remote.

Other limitations on challenging the character or motives of witnesses are tactical. Trust or distrust in witnesses as the sources of evidence is crucial for belief or disbelief. Cross-examination confined to character or motives rarely establishes in itself that a witness is lying, but although it may not be decisive, it can still make a contribution, by creating doubt or distrust.

The effects of distrusting a witness may vary. Distrust of a Crown witness who testifies to some essential element in the case, eg a police officer's visual identification of the accused, could be fatal to the prosecution.

But mostly, doubt or distrust of a witness's veracity, is only conclusive when the evidence given is also shown to be defective, in the context of all the evidence in the trial.

Leaving aside the dubious polygraph, if psychology had discovered any reliable method of diagnosing lying, by purely mental means, the legal profession would have seized on it long ago. Psychology has not done so.

In the courtroom, lying cannot be diagnosed with confidence or exposed, simply by considering the character and motives of a single witness. Much more is necessary.

The superiority of the criminal trial, over a psychological interview, is its massive approach to questions of credibility which requires study of all the evidence from all the witnesses, and from all points of view after thorough testing. This is what makes a sound and integrated holistic judgment possible.

A witness's personal qualities and relationship to the situation are usually clearer from his answers about the issues than his answers about himself. But personal questions are usually asked first, to colour the rest of the evidence. The aim is to insinuate these personal doubts into the context of an objective attack on the accuracy of evidence, so that the flaws are attributable to dubious motives.

A cross-examiner who intends to show that a witness is, or may be, lying, should not attempt too much by way of a personal attack beyond drawing out the main facts about his character and circumstances, from which the court may infer his lack of scruples, and motives for lying, despite the witness's denials.

The cross-examiner should create a background of scepticism or distrust of the witness's evidence on the issues which he will attack.

In practice, after the main personal facts are elicited, suggestions to the witness that he is lying may be interwoven with questions on the issues.

The evidence-in-chief should have given a cross-examiner a view of the witness's personality, character, motives and demeanour and should have enabled him to decide whether to challenge harmful evidence as mistaken or untruthful.

This decision should be unambiguous. Witnesses who know the facts and testify wrongly do so intentionally and can only be lying. But for reasons discussed elsewhere, cross-examiners sometimes suggest that lying witnesses are only mistaken, not untruthful. A cross-examiner should not irresponsibly or without reasonable grounds accuse a witness of lying. But if he can only be lying, a cross-examiner should make the nature of his challenge explicit, even if he chooses to do so diplomatically. It misleads the court to suggest that a lying witness is mistaken, where that is not how he is related to his evidence.

This misleading consists of the invitation to the court to see the witness as honest and his inaccuracies as unintentional. It suggests that inaccuracy should be attributed to a range of possible sources of error in observation or memory—excluding motivation. But a lying witness makes inaccurate statements intentionally, because he is motivated to do so, so that the court would have quite different factors to consider. Cross-examination in which an advocate does not show his position clearly by distinguishing mistake from lying is invariably weak or ineffective, and as a forensic performance it is certainly unimpressive.

On the other hand, a cross-examiner achieves nothing by merely indicating his approach to evidence per se: there is little point in saying to a witness, 'I suggest that you are lying about this', or something similar, without laying some foundation and leading up to it. Few perjurers confess when confronted with such a charge.

The tactics for an attack on lying depend on whether a witness is called by the prosecution or defence, whether he is independent or has personal motives, the subject of lying, viz the crime or the accused's implication, and the form of deception, viz affirmative or negative statements, reluctance and evasiveness, omissions, or false qualifications. These topics are discussed fully in chapter 4 and elsewhere, but some important points are particularly relevant to character and motives.

Prosecution witnesses who are most often challenged as untruthful are accomplices, occasionally victims of some crimes, and police. There are usually grounds for attacking both the character and motives of accomplices.

Where an attack on the veracity of a victim is relevant and material, grounds for attacking his character depend on the individual's history, and for attacking motives on his circumstances and those of the crime. Most victims of most crimes have no reason to lie.

Where police witnesses are challenged as untruthful, there are normally no grounds in their past history for attacks on character. Moreover, the defence usually have difficulty in showing motives for lying where there are no obvious reasons for doing so, and especially in view of the disastrous consequences of discovery for the witness. Two kinds of motive arise frequently in challenges to police evidence.

One is that a mistaken belief in the accused's guilt leads them to exaggerate or even invent evidence to secure a conviction. Malice is the other motive which is often suggested. Such malice may have arisen out of previous contacts of an unpleasant nature between some police witnesses and some accused.

Cross-examination as to the character or motives of the police witnesses is unlikely to help the defence here. Challenging them may only make progress if serious inconsistencies emerge in the evidence of two or more police witnesses about the issues, or as a result of other significant evidence.

If the accused gives evidence, he is the defence witness who is invariably attacked as untruthful. The same approach will usually apply to any of his close associates who give direct evidence about the main incident.

Generally, the attack on the credibility of the accused's testimony cannot be on the basis of his poor character. Attacks on a defendant's character, eg reference to his previous convictions, are prohibited by law, except in special circumstances, which are infrequent. Of course the defence evidence may concede facts which put the accused in a bad light, while denying that he committed the offence. For example, when charged as the driver of a stolen motor car which killed a pedestrian, the accused might claim that he was only a passenger. Whether or not he also denies that he knew that the vehicle was stolen, his admitted presence in a stolen motor car, whether as driver or passenger, is unlikely to help him.

It is interesting to note, in this illustration, the narrowing effect of commitment to any line of defence, irrespective of whether it is true or false. Since the accused denies that he was the driver, he can hardly claim that he, personally, was driving carefully and that the accident was caused by the fault of the deceased who stepped out into the roadway from behind a parked lorry. It would, of course, be open to the accused to testify that this is what happened to the real driver.

If so, this would be one of those rare situations in which a double defence is presented, viz the crime was not committed and, in any event, the act in question, whether it was a crime or not, was not the act of the accused. Such situations are uncommon.

In regard to an accused, obviously motivation may count for more than character. Whether he is innocent or guilty, he is probably the most motivated witness in any trial. But, as was said, this should not determine the verdict, even if it affects the weight of his evidence.

Other defence witnesses, deemed to know the facts because of their association with the accused, eg those who speak to his alibi, are also commonly charged with lying. If they have criminal records, as is not uncommon, these will usually be brought out in cross-examination. Association with such witnesses is not favourable to the accused. Their motives stem from their connection with him.

It would be unusual for obviously independent witnesses called by either the prosecution or the defence, to be challenged as untruthful, or for their characters or motives to be criticised.

An exception, where an independent witness might be challenged as untruthful could arise where he is not directly concerned about the situation or the outcome of the trial, but has some personal motive for falsifying his evidence, eg to avoid the embarrassment of admitting that he saw the event in a gay bar, or that he was in Sheffield at a time when he was supposed to be on a business trip to Leeds.

Hoping to avoid the need to give evidence, such a witness may have qualified his account of the facts to the point of uselessness— which he then feels obliged to maintain in court.

Generally, subjects about which lies are told concern the commission of the crime and facts implicating the accused including visual forms of identification. In each of these main issues, eyewitnesses who were involved in the incident in some way and their associates who were present are the main category of those likely to be challenged as untruthful.

This does not only apply to cross-examination by a prosecutor. It is common enough for the defence to attack the testimony of persons who were present at the incident as untruthful. But this type of challenge is usually reserved for motivated witnesses or for police officers who are natural targets for such attacks.

However, with regard to Crown witnesses who appear to be independent, the more common form of defence challenge is to suggest that they are mistaken.

Circumstantial evidence, typically, consists of isolated items which only become significant when they are put together as a basis for an inference. Police witnesses are sometimes accused by the defence, not only of lying about such matters, but of having gone further, eg by 'planting' incriminating real evidence which can be attributed to the possession of the accused. Extreme forms of such defence challenges would go beyond an allegation of perjury into one of a criminal conspiracy to convict an innocent person.

A similar situation is the common attack on police evidence of confessions and admissions as untruthful. Such evidence can arise in any kind of case. The police need not have been observers of a crime. Inevitably they become involved later, in the course of their duties. That is why such challenges are so common. When they are made, the question of suggesting, if not establishing, motives for such criminal conduct by police officers would be a major one for the defence.

Witnesses other than the accused (except in special circumstances) may be cross-examined as to bad character and previous convictions.

A conviction which is denied may be proved against the witness. The attack should be relevant and fair. Restrictions imposed by law should be known. Some convictions should be ignored. Merely to show that a witness has previously been convicted does not prove that he is now lying, but showing this might reduce the trust in him, which is essential to belief in his evidence.

In putting previous convictions to a witness, skill can make a considerable difference. As has been said, the fact of having a previous conviction is inconclusive in itself. However, if the witness can be induced to show that he is evasive and disposed to deceive in the instant trial, this can damage his creditworthiness more than the conviction itself.

The weakest approach is to put the convictions to the witness directly, asking him if he admits or denies them. This offers no opening for lying if he is so minded. A better way of doing this illustrates how indirect tactics can lead a witness into a trap which he helps to create by lying in the present case about his previous convictions. The lies can then be exposed immediately by direct confrontation.

Casual and seemingly unimportant questions as to whether the witness had ever been in trouble, and suggesting ignorance of the position, might start the process.

> Q: 'I won't keep you long Mr Jackson, you probably don't enjoy being here, do you?'
> A: 'No, I don't much.'
> Q: 'Is it a new experience for you?'

A liar, encouraged, by the advocates apparent ignorance, and mild manner, may confirm this:

> A: 'Yes.'

Having embarked on deception, the witness should be made to commit himself to it:

> Q: 'So you've never been in court before?'
> A: 'Never.'
> Q: 'And so you've never been in trouble before?'
> A: 'No.'

Thereafter, only one previous conviction should be put to the witness which he will have little choice but to admit. His lie can then be exploited by such questions as the following:

> Q: 'Why did you say that you had never been in trouble before?'
> Q: 'Why had you forgotten about this?'
> Q: 'You were put on probation for a year, weren't you?'

This process could be repeated for one conviction after another until the witness is ready to admit them all even including some which the advocate did not know about.

The point of such tactics is not just to show that a witness is of bad character. It demonstrates his willingness to lie in the trial, so that the credibility of his evidence will be in shreds.

Even where such a witness admits his previous convictions, the same approach can be used with regard to any aspects which he has not revealed:

> Q: 'So you admit that you were convicted of car theft on that occasion?'
> A: 'Yes, I was.'
> Q: 'Did you plead guilty?'
> A: 'No.'
> Q: 'So you denied your guilt, and the court found you guilty nevertheless?'
> A: 'The court got it wrong.'

These sample questions illustrate the scope for exposing a witness as false, on the basis of irrefutable documentary evidence of his convictions. If they were simply put to him at the outset, little would have been achieved.

The motives of many witnesses are often quite clear, independently of cross-examination, because of their connections with the issues or parties.

The prosecutor should have brought out any such significant facts which he knew about his witnesses. If he suspects that there are undisclosed interests in defence witnesses, he would probe these areas to bring them to light. If any material facts emerge in cross-examination of witnesses on either side, from which a motive on the part of the witness may be inferred, failure to disclose it in the evidence-in-chief will not impress the court.

However, even where motives, or facts from which motives may be inferred, have already been disclosed, in cross-examining any witness such points, which could affect their evidence, may be highlighted and emphasised. So far as relevancy allows, relationships could be put in story or visual form, to make them more striking:

> Q: 'So, since the accused is your foreman, a day never passes without you seeing him at the factory?'
> Q: 'And he gives you your jobs, doesn't he?'

A cross-examiner, knowing of a witness's undisclosed connection with the case, might, by indirect tactics, lead one who lies into denying such facts, with which he then confronts him by direct tactics. This would be similar to the technique used to elicit a witness's previous convictions.

As was seen, it does not follow from the existence of a motive in a certain direction, that evidence to that effect must be untrue. But it may raise questions and weaken the evidence. Apart from this, the handling of the witness and his response to the question of his motive, on which he may feel vulnerable, is a real opportunity for an able cross-examiner.

Alternatively, without elaborating on the facts which might motivate the witness to lie, an advocate might leave this to be inferred by the court, supported by a mere reference in argument, to suggest that the point is self-evident: 'Of course the witness was speaking about his foreman—the man on whom his job depends'. The implication is clear and compelling

The personality of witnesses and the subject of demeanour were fully discussed in chapter 4. Nothing more need be said specifically about their relationship to cross-examination.

Naturally, there is no one way of cross-examining all dishonest witnesses. Various forms of deception need to be handled in different ways. A massive amount of deceit in courts, which could distort the trial process if it were not detected, would not satisfy the legal requirements for perjury.

The kind of lying which could amount to perjury is found when a witness knowingly affirms something which is not true, or denies something which is true. This is lying in its most stark and extreme form. A witness is unlikely to lie in this way without a strong motive, the existence of which may be obvious.

Because of the gravity of such falsehoods, the original motive which led to them will be reinforced by fear of the penalties which may follow from exposure.

A witness who lies like this will resist cross-examination more than others. An advocate should not expect to obtain any retractions, concessions or confessions, from this type of witness, although he uses a whole range of techniques. Sometimes he may appear to make no headway at all with a well-prepared lying witness who tells a consistent and plausible story. It can be counter-productive to persist and to prolong a cross-examination unnecessarily. Not only does this achieve nothing—it also emphasises the adverse evidence by repetition, elaboration, and resistance to attack.

Here, a cross-examiner may have to be content if he manages to weaken the adverse evidence and may make better progress by relying on the contradictory evidence which he leads himself.

False qualifications in evidence, by intentionally colouring it one way or another, or by overstating or understating the degree of confidence in it, are subtle forms of deception which may be difficult to detect.

The same facts may be stated in many different ways even in honest evidence, and witnesses must be allowed to testify in their own natural language. Therefore it may be hard to distinguish deceptive testimony of this kind from a normal variation.

The witness's motive is not strong enough to make him lie outright. This is a compromise form of falsehood. Sometimes false qualifications are found in an advocate's own witnesses. If so, he may grasp this easily, because of the difference in tone between their previous statements and the present evidence.

Where there is any reason to suspect that a witness is falsifying his evidence in this way, close attention should be paid to the exact language which he uses. He may usefully be asked to explain nuances, eg the meaning of 'as far as I recall' or 'to the best of my knowledge' so that he cannot hide behind them.

Exposure of a witness's motives here can also help in showing that an unwarranted gloss is being placed on evidence.

Reference to previous inconsistent statements, if any, can also assist a cross-examiner, eg where earlier certainty about the offender's identity becomes doubtful in the trial.

Witnesses may demonstrate their reluctance to testify, or evasiveness, by their way of answering questions. They may answer with hesitation, in a subdued voice, or repeat questions to give themselves time to think. They may avoid the obvious point, or answer points not asked.

Their evasiveness would be a poor accompaniment to convincing perjury; it would be too obvious to the court. Such witnesses are not prepared to commit perjury although they are unwilling to tell the truth, or all of it.

Suitable tactics for a cross-examiner could include placing emphasis on the witness's evasiveness. This could be done by asking the witness to listen very carefully, asking questions very slowly and deliberately, repeating them for effect, or having the court reporter read questions back. Such measures should prevent a witness from claiming that he did not hear or understand a question, and should make his evasiveness even more obvious.

More forcefully, a cross-examiner could insist on direct answers to important questions, or refer to previous inconsistent statements. Warnings from advocates and from the bench may also help.

If desired evidence cannot be obtained from reluctant and evasive witnesses, the cross-examiner may at least try to reduce the negative aspects of their evidence both in questioning them and in his closing speech.

Omission of material evidence is another compromise in a witness who is motivated not to reveal all the truth, but who is still unwilling to incur the risks of lying. This, of course, refers to intentional omissions, not merely to evidence which is incomplete as a result of limited observation or forgetting. In the previous discussion of this kind of evidence, it was seen that whatever the witness's contribution to it may be, incomplete or badly framed questioning has most of the responsibility for such an effect. The remedy is to put questions which force the witness to disclose the whole truth as an alternative to committing perjury, which he is unwilling to do. Narrow leading questions like the following may allow a witness to escape such a dilemma:

Q: 'Did you see her put the watch in her bag?'
A: 'No.'

This is truthful but omits vital information which could be elicited by wider leading questions:

Q: 'Did she lift the watch from the counter?'
A: 'Yes.'
Q: 'What did she do with it?'
A: 'She gave it to the boy, who put it in his pocket.'

These questions present the witness with the choice of either giving this information or else lying.

Such witnesses may, of course, escape such dilemmas by taking refuge in pretended amnesia. This is very difficult to overcome in cross-examination because there is no material to challenge, and no way of knowing or demonstrating that the claim is false—unless there was no amnesia in a previous inconsistent statement. However, if the court's faith in the 'amnesia' can be shaken, this may contribute to their view about what the evidence might have been if it had been given.

To challenge the claimed lack of memory for the facts, the advocate should note whether the points which are said to be forgotten form a significant pattern. Also the witness's lack of difficulty in recalling one set of facts in evidence-in-chief may be contrasted with the onset of amnesia in cross-examination directed towards a contrary set of facts.

Cross-examination on such lines, supplemented by critical argument in the closing speech, could be persuasive.

Some tactics may be useful with lying witnesses of any kind. Liars, however well they may have prepared, cannot foresee all the possible questions which may be asked. When something quite unexpected is put to them, they may become anxious, hesitant, confused, and uncertain about which direction to take. A cross-examiner can often achieve some helpful result, without incurring any risk, if he asks a few totally unexpected questions.

To avoid objections to their admissibility, such questions, should, of course, have some semblance of relevancy to the issues, they should seem to be reasonable and they should not be too numerous or too frequent.

However, these questions may, indeed, have little real point, except the cross-examiner's intention of disturbing a lying witness, and of producing useful reactions of a general kind to increase the court's distrust in him.

To ask two or more witnesses such questions, especially on topics which are outside the bounds of preparation or collusion, can be particularly effective. They may lead to glaring inconsistencies which could damage the credibility of their evidence more widely.

Examples would be questions about where the witness went for lunch, with whom, what they talked about, what he did on the previous evening, whom he met, when he first told his story, when he was interviewed by the police, whether he has discussed his evidence and, if so where, when and with whom, or whether he knows a particular place or a particular person.

Although such questions may have little or no underlying reality, they would be designed to suit the particular circumstances of the trial. They are mainly calculated to worry a lying witness and undermine his control of a false presentation—but the witness does not know that.

Challenges to lying witnesses are usually insufficient in themselves to do more than weaken their evidence. Even an untrustworthy witness could be speaking the truth on a given occasion. It would not seem reasonable to contend otherwise in a speech.

However, where the distrust sown in the witness as the source of the evidence, eg because of his motivation, is combined with showing that the evidence itself is defective, eg because of its improbability, the basis for disbelief in that evidence is much stronger.

In cross-examining on the issues, personal flaws would emerge naturally, although they are not the immediate target of questions. That a witness is lying is usually revealed most clearly when he is trying to substantiate his version of the facts.

However, even this may not complete the process of destroying evidence. It is completed in most cases by leading contradictory evidence which, together with the closing speech, overcomes the evidence under challenge. A cross-examiner should therefore be content if he can make a significant contribution to the weakening of evidence, and he should not be disappointed if he does not achieve instant and total victory.

VIII CHALLENGING THE EVIDENCE

Whether destructive cross-examination is conducted by the prosecution or the defence, the essential purpose is to challenge evidence about the central issue of fact in a trial, viz whether the crime was committed, or whether the accused was the offender; criticisms of witnesses as mistaken or untruthful, and other issues, are incidental.

A Nature of process

As was seen, for belief in evidence, the witness must be trusted; how trust may be undermined was considered. This section is concerned with how a cross-examiner may attack the basis for the other two requirements of belief, viz that the evidence must be reasonable, and that the evidence must have weight.

To show that evidence is unreasonable, the challenge should expose inconsistency, improbability or lack of realism. Specific areas of evidence where any of these defects are shown sufficiently, would be rejected.

Sometimes other areas of evidence or even the whole case would be rejected as a result of a the defect found in the area where it is exposed.

The aim of the other type of attack on evidence is to reduce its 'weight' which may be defined as 'the value or significance conferred on individual items of evidence by comparing it with all the other evidence'. The technique consists of opposing the acceptance of disputed evidence by reference to other evidence. Its essence is contradiction. This should be distinguished from a common use of the term 'weight' to mean evidence which has already been accepted, and to refer to its effect in deciding a verdict.

Obviously, the comparison of items of evidence cannot be wholly done in cross-examination. It must also depend on the closing speeches. For one thing, witnesses should not be asked to assess the evidence of other witnesses. For another, at the stage of cross-examination, evidence which will enter into the comparative process may not have been given yet.

However, to the extent that he is able to do so, and the witness knows the material facts, a cross-examiner could initiate such a comparison of evidence by putting his case to the witness and confronting him with material which contradicts his evidence. Even where the witness does not make any comparison in his evidence, the court will have the material for doing so.

B Unreasonable evidence

Evidence which is inconsistent, improbable or unrealistic, may be described as unreasonable.

These are mainly inherent qualities of the evidence of a single witness, which can be seen or exposed without depending on comparison with other evidence. However the concept of inconsistency can be extended in order to compare the evidence of more than one witness where they all purport to tell the same story, but, in fact, they deviate from this materially.

1 *Inconsistency*

Inconsistency means that two statements cannot both be true at the same time. The starkest form of inconsistency is self-contradiction in the evidence of one witness.

Inconsistency may also be found on comparing the evidence of two or more witnesses who purport to give similar accounts but do not in fact do so. Normally they are on the same side, but at times some witnesses may testify in favour of the other side, and, for the purpose of this exposition, they may be regarded as belonging there notionally, in presenting the same story.

Inconsistency is a logical flaw, ie in the relationship between statements, irrespective of the underlying facts. If a witness says that he saw a light on in the upstairs bedroom of a neighbour's house at

9pm but later denies that any lights were on throughout the whole evening, logic requires that at least one or other of these two statements must be rejected. However, logic cannot specify which statement this is and, in fact, both statements may be untrue. Inconsistency, then, throws no light on the facts, but it shows that something is wrong with the relevant part of the evidence.

It means that material parts of one report or the other about the particular facts to which they refer must be mistaken or false. The general impression made by all of this evidence would be weakened without destroying any element or establishing the truth.

A cross-examiner's task is to expose inconsistency. It may be self-evident without pointing it out, eg in the example given the lights could not be both switched on and switched off at the same time. At other times inconsistency only emerges as evidence develops, eg medical evidence of stab wounds on a victim who claims that he was attacked with a hammer.

The importance of discovering inconsistency in evidence in a criminal trial cannot be exaggerated. It is perhaps the first thing that most advocates look for or grasp spontaneously, in an opponent's evidence. Where it is not immediately obvious, careful listening, note-taking, which may be verbatim on important points, and detailed comparisons of evidence may be necessary.

Glaring inconsistencies in the evidence of a single witness would generally be eliminated in the course of taking statements for the trial.

If no inconsistency is found, methods of creating it in dishonest witnesses are set out in various parts of this book.

Once inconsistency has been exposed, a cross-examiner's objective will be to exploit it by expanding the effect beyond the immediate area of evidence, so as to inflict maximum damage.

If any apparent inconsistency arises in the course of an examination-in-chief, an advocate will, naturally, try to correct it as soon as he realises this. If a single witness has made two statements which seem to conflict with each other, this difficulty could be met in various ways.

An advocate could try to elicit an explanation from his witness which reconciles the two statements, or he might cause him to reaffirm one alternative while rejecting the other, or perhaps he might modify both statements. But however the difficulty is tackled, if an advocate tries to lead his own witness to the slightest extent in this critical area of the examination-in-chief, his opponent should object at once. In any event, even if the advocate succeeds in patching up this inconsistency, it may still be a vulnerable point for attack by the cross-examiner.

Objection should also be taken to any attempt to undo cross-examination about inconsistency, by leading in the course of re-examination.

The most likely source of inconsistencies is to be found on comparing the testimony of two or more of the opponent's witnesses, but it is unproductive to highlight minor discrepancies which arise from the universal fallibility of observation and memory. This is often done as the basis for unwarranted contentions that witnesses are unreliable, mistaken or untruthful

In cross-examination, it is better to ignore trifling differences between the evidence of several witnesses. People do not register events with the precision of video cameras. Slight differences abound in the accounts of several witnesses to the same scene. They rarely mean that the evidence is unsound on essential facts. An advocate who relies on such trifles may appear to have a weak case.

Such minor differences must, of course, be distinguished from others which become significant because of the context, for example if there is an issue about whether the witness was present at all at the incident which he describes. If a defence witness testifies that he saw police officers attack the defendant brutally, but he differs from other defence witnesses on details, this may not matter much. But if the Crown contention is that the witness was not even there, minor differences may be significant or crucial.

Similarly, in alibi evidence, minor differences about details or collateral facts, may be sinister where a prosecutor contends that the event never occurred.

Facts whose significance is derived from the context include those which are part of a chain of circumstantial evidence, and about which inconsistency may be very important.

Inconsistency about the main facts, eg the commission of the crime or the implication of the accused, and related material facts, should not be allowed to pass without challenge and exploitation.

Generally, any inconsistency which suggests lying rather than error would invite challenge.

Self-contradiction is more significant in this respect. Only one witness is involved so that, unlike inconsistency between two witnesses, the excuse cannot be offered that one witness is truthful and the other is not.

Under close scrutiny, mistaken or untruthful evidence will be found to have no sound basis of fact and must be in conflict with reality somewhere. In cross-examination, inconsistency which is latent can often be made explicit, and with untruthful witnesses who add to their lies, inconsistency can even be created by direct or indirect tactics.

An untruthful witness can be induced to contradict himself by leading him to invent new evidence beyond the relative safety of his prepared story about the main facts, so that he commits himself firmly. He will not do this intentionally. His control must be overcome by direct or indirect tactics.

The cross-examiner should keep the testimony moving and expanding, with the witness off balance or unaware where it is going, until he alters his evidence, until it is inconsistent with what he said previously. This can be done by direct tactics where unexpected questions are fired at the witness quickly and in an unpredictable order so that he finds it difficult to relate his inventions to what was said before. Alternatively, using indirect tactics, the advocate may encourage the witness to testify freely until his over-confidence leads him to develop his false story until it clashes with his earlier evidence. By employing similar direct or indirect methods on several witnesses—the more the better—the same result can be achieved. Questions may be framed so that none of them see the overall aim. The cross-examiner can exploit the typical situation that some untruthful witnesses will be less motivated and less well-prepared than others.

Separate advocates for several defendants could arrange to cross-examine in different directions, but with a common objective.

The cumulative impact of exposing inconsistencies in the evidence of several witnesses may be striking.

A refinement is to put the story told by one witness to another, which may produce unconvincing efforts to reconcile the differences.

Once inconsistency in evidence is exposed, judgment is needed as to whether or not to press the advantage home, explicitly. This depends on whether it is likely that a witness will improve his position by explaining or reconciling the inconsistencies or fail, or even worsen his evidence in the attempt.

The alternative is for the cross-examiner to stop at once. This will deprive the witness of any chance of improving matters and is less likely to alert his opponent to the need for remedial measures.

Cross-examination may also be required where the evidence of two or more witnesses shows an unatural consistency, which suggests collusion in memorising the evidence; this may be suggested by unusual similarities in language, topics and sequence, points remembered or forgotten, and parrot-like ways of testifying.

If such witnesses are asked to repeat their evidence-in-chief, similarities will be emphasised. Also, rapid and random questioning may disrupt false evidence which is memorised. Without a basis in reality they may be led into inconsistencies and improbabilities.

Referring a lying witness to a previous inconsistent statement is a common and useful tactic, and is most effective if an opening is created for the witness to lie about it. He will then be confronted with the statement and the advantage can be pressed home.

Cross-examination in which a large volume of evidence is challenged is often prolonged unwisely because of excessive expectations. It would be improved by brevity, if it were based on the selection of a few material and decisive points, and ended at once when these were conceded or the challenge had gone as far as it could.

The destructive effects of exposing inconsistency vary. It may make evidence about particular facts quite unacceptable. It may weaken the adverse evidence generally, so that at the judgment stage of the trial it is overcome by the cross-examiner's contradictory evidence. Any material inconsistency in the Crown case may well raise reasonable doubts and, if so, it could be fatal. Inconsistencies in the defence case may be less serious. It would depend on their nature and where they occurred.

In his questions and in his closing speech, a cross-examiner should be explicit as to whether he contends that inconsistency which has emerged is due to mistake or lying, as their effects are different and his argument will differ accordingly. He will no doubt elect for lying, if this can be justified. Inconsistency which is seen to arise from lying is the more serious form. If lying is clearly demonstrated in one area of a party's evidence, it could destroy trust in the witness and could taint the credibility of the whole of that evidence.

If an honest mistake is shown in part of the evidence given by a witness, generally that part will not be accepted. However, this need not entail the rejection of all of his evidence, unless the nature and extent of the mistake, or mistakes made by him raise doubts about his general reliability as an observer, his memory, or the soundness of his way of reporting facts. If so, the effect of his inconsistent and mistaken evidence may be wider.

Of course there can be no rules about the effect of exposing inconsistency. This will vary according to circumstances, and judgment and discrimination will be exercised by the court.

2 *Improbability*

For court purposes, and in general terms, probability means the extent to which the existence of certain facts is likely; in criminal trials it refers to the likelihood that past facts were as stated in evidence.

Conviction requires proof beyond reasonable doubt, acquittal does not. The question of what is meant by proof beyond reasonable doubt has exercised the minds of trial judges and appeal courts. Since it is a legal test, this will not be explored here, beyond commenting that it seems to imply both an objective criterion, ie 'proof' and a mental one, by its reference to 'doubt'.

On any view, probability enters into the decision of many facts in criminal trials. 'Absolute certainty', or similar phrases, are not common in judicial charges to juries. One way of looking at the concept—which is not suggested here as a legal analysis—is that, for conviction, probabilities converge until they attain the objective and subjective standards required by law.

Improbability is one of the inherent qualities of evidence described here as unreasonable; where evidence is sufficiently improbable, this would be a bar to belief in it.

The ultimate nature of probability continues to baffle philosophers and will not be discussed here. For practical purposes, as a criterion for judgment in court, probability applies the tests of life experience, intuition and common sense to disputed questions. The commonsense usage is that something is probable when it is more likely to happen than not; otherwise it is improbable.

In its everyday sense, the quantum of probability does make a difference to judgment, although it is unquantifiable. Evidence may be evaluated by reference to a spectrum which ranges through near certainty, highly likely, likely, odd, or totally absurd. Obviously other adjectives or adverbs could be used to show the gradations of probability, but this would not help.

The extreme of impossibility in evidence is hardly a problem for cross-examination in practice. The allegation of facts which are clearly impossible would be unacceptable per se and would not be expected to survive preparation for trial or the evidence-in-chief. If it emerges that alleged facts are impossible, when evidence is compared, this could be treated as inconsistency or contradiction.

Mathematical and non-mathematical probability are distinct, at least in the use of language. Mathematical probability is the degree to which an event is likely to happen as measured by a ratio ranging from 0, meaning impossibility, to 1, meaning certainty. The probability of a six in tossing dice is 1/6 which equals 0.167. In theory, any event, however unlikely, has a degree of mathematical probability.

In criminal trials, questions of mathematical probability are usually confined to technical evidence, eg evidence of the distribution of blood groups in the population. Otherwise the non-mathematical view of probability prevails in courts, viz the likelihood that past facts were as stated in evidence. Although this could be reformulated in various ways, it would add nothing to the precision of the test. Ultimately it is a human evaluation.

To challenge evidence as improbable is more difficult than to show that it is inconsistent. Inconsistency needs only the self-evident test of logical contradiction when two or more statements are compared. Improbability depends on an evaluation for which there are neither rules nor logical procedures; it is a matter of a judgment based on experience of life outside the court.

A judgment that something is probable or improbable is really an inference from facts, not certain knowledge of them.

To be admissible, questions which are directly concerned with probability, can only be put in cross-examining certain witnesses and in regard to certain kinds of evidence. In other cases, witnesses can only be cross-examined as to facts which the court will take into account in evaluating the probability or improbability of an event.

Expert witnesses who give opinion evidence may be cross-examined as to the probability of their conclusions. Lay witnesses who, in special circumstances, are permitted to give impression evidence, eg as the only way of communicating their observations, might be challenged about their interpretations of ambiguous or obscure happenings, such as the actions of someone charged with taking part in a theft as a look out. Borderline questions of probability may be involved here.

Inferences drawn from items of circumstantial evidence involve issues of probability, but although such inferences may be contradicted by direct evidence, witnesses to the facts on which they are based should not be asked for opinions about the inferences to be drawn from them.

Typically, criticisms of evidence as improbable involve matters of human nature and conduct, which perhaps refer to the witness, but more commonly refer to the accused. Lay evidence can be attacked directly as untrue, and facts and circumstances may be put to such witnesses, from which a different inference is more probable. Such evidence may consist of separate facts with some relationship to each other, or a connected story as an account of the event.

A cross-examiner who intends to challenge evidence as improbable has options. He can dispute any fact on which the story is based, he can attack the alleged relationship between facts, and he can assert a different relationship, as in cross-examining the accused in the following case.

A man was charged with abducting a 12-year-old girl, and with taking her to his home where he assaulted her indecently. He claimed that as she was abandoned, he had to take her home, and he denied the indecent assault. The prosecutor disputed some facts, and suggested a different relationship between others, viz that the girl was not abandoned, that the accused knew of a nearby police station, and that all his actions showed criminal intent. His improbable story was rejected and he was convicted.

A prosecutor's cross-examination of a defendant will often challenge the probability of his denials that he acted as charged, or with criminal intent, or that he was the person implicated. In addition to confronting the accused with direct Crown evidence which contradicts him, he may also ask him to explain facts which constitute incriminating circumstantial evidence.

However, although such cross-examination raises questions of probability, this is for the court to decide. The accused is being asked about facts which are put to him directly.

The position is similar with many witnesses. A good deal of cross-examination which is directed to showing the improbability of their evidence does not raise that question directly with the witness who is giving evidence. The court, when deciding the verdict, will consider the evidence assembled from all the witnesses.

Probability is a matter of degree; the greater the improbability, the more the accuracy of evidence is in doubt.

Facts never exist in isolation; they are embedded in a context with all sorts of connections, eg what occurred before, during and after a main incident, collateral circumstances, motives and actions, or causes and effects.

One technique for exposing improbability is therefore to expand the evidence to include this context so far as this is helpful. If the evidence is true, the facts put forward ought to fit in to other facts and reality. But if the evidence is untrue, discontinuity should emerge to show this. Thoroughness of preparation here would help a cross-examiner in knowing which direction to take.

One way or another, the aim is to extend the contact of an unlikely story with reality, so that it becomes increasingly improbable to the point of absurdity, as it is seen how the story does not fit together, and its discontinuity with reality becomes obvious.

Where admissible evidence contains any element of interpretation, counter-probabilities may be suggested as more acceptable than what the witness states, and built up into a story.

As always, judgment is needed on where to end such cross-examination. Doing so as soon as the aim is achieved has the usual benefits: it prevents the witness from undoing gains and reduces the risk of adverse re-examination, or further evidence from the opponent's witnesses.

3 Lack of realism

As an impressionistic guide to assessing evidence, lack of realism was discussed in chapter 4. Typical unrealistic features of false stories are lack of factual detail and colouring, lack of personal involvement and a tendency for evidence all to be in one direction. It is mentioned here to complete the list of unreasonable qualities of evidence, but it is merely background material for cross-examiners to understand, and draw out. It does not lend itself to a specific technique.

C Weight of evidence

Evidence may satisfy two of the requirements for belief, namely a degree of trust in the witness and the absence of probative defects, and yet be unconvincing. Without further support, it could appear to be no more than plausible, ie it could be true.

For evidence to be believed and acted on, a court will see how it fits into the whole of the evidence in the case, after it has been assembled and considered holistically. This will show the relationships of support and contradiction between parts of the evidence.

In closing speeches, advocates should also take this comprehensive approach, which determines the 'weight' of any given piece of evidence, as defined here. But in cross-examination, an advocate is concerned with putting to witnesses whatever contradicts their own evidence, not evidence which supports it. His aim, then, is to reduce the weight of the witness's evidence.

The principle of contradiction is the essence of the adversarial process. It is put into effect in cross-examination where an advocate must put so much of his case to a witness as is within the witness's knowledge, and confronts him with contradictory material derived from other evidence.

As has been said in various parts of this book, it may be better to do this with one or two comprehensive questions, to minimise the damage which repeated and detailed denials may do. In many cases, the more quickly a case is put to the witness and denied the better.

In confronting the witness with contradictory evidence, a cross-examiner should comply with proper practice. He may ask about facts spoken to by his own witnesses, but not for an opinion on other evidence, or its credibility or reliability.

The cross-examiner should not argue with the witness or, in effect, give evidence himself by such statements as 'My information is ...' or 'My client will say ...'

A cross-examiner should be careful to quote accurately, or summarise fairly, any admissible reference to other specific evidence, eg in questioning an expert witness.

The effect of putting his case and of confronting the witness with contradictory evidence or even undisputed facts varies. The minimum gain is to show the court that a view is possible which differs from the evidence of that witness. The greatest gain would be acceptance of the case put to the witness. Something intermediate may be achieved.

The final effect of this attack on the weight of a witness's evidence, may not occur at the stage of cross-examination. It is usually completed when the court makes its comparison of all the evidence, and prefers the contradictory evidence which the cross-examiner put to the witness.

CHAPTER 9

Cross-examination:
common problems

I   Problems arising from issues
II Problems with witnesses

E very situation which a cross-examiner encounters is unique and
the problems which arise may vary widely. Yet observations of
general application may be made about many recurrent patterns.

Some common problems in cross-examination are considered in
this chapter, in the light of the principles discussed in previous
chapters.

These problems fall into two main categories, viz those arising
from the type of issues, and and those arising from the type of witness.

I PROBLEMS ARISING FROM ISSUES

As was seen, where the defence offer a positive version of the facts,
this will generally restrict the real issue in the trial to the question of
whether the crime was committed, or the question of whether the
defendant was the offender. It would be exceptional for both of these
questions to be live issues.

A   Crime as the issue

Crimes were analysed for practical purposes into result-crimes,
conduct-crimes and object-crimes. Each class of crime involves typical
problems for cross-examiners.

1   *Result-crimes*

A result-crime is one which is constituted by a forbidden act and the
result which it causes.

By definition, the result will be something physical and tangible,
eg a person's physical state, including injury, death or sexual
violation, or the location of the stolen contents of a house in a hiding
place, or damage to property caused by vandalism.

As such results are visible and durable, abundant and compelling evidence is usually available to prove them. Therefore such facts are usually admitted or are not disputed.

They may, of course, not be admitted because some defence advocates believe that the most effective tactics are a total refusal of any co-operation with the prosecution. This may impress their clients especially if they are guilty. But it rarely impresses any type of court.

Where some crucial but obvious facts, like the burglary of a house or the theft of a motor car, are not admitted by the defence, the law requires that, for conviction, the prosecutor must prove them by sufficient evidence. This is easily done, but it takes time, which — essentially—is wasted. Fact-finders are unlikely to welcome this. Where no harm would be done to the defence by co-operating, their refusal may seem to be pointless and unreasonable. If so, this might tend to colour their impression of the advocate, his presentation and his case, unfavourably.

While in no way condoning any deviation from a proper judicial attitude, it is appropriate to point out that undisclosed resistances may be built up in jurors who believe that lawyers profit by prolonging proceedings, who see an endless number of fellow-citizens called as witnesses unnecessarily, and who find that their own time and that of the court is spent on wasteful proceedings.

In result-crimes, advocates would usually improve their presentations by conceding crucial and obvious facts, proof of which will be inevitable in any event. If they decide to do so, there are different ways of doing this.

The most effective way to concede facts is by means of the procedure provided by law for formal admissions, which exclude the need for evidence to prove the facts admitted. It is less impressive to concede facts at the bar, or by implication in cross-examination, or, belatedly, in a closing speech.

In result-crimes, the problems which arise for cross-examiners are those concerned with intangible questions. These include states of mind and the quality of acts. Indeed, where the result of a result-crime is uncontested, and no such intangible questions arise with regard to the commission of the crime, it would seem that the accused's identity as the offender, is the only possible defence. However, intangible questions do arise in some result-crimes.

Self-defence illustrates both aspects of this situation, viz issues about states of mind and the quality of acts. Where the accused's attack on another person, and the injuries which this caused, are not in doubt, the accused may claim that he was merely defending himself, as he was entitled to do by law, and thus committed no crime. His state of mind, eg whether he had a reasonable apprehension of sustaining injury himself, would be a crucial and intangible issue.

Also the nature and quality of the acts of each party would be essential facts which would contribute to the decision of the issue. If the victim was brandishing a bottle and threatening to strike the accused, this would support the defence, but if the victim was silent and had his hands in his pockets, that would be another matter.

Rape also illustrates the point, eg where the female's consent to sexual intercourse is the pivotal question. Here, the states of mind and the quality of the conduct of each party are crucial matters of fact.

Where death was caused in a traffic accident, the question of whether this was just an unfortunate accident or arose from careless or dangerous driving would involve crucial questions of states of mind and the quality of acts.

Indeed, in any case where the result may have been caused by accident, the accused's state of mind, including his guilty intention or otherwise, will be a crucial intangible issue.

Disputes about intangible elements on which the constitution of the crime depends usually involve sharp conflicts of direct evidence and of credibility.

But in a murder charge, the elimination of the deceased participant as a witness usually does not help matters.

Cross-examining witnesses in such a situation can be difficult. Advocates should not allow it to deteriorate into patterns of assertion and counter-assertion, or arguing with witnesses, without making any progress, as so often happens.

In the court's evaluation of the clash of evidence between the main participants or eyewitnesses, and in the approach of parties, it is generally assumed that they must know the facts, and that if their evidence is inaccurate, they can only be lying.

This is the usual line which is taken by a prosecutor with an accused person and his eyewitnesses who are close associates such as relatives, friends or workmates, and is often the defence line with alleged victims.

Here, it may be expected that witnesses are strongly motivated, and whether genuine or not, they may give impressive performances.

A conflict of direct testimony is often inconclusive in itself. To reach decisions on such a basis, without additional facts, may be dangerous.

This can be an effective argument for the defence. Because of the presumption of innocence and the burden on the prosecutor of proving guilt, if the court is left with a reasonable doubt about essentials, an acquittal should follow.

Additional facts can put those which are in issue in quite a new and significant frame which defines their meaning.

For example, if an accused person is stopped by police while driving a friend's motor car he may be charged with possession of prohibited drugs which are found in the unlocked boot. Presumably the accused denies any knowledge of the presence of the drugs in the vehicle, while not disputing that the police found them there.

For the prosecutor in cross-examining the accused, to insist that he must have known about the presence of the drugs and that they were for his own use, might be unconvincing unless he has other facts to back this up.

Such facts could be that the bag containing the drugs bears the accused's initials which differ from those of his friend, that his friend has been abroad for two months, leaving his car with the accused and that equipment used by drug addicts were found in the accused's bedroom.

As a general principle, it may be said that to succeed in cross-examining a witness in a conflict of direct testimony about an intangible element in a crime, will be difficult without extrinsic material. A resistant witness may be confronted with this, both to weaken or destroy his evidence and to set the direct evidence in a new frame, as in the above example of the driver who was charged with possessing prohibited drugs.

Three main sources of such material are:

(1) the results of the acts;
(2) collateral facts; and
(3) previous inconsistent statements.

(a) *The results of the acts.* In a vast number of result-crimes, the crucial intangible facts can be inferred from the results alone.

For example, the guilty mind of a person who broke all the windows in a house by throwing stones at them is self-evident.

Again, 20 stab wounds on an unarmed victim are unlikely to support a plea of self-defence by the person who inflicted them.

The success of such an approach depends on the strength of the results. The prospects are lower where the results are neutral or ambiguous.

For example, taking another person's coat from an unattended cloakroom may be due to a simple error. But this is less likely if the accused was not at the business conference for which the cloakroom was provided, and the article is a mink coat.

(b) *Collateral facts.* Only a few examples of the infinite variety of possibilities can be given. This category refers to relevant but not central facts. In this area, motivation and conduct are prominent.

For example, the defence advocate may ask the alleged victim of rape why she went to the accused's hotel bedroom at 1am after drinking steadily with him at the dance for two hours. The prosecutor might ask the person accused of rape to explain the signs of struggle, injuries, torn clothing, and evidence of screams heard in the next room of the hotel?

Why was the person accused of murder, and who pleads self-defence, carrying the stiletto which was used to stab the deceased? Why did the accountant accused of embezzlement have a duplicate set of account books at home?

Such facts are not conclusive in themselves, but are invaluable for confrontations.

In preparing or presenting their cases, advocates should lose no opportunities of discovering objective facts, which are difficult to deny or to explain. They should do this for two reasons. One is to have the benefit of their effect on the witness who is confronted with them, which may weaken or destroy his story. The other reason is the intrinsic value of these collateral facts as elements in his case. There is no need to repeat here the tactics of exposing and exploiting inconsistency and improbability, which were discussed earlier. Facts which amount to circumstantial evidence would obviously be included in this category.

(c) *Previous inconsistent statements.*   Witnesses who deny facts in court have often admitted them previously, mainly to the police.

A wise provision of the law allows their previous inconsistent statements to be put to witnesses in order to discredit the testimony which they are giving in court.

Cross-examiners often have openings for exploiting this technique in issues of credibility about intangible facts in result-crimes. As was said, some ways of doing this can magnify its effect in discrediting a witness.

2   Conduct-crimes

Since conduct-crimes are committed by forbidden acts alone, whatever their consequences, they are essentially intangible. The range of such crimes is wide, covering a variety of acts from indecent exposure to soliciting bribes. What they all have in common is that nothing tangible need be left after the crime is committed and the issue would depend on a conflict of credibility of eyewitness evidence coming from each side, were it not for the help provided by collateral facts and previous inconsistent statements.

Accordingly, the cross-examiner's problems, role and techniques are similar to those which apply to the intangible elements of result crimes, and they need no further elaboration.

Attempts to commit result-crimes may either fall into that category, or into the same category as conduct-crimes, depending on how far the attempt has gone in its objective effects.

3 Object-crimes

The problems met in result-crimes or conduct crimes also arise in object-crimes.

These crimes are constituted by a forbidden relationship to some object. Here, the object is tangible, and the relationship may either be physical, eg a suspect with a flick knife in his anorak pocket, or intangible, where the suspect is a resident in a flat occupied by several people, which contains an unlicensed television set.

The variety of such charges and surrounding circumstances limits any generalisations about forms of cross-examination.

The object ought to be produced in court as an exhibit. The nature of the object is crucial, and since this is usually obvious on inspection, few problems arise about this in cross-examination. This could happen, however, eg where an article like a cutlass is alleged to be an offensive weapon and the defence allege that it is merely a decorative article, en route to a friend as a Christmas present. A hammer and other tools in a bag, when returning from work, is one thing. In the inside pocket of a jacket, in a pub, it is another. In either case, the nature of the object would not determine guilt or otherwise. The sword may seem to be sinister per se. A hammer is a neutral article but in a public place, intention becomes a crucial issue.

Material produced as an exhibit in court and identified as cannabis resin by a forensic scientist usually offers little scope for cross-examination in itself. The usual subjects of enquiry are the location and circumstances in which it was found.

Cross-examination which probes collateral facts may be required in connection with ambiguous objects, or the intangible relationships of a suspect to the object. Whether he is in possession of it is a typical example.

It is very common for the defence to attack the credibility of police evidence about where and in what circumstances articles were found. To succeed they have to tackle the difficulties of showing reprehensible motives in a class of witness who are supposed to be of exemplary character. Cross-examiners who undertake such a challenge should be well prepared for this, and should lead substantive evidence to support their attacks. They should also be careful to ensure that police witnesses who are challenged like this should have an opportunity of answering the charges. It would not do to criticise a witness whose evidence is over, only by cross-examining his colleague.

B Identification as the issue

In discussing the issue of identification, it is assumed that the commission of the crime is admitted or proved.

Various forms of identification, viz visual identification, circumstantial evidence and confessions are considered here separately, although in practice one such form of evidence often reinforces another.

1 *Visual identification*

In the visual identification of a person whom the witness knows, familiarity with the suspect, and the question of his identity with its personal associations, rather than perception and comparison of the patterns of faces, is the subject of the evidence.

Nevertheless, where the circumstances of observation were adverse, a cross-examiner might still succeed in weakening such evidence, even if the accused was well known to the witness.

As was seen, visual identification of a stranger as the offender may consist of evidence of recognition, resemblance, or recall of some special characteristic.

Only recognition, ie where the witness says 'That is the man' or words to that effect, proves the accused's guilt if it is accepted.

Resemblance, ie 'He looks like the man', is only one item of evidence among others. Even if it is accepted, this alone does not prove that the accused was the offender. Many people other than the offender may look like him.

The most common defence contention about the accused's implication in the crime is that identifying witnesses for the prosecution are mistaken. The cross-examiner may probe sources of error in observation and suggest that a witness's memory was weakened by delay, or that his identification has been influenced by factors such as discussion between witnesses or irregularities in an identification parade. Even a large number of witnesses have been known to make the same mistake.

At best, cross-examination of this kind may weaken confidence in an identification, so that it is held to be unreliable, and may become unacceptable because of the burden of proof on the Crown. But by itself it is unlikely to show that the identification is wrong.

A cross-examiner should focus on a witness's exact words if recorded in pre-trial identifications, or in court, to see if there is any room for doubt about whether they mean recognition or resemblance. The two although different in meaning, can blend into each other.

If a witness can be brought to concede any uncertainty about his identification at all, the door is opened to increasing this progressively to the point where he is only speaking to a resemblance. If so, the cross-examination has succeeded to the extent that the witness is not now saying that the accused is the offender, but only that he looks like him.

In leading the witness to concede some uncertainty, cross-examination about difficulties of observation and memory may have some persuasive effect on him as well as the court, if he is impartial and fair.

Defence cross-examination may also be helped by the common fear of responsibility for convicting the wrong person. Moreover, some people doubt their own perceptions and memory to such an extent that they are hesitant about many things. On the other hand, some witnesses may be reluctant to retract or qualify earlier positive identifications.

A useful line of enquiry is to ask the witness about the basis of his identification, eg facial features and if so which, build, hair colour and so on. Faces are really perceived as a whole pattern, and a witness who is drawn into such an analysis and into listing the features on which he relies becomes vulnerable to further questions asking what is unique about them. He is also exposed to the possibility of converting evidence of recognition not only into evidence of resemblance but also, even more destructively, into evidence of individual features.

But a witness who resists any questions which are aimed at having him analyse his identification may seem to be dogmatic and uncooperative, which can, in itself, introduce some doubt about his testimony. This would also be the case where the circumstances of observation were such that dogmatism is inappropriate.

Evidence of visual identification may be reinforced if similar evidence is given by a number of unconnected witnesses, or if it is supported by circumstantial evidence, or confessions, or it may be weakened or overcome by the defendant's testimony and alibi evidence.

Defence cross-examination may challenge Crown identification evidence as untruthful, ie where the serious allegation is made that police witnesses are lying, or even conspiring to secure a conviction. If so, this is not a question of visual identification at all. It is a matter of challenging the credibility of evidence. The approach would then be different. The tactics required would be those discussed in relation to untruthful witnesses.

2 Circumstantial evidence

Circumstantial evidence pointing to the accused as the offender may take various forms. A cross-examiner's problems will differ accordingly.

Often, an offender leaves personal traces at the locus or on a victim, or carries signs away with him on his person or on his clothes. The findings of forensic medicine or forensic science may link him with the incident unless these traces can be accounted for in some innocent way, eg that his jacket on which the victim's bloodstains are found was stolen from him several days before the crime. Fingerprints or DNA samples are classic examples of this type of identification.

Little is usually achieved by challenging such evidence, unless there is some scope for a battle of experts, or some alternative explanation for the connections.

The possession of recently stolen property can incriminate the accused as the thief, unless it can be explained satisfactorily. The most common chestnut here is that the accused bought the article from a man in a pub whose full name and address he does not know. Whether the story is true or not, it cannot be investigated.

Another common form of circumstantial evidence is an account of the accused's conduct before and after the incident, which may give rise to incriminating inferences. Here there may be some scope for offering another version of the facts which is consistent with innocence.

A number of unconnected and independent witnesses may each speak to details, each of which is apparently of little significance until, on being assembled, they have the effect of incriminating the accused.

It would seem unreasonable to suggest a lying conspiracy between persons who do not even know each other, and who would have no reason to seek the accused's conviction for a crime which he did not commit.

It may also be improbable that such witnesses are mistaken. But since they are likely to be impartial, there may be scope for constructive techniques of cross-examination to modify the factual basis of items of circumstantial evidence, without a stark challenge.

These techniques, which have been discussed, include emphasising some facts, suggesting new meanings, or eliciting new helpful facts. The objective would be to change the balance, even slightly so as to replace a sinister picture with a more favourable one. The defence cross-examination is usually confined to subtle adjustments of circumstantial evidence in this way, although the defence can, of course, lead evidence themselves to contradict any incriminating inference with a different and direct account of the facts.

The defence cross-examiner's real aim is to replace the incriminating inference from the circumstantial facts with an innocent explanation. The facts themselves are only the basis for this and they are all that he can tackle. The inferences to be drawn from them are not matters for any witnesses. They are questions for the court which can be argued in closing speeches.

3 *Confessions and admissions*

In the present context, although not in legal terminology generally, 'confession' is intended to mean a full confession of guilt, and 'admission' means an incriminating statement, which falls short of that. Both are normally recorded in writing. Confessions are generally taken in the controlled circumstances of a police station. Admissions may be made spontaneously or in answer to caution and charge, in a police station, but are frequently made in uncontrolled circumstances, eg, at the locus of the crime, at the accused's home, or in a police vehicle.

Admissions which are implied by conduct or by silence are possible but are only found exceptionally.

Defendants are often implicated by confessions or admissions, if they are accepted by the court. There can be few more convincing reasons for finding that a person committed a crime than that he said that he did it—although it is known that people sometimes confess to crimes which they did not commit.

Where other evidence is weak, a genuine admission of guilt can make the proof conclusive.

Because of the crucial effect which confessions or admissions will have, if it is proved that they were made, they are often contested strenuously by the defence.

This opposition takes various forms. It may be argued that the evidence is inadmissible because it was obtained improperly. If however it is admitted, it may be contended that the evidence of the confession or admission is mistaken or untruthful in whole or in part. Again, if its accuracy is accepted, or proved, the defence may argue that the words are being interpreted wrongly and that they do not prove the implication of the accused as the offender. Finally, even if none of these contentions succeed, the defence may still argue that they create a reasonable doubt about the defendant's guilt, and that he ought therefore to be acquitted.

The admissibility of evidence of confessions and admissions belongs to the law of evidence, for which suitable texts should be consulted. Reference is only made to this question of law here, briefly, since the procedure for determining admissibility may involve cross-examination in some circumstances.

By statute, such evidence is inadmissible where it was obtained by oppression or in circumstances likely to have made the confession unreliable. On defence objection being taken, or on the court's initiative, the evidence will only be admitted on prosecution proof beyond reasonable doubt that the statements were not so obtained. The question is decided in a 'trial within a trial'.

In cross-examining police witnesses, the defence may construe 'oppression' widely to cover anything which tends to deprive a confession of its voluntary character, eg not only torture, violence, threat of violence, or intimidation, but also more subtle forms of pressure such as prolonged questioning, or lack of refreshment or of an opportunity to sleep, taking into account the suspect's character and circumstances. 'Unreliability' may include various types of threat, eg threatening to charge a suspect's wife with a crime, or inducement, eg a promise to facilitate bail.

Whether or not the more serious allegations of misconduct by police officers are true, those concerned may be expected to deny them. Consequently an issue of credibility will have to be decided.

Less serious defence suggestions, whatever their truth, may meet less or no resistance from police witnesses, eg questions about times of arrival or questioning, or provision of meals, whether the suspect complained about illness or injury, whether a doctor attended to examine him and so on.

Even if the information given by the defendant to his advocate is genuine, the defence cross-examination of police witnesses is still likely to be difficult.

In the trial within a trial, the defendant may call other witnesses, and should do so if they would be helpful, eg a doctor to testify to his condition on release from the police station, or to his wife's advanced pregnancy and dependence on the accused for help. But the most usual situation is that the only defence evidence is that given by the accused, and that this is contradicted by the evidence of several police witnesses.

The defence advocate must therefore be alert for any weaknesses in the prosecution evidence. In a situation like this, inconsistency between police witnesses may be very significant and this, and any improbabilities, should be exploited where possible.

In closing speeches, the defence should emphasise the burden of proof beyond reasonable doubt which is borne by the prosecution.

If it came to a prosecutor's knowledge that there was real substance in the defence objection, it would be proper to concede it. Otherwise, he is likely to cross-examine the defendant on the basis that any serious allegations of police misconduct are merely inventions. Whether complaints of a more minor character, even if established, would justify exclusion of a confession may be arguable.

The next stage of possible attack is that where evidence of a confession or an admission is allowed, it may be challenged on the basis that it is mistaken or untruthful.

A spontaneous and brief admission made in informal

circumstances, and not noted at once, or at all, is more likely to be mistaken than a full confession made in controlled circumstances, and recorded in writing at the time.

Police witnesses may say that an accused made an informal statement against his interest at the scene of the crime, his home, in the police vehicle, or somewhere other than a police station.

A defence cross-examiner might challenge this evidence as mistaken because what the defendant said was misheard, as a result of the kind of impediments considered earlier.

The following are some of the ways in which it might be contended that such evidence could be mistaken or could be subject to unreliability: nothing was said; something was said, but not the statement attributed to the accused; the statement was made, but parts of it were wrongly reported; the statement was made by someone other than the accused; the statement was made but meant something different in the situation, which opens up enquiry as to the context; the statement was made but should be interpreted differently.

But it is inept to suggest that the inaccuracy of police evidence is due to mistake, where the police witnesses must know the real situation. Where this is so, the only possible explanation for any inaccuracy is that they are lying.

A great amount of cross-examination of police witnesses about admissions by an accused is of this unimpressive kind. There may be several reasons, including those which follow, for the reluctance of cross-examiners to call a spade a spade and to accuse the witness of lying.

Notwithstanding the professional duty of an advocate to present a case on the basis of the information and instructions given to him by his client, without forming any judgment about them, this may sometimes fly in the face of human nature.

The advocate may accept the obligation to charge police witnesses with giving false evidence, on the basis of his written information. However, their evidence-in-chief may be so impressive that he feels some embarrassment in putting forward allegations which may appear to him, and to the court, to be unreasonable, absurd, or even outrageous. He may then try to achieve a compromise between this impression and his duty, by a lame 'suggestion' that the witnesses are mistaken.

Another compelling reason for caution in accusing police witnesses of lying is that the prosecutor may contend that the cross-examiner has gone beyond the bounds of what is necessary for the purposes of the defence, and is attacking the character of Crown witnesses. If so, the accused may lose his statutory 'shield' against cross-examination as to his previous convictions. If he has any, he will be vulnerable.

Other contributory factors may lead to this kind of half-hearted challenge, where it is suggested that evidence which could only be untruthful if it is inaccurate is merely mistaken.

There may be false notions about appropriate style in advocacy. It is true that an advocate should maintain professional detachment, should avoid any impression of personal involvement and should be courteous to witnesses. He may also allow a witness to save face, in order to obtain his co-operation in providing favourable evidence. But none of these desirable features of advocacy should be adopted to the extent of causing an advocate to descend into self-evident hypocrisy. To call what could only be a lie a 'mistake' is an example of this. It merely creates an impression of polished insincerity.

An advocate will maximise his presentation by showing that he does not allow his duty to his client to impair his duty to act as a sincere guide to the court. The methods of cross-examining police witnesses which have been criticised give a harmful impression. There is no reason why the credibility of police evidence should not be challenged. But if so, it should be done explicitly. The ambiguity which has been described is a common problem to-day.

Because of its importance in current practice, this whole question should be looked at squarely. It is a central issue in evidence. If a suspect tells police that he committed the crime, is it likely that they would often be mistaken about this confession? Whether the police might lie about it is another matter.

Is evidence about an informal admission likely to be mistaken where this would mean that several police witnesses have made the same error? Unlikely though this may be, it is a common suggestion.

More cogently, where the evidence refers to a full confession, in controlled circumstances, in a police station, recorded in writing, read over to or by the defendant, and signed by him, and this is confirmed by several police witnesses, it is difficult to see how any mistake can be made, apart from the odd word or two. The more reasonable inference would be that either the police witnesses or the accused are lying. (It would be exceptional for other defence witnesses to be present at such an incident.)

It is therefore recommended as a sound working guide for cross-examiners that disputes about the accuracy of admissions or confessions nearly always raise questions of credibility not reliability.

Where this is clear, it is more impressive for the defence to cross-examine police witnesses realistically on the basis that they are untruthful, than to make suave suggestions about mistakes, which are an affront to common sense and deceive nobody.

Cross-examination of police witnesses which suggests that they are lying about an admission or confession may have little or no effect unless it is supported by persuasive testimony from the defendant, which resists his own cross-examination successfully.

Confining the discussion to full confessions, this issue of credibility raises major questions of motivation for the court to decide, viz:

(1) Why would the accused confess to the police?
(2) Why would he deny his confession in court?
(3) Why would police lie about his confession?

The prosecutor and the defence advocate must keep these questions in mind in their respective cross-examinations, although they could not put some points to witnesses, eg the defence could not ask a police witness to explain the accused's reasons for confessing, although he might elicit evidence of facts and circumstances known to the officer from which this could be inferred.

Why do suspects confess? Naturally, the reasons vary according to the individual and the circumstances. However, some general considerations may guide cross-examination in particular situations. It may be advantageous to the defence to keep this question to the forefront in cross-examination and argument. Often, it is not given the prominence which it should have.

If the defence cross-examination can elicit facts to suggest that there was no reason for the defendant to confess, this will support the defendant's evidence that he did not do so, and may put the police evidence in a critical light.

The point to be emphasised is that this must be a genuine question in every case, even where the defendant is guilty of the crime charged. People do not normally commit crimes with a view to conviction and punishment. Why then do they change their intention in a police station?

The defence, in cross-examining police witnesses, may explore the situation to show that they know of no facts which would explain why the accused confessed. The cross-examiner is assisted by the inadmissibility of any speculations or opinions about this. These witnesses can only speak to facts.

It would, on the other hand, be open to a prosecutor to cross-examine the defendant directly about his reasons for confessing, and to argue the matter in his closing speech.

Police evidence of facts which would explain the accused's decision to confess may not be impressive. However, based on the evidence, the court may have certain considerations in mind.

In unpremeditated crimes committed in hot blood, such as some assaults or even murder, it is conceivable that when the blood cools, remorse in itself may lead to a confession. But this is unlikely in the vast majority of crimes.

States of mind such as exhaustion, stress, a wish to get the whole thing over, and so on, by themselves, or in association with remorse, might play a part, but may not seem generally to be compelling reasons for confessing to a crime, especially where the consequences for the accused may be serious.

Even in criminal situations, confessions do occur from motives of loyalty, where one person takes the blame to protect another, perhaps where the one who confesses has little or no criminal record, and the offender has a bad one. Again, parents might do this for their children.

Other reasons for confessions may arise from pressures or inducements which influence the suspect.

However these are not the most common situations. It is suggested that the key to voluntary confessions by criminals is usually something else. It is the belief that denial is useless because the incriminating evidence is overwhelming, ie metaphorically where the accused has been caught with his hand in the till.

This situation raises two distinct questions: (1) what evidence the police have, and (2) what evidence the suspect thinks that they have. This may depend on what the police tell him.

A suspect could be interviewed by the police or arrested in various situations, from being caught red-handed to being traced by forensic evidence.

If, at that time, the defendant knew or believed that there was incriminating evidence which would prove his guilt inevitably, this would increase the probability that he confessed. He might have thought that he had nothing to lose, or he might have hoped that if he co-operated, he might be treated with leniency.

Obviously, where there was indeed strongly incriminating evidence, it would not be in the interests of the defence advocate to explore and emphasise this. To refer to it in cross-examination would strengthen the Crown case, and would increase the probability that the accused confessed.

On the other hand, if there was little or no incriminating evidence when the confession is said to have been made, the defence would be in a position to contend that it was obviously inadequate and that, even if the accused had been guilty of the crime, he would have had no reason to confess.

The defence cross-examination should bring this out from the police witnesses who speak to the confession, and any other police officers who were engaged in the enquiry. If a number of them speak to single elements of evidence, the significance of which they cannot explain, the cross-examiner may exploit their limitations.

A prosecutor who foresees an attack on police evidence of a confession as untruthful should reinforce that evidence-in-chief. He will emphasise the strength of the incriminating evidence as a reason for confessing, as well as pointing to guilt in itself.

He should take a similar line in cross-examining the defendant if he gives evidence, by demonstrating that he knew the strength of the evidence against him, and that denial was hopeless.

The second main question, as to why a guilty defendant who confessed initially should deny it later in court, is not difficult to answer.

After rest, time to reflect, discussion with others, arranging for witnesses to give false evidence, and so on, the situation may seem to the accused to be less hopeless. He may then invent a story to explain the incriminating evidence, and denial of his confession would follow from this. He may receive legal advice to the effect that there may be grounds for holding the confession as inadmissible as a question of law, or of mixed fact and law. He may also be advised, on the basis of the false information which he gives to his lawyer, that legal aid will be available and that he has a possible defence to the charge.

The credibility of police evidence of a confession is attacked regularly. The court must decide whether police witnesses are reporting the confession truthfully or committing perjury.

This involves the final question of why the police would lie about the accused's confession. It raises the matter of the motivation of police witnesses for doing so. Since there are many obvious reasons why a police witness would be truthful about this matter, a defence challenge which fails to suggest a realistic motive for lying may not be persuasive.

A police officer found to have committed perjury in a criminal trial would be exposed to conviction for a serious crime, severe penalties, loss of career and pension. Police officers would presumably know of the risk of detection. Even if the witness was careful about his deception, he might be concerned about whether he can trust his associates who are also lying about the confession. Internal police enquiries might expose the falsehoods. Again, as sometimes happens, the truth could emerge later as a result of a public enquiry, or the confession of the real offender.

If the defence suggest that malice towards the accused motivated some police witnesses to incriminate him by lying about his confession, they face the problem of probing past relationships without revealing previous convictions. This weakens such challenges.

The defence sometimes suggest that police witnesses, who genuinely believed in the defendant's guilt, have exaggerated the weight of certain incriminating evidence in some way.

This could happen, for example, where one police witness identified the defendant, genuinely so far as he was concerned, and another one exaggerates his own dubious identification insincerely, under the influence of his discussion with the first witness.

However, the topic under discussion here is not a matter of exaggerating evidence. The issue is whether or not police witnesses are truthfully reporting the accused's confession —a matter which does not easily lend itself to exaggeration. It would appear to involve allegations of deliberate perjury.

In making such an extreme charge, with the risks which untruthful police witnesses would incur, a defence cross-examiner might find it difficult to elicit evidence of facts which point to such conduct, even where the allegation is true.

Many police officers with court experience are more or less professional witnesses, and if they are indeed launched on a false story, they would persist in it.

Cross-examiners should bear in mind that strong incriminating evidence is more likely to persuade a guilty accused to confess, and less likely to make police invent an unnecessary confession.

But if the evidence of guilt was weak, an accused has less reason to confess, and only an invented confession could lead to conviction.

So the state of the evidence against the accused at the time of his arrest merits close consideration for its implications in any direction.

Apart from the motivations of the accused and the police, the defence cross-examination can apply other tests to evidence of a confession.

Notwithstanding the general advice that an advocate should not ask a question to which he does not know or cannot reasonably predict the answer, a certain amount of exploration of the circumstances surrounding an alleged confession, with a purpose, may sometimes be productive.

Such topics as the following may be probed: whether the accused was cautioned before he made the statement; whether it was voluntary or made as a result of any pressure or inducement; and whether the officers who noted it were also involved in the enquiry.

The following additional questions might be asked: what was said to the accused before he confessed; who was there; who wrote down the confession; if it was not the accused, whether the confession was read over to him or he read it over himself; whether he was told that he could alter anything in it; whether it contains any corrections and if so, how these came about; whether his signature is genuine; whether the confession was dictated by the accused and recorded verbatim or obtained by question and answer; whether the accused was interrogated; whether the language is natural to the accused or contains police jargon; whether the spelling gives any clues; how long it all took, or whether it was hurried.

Despite the number of questions listed, they are not necessarily exhaustive although they cover many situations in practice. Here, they are intended to be suggestive. Appropriate questions would be selected, or framed, according to the cross-examiner's objective. It is not suggested that such questioning should be random and aimless.

Such questions put to any single witness to the alleged confession may create various openings for helpful lines of enquiry.

If the evidence of the confession is false, comparison of the answers to such questions by two or more police witnesses may yield significant inconsistencies which can be exploited. However well prepared liars may be, it is impossible for them to foresee every possible question. Having no memory of reality to fall back on, they must invent answers to unforeseen questions. If these are put rapidly in unpredictable sequence, lying witnesses may be led into self-contradiction or inconsistency with each other.

By such means, evidence of a confession may be impaired by cross-examination in various ways which can cast doubt on it. Naturally, whatever is put to the police witnesses should be consistent with the information given to the cross-examiner. Whoever else may indulge in invention in a criminal trial, it should never be the advocates. If the defence deny the confession altogether, this involves a serious attack on the police witnesses and it would be expected that the defendant would testify to that effect. His denial of the confession, in evidence, may at least raise a reasonable doubt about it, and lead to an acquittal.

4   Alibi evidence

It is to be expected that an accused who is insisting on his alibi will testify in support of it.

In error, an alibi witness could identify the accused as having been at some place other than the scene of the crime when it was committed, or he could be mistaken about the date of an incident when he made an accurate identification. But prosecutors do not challenge alibi evidence very often as mistaken; they usually allege that the accused and alibi witnesses are lying, as they know the facts.

When alibi evidence is given, a prosecutor might at first explore the character and motivation of each witness, where something is to be gained by this. He should ensure that the witness's link with the accused is made explicit. The closer this is, the more vulnerable the evidence may be.

Standard tactics for the prosecutor, thereafter, are to probe the story in detail, to explore collateral facts, to seek both minor and material inconsistencies between alibi witnesses and to exploit any improbabilities.

Under such scrutiny, it would be an exceptional story which did not present some flaws, although they might be minor.

Probing the story in detail involves questions of the 'what was on the television?' type for which lying witnesses have probably prepared. But it is noticeable that the motivation of lying alibi witnesses varies in strength; some may be word-perfect in their stories, whereas others may have prepared with less care. Moreover, lying alibi witnesses are not always conspicuous for their intelligence. So such probing may be productive.

Exploring collateral facts generally uncovers some area for which lying alibi witnesses are unprepared, viz the circumstances which preceded, accompanied or followed the alibi situation. Rapid and unpredictable questioning in a random sequence, may defeat the witness's capacity to invent facts for which he has no basis in memory. While such a witness might be hesitant or claim amnesia for some essential detail in the alibi situation, if he feels threatened by questions, he may be less concerned about points which seem remote from the central facts, and this may lead him to lower his defences in the peripheral area.

If this lowering of defences occurs with a number of witnesses, it may be exploited so as to build up a network of surrounding facts which are in conflict with the alibi situation as described and with each other.

By such methods, a prosecutor would try to lead or drive false alibi witnesses into inconsistencies. These too may be developed further. One witness might be asked about unexpected facts to which another spoke. His hesitation or reluctance to commit himself may be transparent. If he does make a definite statement he should be led into asserting it as dogmatically as possible. This will intensify the effect of inconsistency. Alternatively, after leading various witnesses to commit themselves in different directions, the prosecutor may simply leave this mixture of statements for a forceful closing speech so that it is beyond correction by the defence.

Since a false alibi must often be constructed within the parameters of certain facts which cannot be disputed, or other limits, it may seem to be strained and improbable. A prosecutor would, again, exploit any such improbability by expanding it to the point of absurdity, where he could.

Some recurrent patterns of alibi evidence and how they may be handled should be mentioned.

Where it seems that an alibi has been memorised in detail, a prosecutor might start by asking the witnesses to repeat their evidence in-chief. Any identity or excessive similarity of phrases or wording might show collusion.

To ask alibi witnesses if they have ever discussed their evidence often yields improbable denials which tend to discredit them. Since even honest witnesses are sensitive about the subject, lying witnesses may well respond in an even more significant way which makes them suspect.

Under pressure, lying witnesses to an alibi may take refuge in 'amnesia' claiming that the event happened so long ago that they cannot recall certain details about which they are asked as a form of test. Here, the prosecutor might note facts said to be forgotten and how often this occurs, and he may compare this 'amnesia' with the claimed sharpness of recollection for other facts, by asking the witness to comment on this.

It can be difficult to weaken or destroy some alibis which refer to real events but on a date other than the date of the crime.

To challenge this, the surrounding elements which are related to the date would have to be probed. If the alibi is false, and the witness is dogmatic about the date, the grounds for his certainty may be investigated. People do not normally recall the dates of unimportant incidents, without good reason. Also, the Crown evidence will contradict the alibi witnesses by implicating the accused.

Any challenge to false alibi evidence should not, realistically, be expected to lead to its retraction by the witnesses or to its immediate destruction. The aim is so to weaken the alibi evidence that it succumbs to positive and contradictory evidence led by the prosecutor which points to the accused as the offender.

Destruction of an alibi does not per se place the defendant at the scene of the crime or establish his guilt; an innocent person may resort to a fabricated alibi in lieu of a weak defence. But generally, to show that an alibi is false would affect the defence adversely.

II PROBLEMS WITH WITNESSES

Typical problems are associated with cross-examining various kinds of witnesses.

A Prosecution witnesses

1 *Police*

Police evidence has been discussed in various contexts, but a reminder of some salient points may be helpful for cross-examiners. Police witnesses testify in most criminal trials, and are often very important. They have no special status as witnesses. Their evidence may be challenged as mistaken, unreliable or untruthful like that of any witness.

Errors of observation or memory of the kind which can affect the testimony of any witness are also attributed to police witnesses, quite commonly by the defence. Two features related to mistaken evidence are of special interest to defence cross-examiners, viz discussion of evidence, and the possibility of occupational bias.

Teamwork and pooling of information are typical in police enquiries. Many written records must be kept, eg notes of interviews, or reports which may be circulated or made available to colleagues and senior officers.

Police duties oblige officers to discuss their cases, and they often work in pairs.

Sometimes, such discussion may be capable of influencing and modifying police eyewitness evidence by suggestion, although the witness sincerely believes that he is reporting his original observations accurately and independently.

An illustration is the risk of error where police witnesses see a group of youths in a riot, and, influenced by later discussion, albeit in good faith, they implicate an uninvolved person who was merely present and who committed no offence.

As has been pointed out, to ask witnesses if they have discussed their evidence is an excellent test of their sincerity. Generally, they are reluctant to admit it or, if they do admit it, they frequently deny that their testimony was influenced thereby, in any way. Sometimes this reluctance leads to manifestly insincere statements.

The defence often fail to grasp the opportunities for cross-examination which arise from the routine discussion of the case and the evidence, which police witnesses are obliged to undertake, and which may be responsible for mistakes or unreliability.

The evidence which would be most vulnerable to such sources of error would be that relating to intangible crimes, or intangible elements in crimes, and visual identification.

Any occupation may create typical attitudes and there is no reason why police should be an exception. Indeed, some habits of mind are desirable in their work, eg curiosity, alertness to possible wrongdoing, suspicion, scepticism, determination in tracing and apprehending offenders and, when they assist the prosecution, the expectation that the suspect, if guilty, will be convicted. Of course, police officers are expected to carry out their duties with impartiality and fairness, especially when they testify, but human nature may be moulded in various ways of which people are not always aware.

At times, a defence cross-examiner might suggest that bias has led to mistaken police evidence or has contributed to mistakes in the evidence of lay witnesses with whom police witnesses came into contact. Such mischief may seem more likely in evidence of a marginal kind, eg reports of ambiguous or obscure situations, such as the actions of a person suspected of acting as a lookout.

If the cross-examination is carried out diplomatically, showing that the witness's sincerity is accepted, a fair-minded police officer who has not committed himself irrevocably to some stark statement might make concessions, eg that he would naturally be suspicious about youths lurking about in the darkness of a car park and that perhaps the accused was just holding the door handle to steady himself because he was drunk.

Biased police officers, without intending it, may influence the evidence of lay witnesses with whom they come in contact during their enquiries. Visual identification of the accused would be particularly vulnerable to this in the range of pre-trial identification procedures, eg giving descriptions, confronting suspects, being shown photographs, or taking part in identification parades.

If he has established a foundation for this, a defence advocate may argue in his closing speech that the bias of a police witness is so extreme as to amount to partisanship. To create that foundation he can challenge the evidence openly and directly, in cross-examination to that effect. But merely to assert this, albeit in question form, is insufficient without material.

Alternatively, a cross-examiner may conceal his doubts and encourage the witness to become more and more one-sided and dogmatic until he discredits himself by showing how untrustworthy he is.

Evidence of visual identification is particularly sensitive to any possibility that it is influenced by bias. In view of the burden of proof on the Crown, an identification may be rejected if the cross-examination can persuade the court that the identification is tainted or unreliable, for such reasons, even if it cannot show that it is wrong.

The credibility of police evidence has been discussed, eg in relation to confessions. A few reminders will suffice here. The defence are free to attack the veracity of police witnesses, but should only do so on responsible information, which will normally be supported by the accused's evidence; otherwise the challenge may be open to criticism. Defence advocates often seem to shrink from such confrontations by suggesting that police witnesses are mistaken about facts which they obviously know, so that it is veracity which is in question, not the possibility of a mistake.

If the accused has a criminal record, the defence advocate should consider carefully, whether any challenge to police evidence may amount to an imputation against police witnesses which may expose the accused to cross-examination on his record. The advocate may understand that the accused has no criminal record or only one which is insignificant, but it would be prudent to obtain confirmation of this, to avoid unpleasant surprises.

Common weaknesses in any attack on the truthfulness of police witnesses are the suspect motivations and, perhaps, poor character of the accused, the exemplary record of the police officers, the serious consequences of such misconduct, and the lack of explanation for it.

The defence advocate must be prepared for such difficulties and should try to meet them where he can, in the course of cross-examination and, if possible, by leading supporting evidence, in addition to that of the defendant.

2 Complainants

The evidence of complainants is normally led to support the proof that the crime was committed or the identification of the offender, or both.

Although the complainant saw the whole incident and will testify to both the crime and the identity of the offender in examination-in-chief, as has been seen, only one of these matters is normally disputed. This alone will be the subject of defence cross-examination.

Of course a complainant need not necessarily have been an eyewitness to a crime, eg a householder where a burglary occurred in her absence and the family silver was stolen. She might be cross-examined on some relevant point, eg her identification of a candlestick discovered in the accused's possession.

In cross-examining a complainant about the crime, the challenge may either be that his evidence is mistaken or untruthful and the advocate should be specific about this.

If the complainant was an eyewitness to the whole crime, crticising his evidence as mistaken may only seem reasonable in regard to obscure or ambiguous facts where errors are possible, eg whether a nocturnal trespasser in his garden was trying to force the french windows.

But if the facts were stark, eg in a charge of menacing the householder with a hammer inside the house, the complainant could hardly be mistaken.

On the other hand, if a cross-examiner accuses a complainant of lying about the crime, he will have to suggest a motive for doing this to make his challenge reasonable.

The most obvious motives for inventing or exaggerating a crime would be hostility and malice towards the defendant. Such animosity might arise from prior relationships or from the incident itself.

A rejected wife might claim that her husband attacked her when she was visiting her children in his house. This could be part of a pattern of relationships in which she is trying to recover custody of the children.

Another example of a malicious fabrication of a crime might be where schoolgirls make a false complaint of indecency against a male sports instructor because he had reported them to the headmaster for smoking in school.

However, even where there has been no previous relationship between the complainant and the accused, hostility between them may arise from an incident and may lead to a false charge that a crime was committed, eg a bus driver may stop the bus to tell two rowdy teenagers to get off. They lie at the police station, by claiming that they were thrown off the bus violently.

They exhibit minor injuries which they say were caused by being pushed off the deck of the bus on to the pavement. In fact, they sustained these injuries in a fight with a gang before they got on the bus.

A cross-examiner, in defending a motorist charged with careless driving and colliding with another vehicle, may accuse the other driver of inventing or exaggerating the crime to exonerate himself from blame.

A cross-examiner may suggest that a complainant is exaggerating a crime for gain, eg that a householder is adding false items to the list of unrecovered stolen goods to increase his insurance claim.

In a charge of rape, it may be alleged that the complainant consented to intercourse but then decided to lie about this because of fear of her parents.

Sometimes, police officers become complainants when they charge a man with resisting arrest and related offences. It may be alleged that they had no grounds for arresting him in the first place, and that they have superimposed this false charge out of malice.

In such cases, the cross-examiner should try to expose the motive for lying about the crime.

Examples, which are not exhaustive, have been given of false accusations or exaggerations of crimes, from motives of malice, hostility, self-exoneration or gain.

Complainants who lie like this will not admit it under cross-examination. It will be necessary to establish facts and circumstances from which the falsity of their account may be inferred, or which raise a reasonable doubt about the commission of the crime.

This may require some probing of previous relationships or the collateral facts of the incident, within the bounds of relevancy.

Of course the complainant's motive for lying about the crime will not be the only target of cross-examination. Objective defects in the complainant's evidence such as inconsistency or improbability should also be exposed in order to weaken them, so that this Crown evidence may either be defeated by contradictory defence evidence or, at least, tainted with reasonable doubt.

In any event, proof of the crime or otherwise will not be determined by cross-examination alone. It will depend on the whole of the direct and circumstantial evidence, given by all the witnesses, who may include the defendant.

Where the real issue in a trial is the identification of the accused as the offender, the most common challenge to complainants who were eyewitnesses is that they are mistaken.

The possibility of such a mistake must always be taken seriously. Courts have become increasingly sensitive to this, following miscarriages of justice which attracted wide publicity.

While the risk may be greater in fleeting glimpses of unfamiliar faces, it is not absent in identification of well-known persons, if the conditions are adverse.

There are, of course, other ways of proving a suspect's implication, but where a complainant's visual identification of the accused is crucial, the defence should strive, at least, to sow reasonable doubt about its reliability, even if they cannot establish misidentification firmly. The cross-examination would follow lines already discussed.

It is less usual for cross-examiners to accuse complainants of lying about the offender's identity than to claim that it is mistaken. To lie in this way a complainant would have to be strongly motivated in various directions which are far from commonplace.

Such a lie would amount to the commission of perjury and might make the complainant responsible for convicting an innocent person and for allowing the real offender to escape detection.

However wicked such lies may seem, they are sometimes attributed by the defence to police eyewitnesses who are so involved in an incident that, in effect, they become complainants.

For example, it may be suggested that in a riot at a football match, the police decided, improperly, to charge every member of a group, who was wearing a fan's tee-shirt, without knowing what the defendant did personally, if anything. In evidence, they might lie by saying 'they were all doing it.'

Occasionally, defence allegations go even further by alleging a police conspiracy to convict the accused, including the 'planting' of exhibits to incriminate him, although the real offender is someone else. Such grave charges will not be established by cross-examination alone. Substantial supporting evidence would be required. Although such things have been known to happen, fortunately they are rare and uncharacteristic. The are mentioned here for completeness of exposition.

In attacking the evidence of police complainants as untruthful, defence cross-examination would consist of techniques discussed already.

The character of serving police officers is unlikely to be blemished or vulnerable to challenge, but evidence of facts may be drawn out from which improper motives could be inferred. Inconsistencies or improbabilities should be exposed and exploited.

Serious imputations against police witnesses would deprive the accused of his statutory shield against cross-examination as to his character including his previous convictions.

Where a crime has in fact occurred and a complainant is said to be lying about the offender's identity, it is to be emphasised this would not only be perjury leading to the possible conviction of an innocent person; it would also help the real offender to escape detection. There would have to be unusual reasons for a complainant to desire such an outcome, where only the defendant is accused of the crime. Yet if a complainant was attacked by only one member of a gang, while he might identify the offender correctly, he might include another member of the gang as one of the assailants, out of malice.

Mistakes and lies in identifying the offender have been discussed. There is also a twilight zone between the two which involves subtle psychological processes.

To illustrate this, complainants may be vulnerable to influence, eg the elderly lady whose house was burgled, and who appreciates all the consideration and trouble of the police in recovering her valuables and in catching a suspect.

She thinks that the man in the dock, whom she picked out at the identification parade, with some hesitation, is the man she saw climbing out of her window. She would not lie about this intentionally. Nevertheless, out of gratitude to the police, the feeling that they know what they are doing, and reluctance to cause any trouble, she confirms her identification firmly in court, although she has lingering doubts about it.

Such motivational patterns are often not far from intentional misstatements, which can matter greatly. Degrees of confidence in identifications can range from certainty at one extreme to no more than thinking that there is some resemblance at the other. Because of the subjectivity of visual identification and its role in the criminal process, doubts like this may be crucial to a verdict.

A thorough defence cross-examination of identification evidence given by complainants would cover this intermediate zone and would be aimed at exposing unstated qualifications.

As always, when private psychological processes are in issue, direct questions about them may be unproductive although they have to be asked, if only to inform the court of the cross-examiner's contentions. However, he should support his allegations by eliciting facts from which influences on identification evidence may be inferred. This may cause the witness to modify that evidence until it is more accurate.

3 Accomplices

The class of prosecution witnesses, denoted by 'accomplice' and the circumstances when warnings or corroboration are required, are governed by rules of evidence. Here, since the concern is with tactics, the term 'accomplice' is used in the general sense of the word and not in that legal sense.

The testimony of such persons has always been viewed with caution. Their characters and motives are usually suspect. They may be as culpable as a guilty offender.

A self-confessed offender, may testify against the accused with a view to achieving immunity from prosecution or, if that is not possible, a lighter sentence.

Often, an accomplice may have an interest in the verdict. For his own purposes, he might incriminate the defendant falsely, eg to exonerate a friend, or he may minimise his own role in a crime, and exaggerate that of the defendant.

As the witness is designated here as an accomplice, this implies that the crime has been established. The accused's implication in committing it will be the issue.

Defence cross-examination of an accomplice usually has a flying start: his involvement, and perhaps his criminal record, would be revealed in his evidence-in-chief.

The cross-examiner will emphasise the witness's motivations, aiming to discredit him and to make his protestations of truthfulness sound hollow and unconvincing. Hesitancy, reluctance, inconsistency or improbability are often seen in such evidence. This may be because the witness is caught in a dilemma between what he hopes to gain from his evidence, and the risk of reprisals.

A competent cross-examiner has good grounds for hoping that, as a result of his efforts, the court will hold that such evidence, by itself, is too unreliable to be a basis for conviction or even to support it, although of course there may be other trustworthy evidence to implicate the defendant.

4 Children

Children are often called as witnesses for the prosecution. This often occurs in trials where some form of indecency is charged. This section refers to those who are competent witnesses.

Psychological research has yielded no established body of knowledge to help cross-examiners in testing the reliability or credibility of children's evidence. This must be said because of the current public concern about this subject and innovations in criminal procedure where children are involved. In any event, where a witness is accepted as competent, it is inappropriate that any general findings should have any significance for courts. The quality of the evidence of a particular child in a particular case is what a particular court must evaluate, without reference to statistics.

Today, public feelings about issues involving children are so intense that cross-examiners ought to take into account their possible effect on the views of jurors or lay magistrates. Mounting concern about the incidence of child abuse, the need to prosecute it, the widespread anxiety about the psychological effects of the trial process on child witnesses, and the need to protect an accused's right to a fair trial, create a merry-go-round of views, proposals and counter-proposals. All these considerations do not coincide, and may lead to procedural innovations in different directions. That is not the concern of this book. However it would be difficult for lay jurors or magistrates to remain uninfluenced by the ferment of ideas which are being generated. Advocates ought to know this.

In court practice, the immediate difficulty with child witnesses is neither the reliability nor the credibility of their evidence: such problems arise and are dealt with constantly in adult witnesses. The real obstacle is that child witnesses are so often inarticulate and tongue tied, especially in the sensitive areas of their testimony, that it is difficult to extract any coherent evidence from them at all.

Despite all the steps taken by the court and advocates to put children at their ease, and the presence of a parent, frequently they are subdued, their speech is inaudible, and they may even not answer some questions at all. This can only be met by encouragement and sometimes by a little harmless humour, but not by threats or any pressure which makes them even more anxious.

In examination-in-chief, unless a certain latitude about leading is allowed, with defence consent, it might often be impossible to obtain any coherent account at all. Moreover, the quality of the evidence given by a child in response to leading gives a court very little guidance, either in regard to the content of evidence, or the manner in which it is given. The evidence is often limited to 'Yes' or 'No' answers.

The defence have to conduct a cross-examination in these difficult conditions, and usually in an atmosphere which is unsympathetic to any possibility of harassing or upsetting the child, and perhaps hostility to the defendant. Above all, patience, tact and consideration are necessary in this area. This is not an ideal forum in which the classical art of cross-examination can flourish.

Accordingly, while the defence advocate is entitled to, and is often bound to, cross-examine on some topics in the interests of the accused, he should make the most of any measures other than forceful cross-examination which are open to him. It may upset a child, and may be unnecessary, to drive a point home in cross-examination such as inconsistency or improbability, or to insist that something unpleasant is said explicitly.

Moreover, any harassment may invite the intervention of the bench, or have an unpredictable effect on a jury's verdict. Very often, points can be made in argument, if sufficient foundation has been laid.

If as much as possible is left for a forceful closing speech, the court is likely to appreciate this and to take the defence advocate's tact and restraint into account. He should certainly emphasise the burden of proof borne by the Crown, the exacting standard of proof beyond reasonable doubt, and the grave danger of basing a conviction on the testimony of a relatively inarticulate child witness. Unconvincing Crown evidence about essential matters is bound to favour the defence.

Other courses open to the defence are, of course, to cross-examine prosecution witnesses other than children, as forcefully as may be necessary, and to lead evidence, including, if so advised, that of the defendant.

Having set up the framework within which cross-examination of child witness generally occurs, some comments on the process may be helpful. The cross-examiner's task may vary greatly according to what exactly is in issue.

If the question is whether the crime was committed, medical evidence of physical signs, such as the effects of sexual intercourse, may reduce the evidence required from the victim, but may not be conclusive by themselves, eg where physical signs on a mature female child could have been caused either by intercourse or by using a tampon. Here again the child's evidence may be vital, although sometimes a mother can give relevant and admissible information.

But if the disputed crime consists of alleged acts of indecency, which left no physical traces capable of confirmation by expert evidence, it is generally very difficult to take a child's evidence in the form of an exact description of such acts, or to cross-examine about it.

Within the limits of admissibility, resort may be had to diagrams, gestures, anatomical dolls, and euphemisms or popular terms for sexual parts or acts.

In such intangible conduct-crimes, which leave no physical signs on the victim to confirm what was done, the direct evidence is crucial and often stands alone more or less, since it is unlikely that there would be eyewitnesses to what took place between the complainant and the defendant. Unfortunately, here, where the child's evidence has great importance, both the prosecutor and the defence advocate may face difficulties in extracting testimony.

The situation may sometimes be less tense for the child where the issue is one of identification, but again difficulties could arise if the defendant is a close relative towards whom the child has mixed feelings, or perhaps a stranger of whom the child is still afraid.

Whether the commission of the crime or the defendant's implication is the issue in cases involving children, a cross-examiner should strive to obtain whatever help he can from collateral facts.

Although the commission of indecency with a child is likely to have taken place in private, it is always important to take into account when the first complaint was made, the opportunities for making it, to whom it was made, what was said, and in what circumstances.

One qualification to everything said here on this subject would be appropriate. The age and individuality of a child witness can make a difference to performance in court. Some children do sail through the proceedings with the aplomb of adult witnesses, in which case the cross-examiner may not encounter the difficulties mentioned, to such a great extent or at all.

But generally, the root and focus of the problem is the leading question. If it is not allowed in examination-in-chief, as indeed it should not be according to the general rule, incriminating evidence would be hard to obtain. But when leading questions are asked, at any stage, they often elicit monosyllabic or limited answers which are a poor foundation for the court's judgment.

Innovative procedure in taking the evidence of children, eg by video or short-circuit television, is not discussed here.

However, in view of the problems connected with the evidence of children, these and other progressive measures certainly merit investigation.

5 Expert witnesses

An expert witness is one whom the court recognises as having special knowledge of a subject through qualification, training or experience so that he is allowed to state opinions on matters outwith the knowledge or experience of the ordinary lay person.

With the advance of science, increasing use is being made of expert witnesses, mainly by the prosecution who are better able to bear the expense. They have been included here as prosecution witnesses, but substantially this section also refers to cross-examination of expert witnesses called for the defence.

Expert evidence may support proof of the crime, eg evidence given by experts in fireraising or explosions. Medical evidence of a victim's injuries is common.

Expert evidence may help in the identification of the offender, eg fingerprint evidence.

Forensic science is developing rapidly and can often establish traces left by the offender at a locus or on a victim, or traces on the offender or his clothing, of the victim or the locus.

An advocate should prepare for any technical cross-examination of an expert witness by such study of the subject as is necessary. He should master the contents of reports provided by expert witnesses on either side, whether they are disputed or not.

Questions of the admissibility of expert opinion evidence belong to texts on the law of evidence. It is assumed here that the witness is accepted as an expert, but that does not necessarily end the matter. He should not be asked for an opinion on a point which is outwith his field. He may be an expert on some aspects of the facts in issue, but not on others, eg a neurophysiologist should not give a psychiatric opinion. Objection should be taken if boundaries are overstepped.

An expert's qualifications may affect the weight of his opinion, especially if other experts disagree. These qualifications are usually excellent in themselves, but sometimes a witness's status in relation to the fact in issue may be undermined.

One technique for doing this is the following—but only where the circumstances are appropriate. A cross-examiner may explore some aspects of an expert's qualifications systematically, with the witness's willing co-operation, eg degrees, training, positions held, membership of professional associations, or his special field of expertise and how he acquired it, all with apparent approval. But he may do this, not to enhance the witness's status, but in order to build up a picture of his experience which shows that he is not qualified as an expert to give the opinion which he has stated, or any other opinion on the facts in issue.

To do this well can be impressive, but the cross-examiner should be sure of his ground and of the demarcation lines between fields of expertise. He should consult any expert witness whom he intends to call himself about this.

A similar type of question, which may be risky unless a favourable answer is reasonably predictable, is to ask the witness how many times he has had actual experience of an identical situation—especially if the technical issue is something very exceptional.

Such cross-examination, which suggests that the expert witness is stepping out of line, need not be pressed to the point of raising a belated objection to the admissibility of the opinion which he has stated, especially if he may be marginally entitled to give it. But these tactics are designed to weaken its effect.

It is unusual to attack expert evidence as untruthful, although such a possibility cannot be excluded.

The usual grounds of challenge are that the expert has based his opinion on facts spoken to by lay witnesses, which are inaccurate, or has drawn the wrong inference from them.

In support of the criticism of his inference, facts suggesting one-sidedness or bias may be suggested tactfully. Of course if the opinion is correct, a cross-examiner should not expect to destroy it, but that is for the court to decide.

Moreover, even if the opinion is wrong, as is the case with all evidence it may be weakened but not destroyed at the time, and could then be defeated by contradictory evidence. But if the expert evidence is crucial to the Crown case, this may be defeated by cross-examination alone, which raises a reasonable doubt about some essential fact.

Apart from challenging an expert's evidence in the ways stated, a cross-examiner would incur a risk in opposing technical points in the expert's field and which the witness has prepared himself to deal with in the trial. Here, an experienced expert witness could intensify the damage to the defence case.

But it could help a cross-examiner to ask the witness to explain technical terms and concepts, or jargon, in plain language. Once the mystique and fog of terminology are removed, ordinary facts may be revealed which a jury can assess on a commonsense basis, with less reliance on the expert.

Before embarking on any form of destructive cross-examination, it would generally be best for the defence advocate to cross-examine constructively, viz by emphasising helpful facts, or eliciting new facts which could assist his case. It is best to do this at the outset when the witness, not yet having been challenged, is likely to be at his most co-operative.

Expert witnesses may give evidence of both facts and opinions. They may report facts which are inaccessible to lay witnesses, eg the alcohol content of the deceased's stomach.

But cross-examination is often aimed at changing inferences from facts to which the expert has applied his special knowledge, rather than the facts themselves.

In the examination-in-chief, the prosecutor should have caused the expert witness to state the facts on which he based his opinion, and which must be proved by admissible evidence given by the expert or lay witnesses. The court can then evaluate the expert's opinion. But any information given to an expert witness out of court is not evidence, and neither are hypotheses put to him in the trial.

In cross-examining an expert witness either the factual basis of an inference or the inference itself may be challenged. To challenge the factual basis, a first step is to establish what it is, unless this was brought out clearly in the evidence-in-chief. This having been done, any such facts in dispute would be challenged in the ordinary way, whether they were facts observed by lay witnesses or by the expert.

The following tactics may be useful. The cross-examiner could ask the expert to accept that his opinion is based on disputed facts to which lay witnesses have testified, but of which he, personally, has no knowledge.

The expert would usually have to agree to this.

If so, he could then be asked whether on the basis of alternative facts, which the cross-examiner puts to him, his conclusions would be different, and, if so, what they would be. To resist this reasonable line of questioning might suggest bias on the expert's part. He may be expected to provide alternative opinions. In this way, the opponent's lay evidence about disputed facts can lose its aura of expertise, and become more vulnerable to attack in the ordinary way.

Cross-examination should expose any inadmissible factual basis for an expert's evidence, viz hearsay or facts put to him out of court, or hypothetically in court. Any confusion should be eliminated which might give a jury the impression that facts in dispute, or which are not the subject of admissible evidence, are somehow validated by the expert's opinion, eg where the expert agrees that his findings were consistent with some version of non-technical facts which are in issue.

The expert could be brought to confirm that 'consistency' here only means that the prosecution version of the facts could co-exist with his findings, but that this did not tend, in any way, to prove those facts.

In cross-examining the expert about the inference which he draws from facts, new meanings may be suggested. The witness's response may range from accepting them to outright rejection.

But however the witness responds, the cross-examiner will usually gain in some way. Merely putting the questions suggests the alternative interpretations to the court. If the witness accepts them, or responds to them favourably, good progress has been made. If the suggestions are reasonable, but he rejects them dogmatically, he may discredit himself as biased. The evidence would only be harmful if the cross-examiner suggested an unreasonable inference from the facts.

Although it would be unusual to suggest that an expert witness was lying, questions of bias and partiality do arise. As a background to cross-examination, the following considerations may be kept in mind.

Expert witnesses, like any witnesses, are expected to comply with the oath which they take. Many of them belong to professions and must conform to their standards and ethics. Expert witnesses are often eminent in their fields. Up to a point, they are independent witnesses.

But they are independent in the sense of having no direct connection with the case. Although experts are generally treated by advocates as persons of integrity, they are often subject to pressures which can introduce an element of partiality to their evidence.

Expert witnesses are not independent assessors appointed by the court. They have entered the arena. They are instructed and paid by one of the parties in an adversarial conflict. An expert may appear in court regularly for the Crown, or for a particular firm of solicitors to the extent that he becomes a professional witness with a continuing relationship with his client. Experts may be consulted during the preparation of the case. Sometimes they may be allowed to remain in court to hear other evidence before testifying themselves. Their time is expensive, and lawyers may try to derive the greatest benefit from this by consulting them during the trial. All this places the expert in the dilemma of being, on the one hand, a partisan adviser in an adversarial contest, and on the other, an impartial witness.

Also, an expert may have committed himself to certain views in a written report provided to the party who instructed him.

This would usually be produced in court, as the basis for his oral evidence. Understandably, the 'freezing effect' referred to earlier might come into effect. The expert might be reluctant to change those views under cross-examination and there may be a risk that he might present information selectively for its persuasive effect in order to support a mistaken opinion.

That this can happen is suggested by the frequency with which equally well qualified expert witnesses on opposite sides often disagree completely, particularly in interpretative fields like psychiatry.

Where expert evidence is influenced in such ways, unintentionally, battles of experts may occur and some of them may be vulnerable to attack in cross-examination as guns for hire.

A cross-examiner's duty is to the party whom he represents, and to the court. He need assume nothing. If he has reason to test or challenge expert evidence on grounds which imply partiality, eg that it is mistaken, one-sided, biased, unreasonable or dogmatic, he should not hesitate to do so, especially if he does it on the advice of his own expert. It would, however, be proper to do this without hostility, and with good taste, courtesy and respect.

Even where no substantial challenge of expert evidence is made, it is often a good tactic to ask just one or two questions to prevent the evidence from appearing to be beyond criticism and so that jurors should not be overawed by the expert.

B Defence witnesses

In cross-examining, a prosecutor's overall aim is to weaken or destroy any defence evidence which may leave a reasonable doubt about the essentials of his case, whereas the defence need only raise a reasonable doubt to succeed.

But a prosecutor not only has a more exacting task than a defence advocate; he is restricted by his role as an advocate, who, in the public interest, merely presents a case to the court for decision. He must be fair, and be seen to be so. He must not cross-examine oppressively, or go all out for victory at all costs. Indeed, if defence evidence is strong enough, he may even not seek conviction.

1 *Defendant*

The prosecutor's reasonable attitude should be most obvious when he cross-examines the accused. In his evidence, if he decides to testify, the defendant will contend that either the crime was not committed or that he was not the offender.

Some techniques of cross-examination have little application in cross-examining a defendant. Constructive techniques whereby favourable concessions are obtained from a witness are rarely of use here. A defendant cannot be expected to concede anything. But the constructive technique in which a party puts his whole alternative case to a witness who knows the facts, must of course be employed by the prosecutor. This is usually done at the end of the cross-examination, often by a brief and comprehensive question containing the essential elements, viz to the effect that the defendant committed the crime charged, which only permits of a simple denial, irrespective of whether he is innocent or guilty.

To put all the incidental facts to the accused, seriatim, will just elicit detailed denials, with repetition and emphasis of unwanted evidence.

It is not beyond the bounds of possibility that an accused person could be mistaken about his innocence or guilt, but this is a situation which is rarely encountered.

Scenarios could be imagined in which the accused had amnesia after a blow to the head in a fight, or in which he was genuinely unaware that the pedestrian was killed by the motor car which he was driving, and not by another vehicle. But such situations would be exceptional and, not surprisingly, prosecutors would be sceptical about them. Normally, the prosecutor proceeds on the basis that the defendant must know the truth, and that his denials proceed from lying. Prosecutors usually take the same approach with eyewitnesses who are associated with the accused, eg relatives, friends and fellow-employees—although, naturally, the possibility of error cannot be completely ruled out in the case of these witnesses.

In cross-examining a defendant, the destructive techniques will normally be limited to those which are applied to a lying witness. The prosecutor will focus on the defendant's motives, and any inconsistencies or improbabilities in his testimony.

It can be persuasive for a prosecutor to start his cross-examination of the defendant mildly, without undue pressure, and giving him every chance to reply.

This has tactical value. To the tribunal of fact the prosecutor presents himself as a reasonable and humane person who is making efforts to be fair. But since, invariably, a guilty defendant will start to be evasive, obstructive or inconsistent, the prosecutor will gain the sympathy of the court as he gradually becomes more and more firm with the accused. The court will see the need for this. Progressively, the cross-examination may become more and more forceful and, if it is well done, this will have the tacit approval of the jury.

Among the destructive tactics for cross-examining a liar, some may not be suitable with an accused. Indirect tactics to lead him into a trap are less likely to succeed with the defendant who, truthful or not, will usually have complete distrust for the cross-examiner.

Direct tactics remain the method of choice but even here there is a major exclusion. A prosecutor may only attack a defendant's character in circumstances which are strictly defined by statute and which do not arise in the majority of trials. This refers only to evidence of bad character in relation to credit, and not as evidence of guilt by showing a prior disposition to act in the way charged. The question of similar fact evidence is not considered here.

As a result of all these restrictions, to which, of course there may be exceptions, a prosecutor's typical method of cross-examining a defendant is usually an open and direct challenge to his truthfulness, which focuses on his motives, his conduct, any improbable facts to which he speaks, and on any inconsistencies which can be found within his evidence, or which arise on comparing it with the evidence of other defence witnesses.

If the accused has made any previous inconsistent statements, for example when he was cautioned and charged, the prosecutor will be sure to exploit this. Admissions or confessions made by the accused to the police will be put to him for acceptance, denial or comment.

The accused may also be confronted with contradictory evidence and facts emanating from Crown witnesses, and with any exhibits or documents which the Crown have produced.

The defendant ought to be given an opportunity of explaining any incriminating circumstantial evidence, in some way which is consistent with innocence. His direct evidence is admissible to counteract inferences of guilt.

Where, as is usual, the accused's character cannot be attacked in the sense of eliciting evidence of previous convictions, unimpressive features of his personality and motives often emerge in the course of probing the evidence objectively.

The defendant's response to inconsistencies in his own or other defence evidence is often significant. An improbable story may be made worse by amplification and exploration of collateral circumstances. The lack of realism in his evidence, on the lines discussed earlier, may become manifest. The ineffectiveness of his denial of contradictory facts spoken to by Crown witnesses, with which he is confronted, may be obvious. But however damaging his cross-examination may be, a prosecutor should not expect it to destroy the accused's evidence there and then, in the sense that he will break down and confess. The realistic aim should be to weaken it as much as possible, so that it succumbs, after final arguments, to prosecution evidence which is accepted and leaves no reasonable doubt about guilt.

Where the crime is in issue, what is in question is likely to be some intangible fact. This might be a question of whether the accused's intention was a guilty one, or some intangible form of crime, eg a threat with a knife. The cross-examination of the accused, and his response to it, may be crucial to the verdict.

Where the issue is whether the accused was responsible for the crime, he may concede that he was at the scene but contend that he took no guilty part in the incident, or he may deny that he was present at all, with or without the added defence of alibi.

In the first situation, the accused's identity as a person who was at the scene is not in doubt; he admits it. However he may have to explain why he was at the locus at that time and what he was doing there. It is one thing to be at a football match where a riot occurred, and another to be seen with companions outside a broken shop window at 3am far from home.

The question in this kind of situation is one of relating admitted identity to observed actions, or to inference, not one of visual identification.

The prosecutor may have led eyewitness evidence which connects the accused with the criminal acts, which he denies.

If the eyewitnesses were police officers on motor patrol duty, the accused might claim that they were lying. If the eyewitnesses were independent lay persons, eg the residents of a flat across the road from the shop, to suggest that they were lying may be so improbable as to impair the defence. Finally, if the accused says that lay eyewitnesses must be mistaken, the outcome may depend on their number, lack of connection, or discussion with each other, and the effect of ordinary obstacles to observation which have been considered. For example it would be adverse to the defence if a second set of eyewitnesses looked out of their window, above the shop, and, by the light of nearby street lamps, saw the accused go through the broken window and come out with a radio.

Special features may be found in such situations, where the accused is charged along with others as co-defendants, depending on whether they incriminate or support each other in evidence.

Apart from this, where presence at that place at that time is suspicious in itself, there is scope for destructive cross-examination applied to the defendant's explanation for this, which often raises questions of improbability.

For example, in the situation described, the accused may claim that when the police car arrived he was simply walking past the broken shop window with a girl whom he had met at a disco and who hid in a lane when she saw the police car come to a halt. The accused is not helped by the facts that she is not a witness, and that he does not recall her surname or the address to which she was taking him.

Where an accused simply denies that he was at the locus of the crime when it occurred, without specifying where he was at that time, this may raise typical problems of visual identification, circumstantial evidence, or confession, of the kinds already discussed.

The prosecutor may also depend on this type of evidence where the accused offers alibi evidence, whether or not it is supported by other defence witnesses.

A significant point for cross-examining the accused is the question of when he first told the police about this alibi. Given such a plea, he would not have been arrested at the time of the incident. Questions will then arise about when the police first contacted him, and whether the accused told them of his alleged whereabouts so that they could check this.

If the accused puts forward a false defence of alibi, he and his supporting witnesses will be exposed to the range of tactics which can weaken or destroy an invented story spoken to by several witnesses, as well as contradictory evidence from Crown witnesses. This has already been discussed.

A prosecutor should not fail to cross-examine a defendant about any confessions or admissions which he made, according to police witnesses.

It is unconvincing for an accused to claim that a report by a police witness that he admitted his guilt is mistaken, where the report has been noted in the witness's notebook, and is also spoken to by another officer. If such a report is inaccurate, it must proceed from lying in collusion. A defendant who relies on this contention undertakes a heavy burden.

2 Special classes of defence witness

Some witnesses, linked in some way with the accused, fall into special classes under the rules of evidence, viz the defendant's spouse, co-defendants and the spouses of co-defendants. The competence and compellability of such persons, as defence or prosecution witnesses, rights of cross-examination, the need for warnings or corroboration, and the extent of judicial discretion, are subjects which are outwith the scope of this book.

From the tactical point of view the significant point about such evidence, is that it is usually highly motivated.

The spouses of defendants or of co-defendants often become reluctant to give incriminating evidence, although what they said previously to that effect is the reason for calling them as witnesses. Typically, they will then come under pressure, and their previous inconsistent statements will be put to them. Sometimes this works, and sometimes it does not. The dilemma in which such witnesses are caught, between loyalties and fear of penalties, becomes obvious to the court. While not condoning any failure to testify as required by law, it must be said that advocates who bully such witnesses, with whom some jurors may possibly identify themselves psychologically, may not gain much favour with the court.

However it develops, the evidence of such witnesses is rarely of exemplary value.

Co-defendants may support each other but a court may be critical of the weight of such evidence. Co-defendants may also blame each other in a 'cut-throat defence' which, again, may be suspect. Cross-examination by a prosecutor is assisted by the fact that the motives of such witnesses are usually obvious, although what this means in relation to the facts will depend on the context of the whole of the evidence.

3 Other defence witnesses

With regard to cross-examination of defence witnesses other than those in the above special classes, a practical division of importance to the prosecutor is into witnesses who are connected with the defendant in any way, and those who are independent.

A prosecutor may probe possible links between the witness and the accused, eg those which may arise from family relationship, friendship, or being neighbours or fellow-employees. If there is some relationship which was not brought out in evidence-in-chief, this may not enhance the court's view of the witness's credit nor the defence advocate's candour.

The existence of a connection between the witness and the defendant may have a bearing on the credibility of the evidence, and on the prosecutor's approach. He is more likely to treat such witnesses as untruthful than to suggest this about independent witnesses.

Where eyewitness evidence about the incident under enquiry is led for the defence from witnesses who are closely associated with the accused, the prosecutor is likely to attack it as untruthful since it is likely to be motivated, for example where a man denies that his brother assaulted a police officer at a football match.

On the other hand it would not be unreasonable for a jury to think that such witnesses could be motivated to support an innocent as well as a guilty accused. Certainly, as has been pointed out, the existence of a motive in a certain direction does not eliminate the veracity of evidence to the same effect. The philosophy behind the comment 'She would say that, wouldn't she', as a ground for rejecting evidence, is untenable.

To maintain rapport with a jury, it may be best for a prosecutor to initiate the cross-examination of such witnesses in a neutral way.

It might be counter-productive to commence in a hostile and obviously sceptical way. An initially mild approach could be the prelude to a direct and forceful attack on the witness's veracity when the need for this emerges from his obviously unsatisfactory evidence, as the jury will then understand.

Usually, the prosecutor accepts independent eyewitnesses as sincere; but he may wish to show that they are mistaken. If so, his approach should be diplomatic. By his manner of cross-examination, he should show that the witness's good faith is accepted. He could probe, gently, to ascertain how mistakes could have arisen and, suggesting this, he might lead witnesses who are impartial to concede doubts or, by means of constructive tactics, to give favourable evidence.

As always, of course, unrealised partisanship and loyalty to the defence who called them may be an impediment.

Circumstantial evidence from which a fact in issue may be inferred is most commonly part of a prosecution case, but in theory there is no reason why the defence should not also seek helpful inferences from such evidence.

Defence witnesses who give alibi evidence tend, mostly, to be persons associated with the defendant which, of course, need have no sinister significance per se. These are the people in whose company he might be expected to be.

There is generally little chance of a mistake in a detailed alibi which has been worked out, checked, and discussed by the witnesses.

Usually, a prosecutor will cross-examine alibi witnesses associated with the accused on the basis that he and they are lying.

An independent witness to an alibi is likely to be challenged as mistaken in his identification of the accused, or about the date or time of the incident.

Untruthful defence witnesses will plan their evidence before the trial. As the trial proceeds, they may then adjust their stories, collusively, to meet difficulties. They can arrange for informants, other than witnesses, to report the evidence to them, as it comes out in court. This can be discouraged. During the day, access to witnesses can be restricted. But for trials which last for more than a day, witnesses who are not in custody cannot be prevented from abusing court procedure like this.

For prosecutors, the discussion and adjustment of evidence by defence witnesses may be either a problem or an opportunity.

The problem is that, in this way, false evidence may be modified and improved, difficulties may be overcome and inconsistencies may be reconciled.

The opportunity is that if collusion can be detected, and the bad faith of the witnesses can be exposed, the credibility of their evidence may be impaired or destroyed. This opportunity may be exploited in various ways. They need not transcend the bounds of relevancy; credibility can always be explored.

The foundation would be for the prosecutor to draw out the connections between witnesses and the accused, and with each other. They may be friends, relatives, or neighbours or they may work together.

The prosecutor may also probe the extent of the contacts between them, before the trial. Eyewitnesses would have been present at the incident; however it would be of interest to know what subsequent contacts occurred between that event and the trial. Questions could be put about how, when, where, why and for how long, such contacts took place.

In this way the prosecutor would begin to assemble material by questions which false witnesses are unlikely to have foreseen, and for which they are not prepared. Some witnesses might answer these questions truthfully; some might not. Untruthful answers would, almost inevitably, create inconsistencies between witnesses, eg if A says that he has not seen B since the incident with which the trial is concerned, and B says that he saw A every other day at the local pub. Something can be made of such inconsistencies:

Q: 'You say that you haven't seen Mr Butler since the day of the accident a year ago?'
A: 'That's right.'

Q: 'But Mr Butler said that he sees you several times a week at the Haystack Inn?'

The witness now has a problem. How he handles it, and how the prosecutor exploits it, may be important.

Witnesses who see the point of this line of questioning, and who wish to dissociate themselves from the collusion which has actually taken place, might deny their contacts with others or with the accused, or they might become evasive, which can start the process of casting doubt on their evidence in other respects.

Going beyond enquiries about contacts, when the the witness is then asked if he has discussed his evidence with other witnesses, a similar situation arises.

He may deny such discussion, untruthfully. This is an opening for the prosecutor, especially if he has just established frequency of contact between this witness and the accused or other witnesses. If, for example, the witness and the accused are brothers, living in the same home, it would be improbable, if not incredible, that they had not discussed some dramatic incident, eg the death of a child who was knocked down by a hit-and-run driver, said to be the accused. This line can be pursued:

Q: 'Did you talk about your brother's trial?'
A: 'No.'
Q: 'Is this just a trifle, something which happens every day, which you didn't think was worth discussing?'
A: 'I never said that.'
Q: 'Well, what are you saying?'
A: 'Maybe it was mentioned once or twice.'
Q: 'Why didn't you say that in the first place?'
A: 'I didn't understand what you asked me.'

The reluctance is obvious and unimpressive.

It is common for some witnesses to admit, and for some to deny, discussion of their evidence. This inconsistency makes them very vulnerable to challenge. It may be exploited by asking for details, eg where, when, and with whom the discussion took place, and what form it took.

This provides a detailed basis for cross-examining the other witnesses and for comparing their evidence.

Even when discussion is admitted, this is nearly always accompanied by a denial that it influenced their evidence in any way. If the prosecutor tries to explore the content of the discussion, unsatisfactory answers will follow invariably.

Collusive discussion of evidence in the course of a trial can also be an opportunity for a prosecutor. This will depend on the information at his disposal.

If it is reported to the prosecutor by police officers that, within the court building, or the precincts of the court, or in the street nearby, defence witnesses were seen in the company of various persons who had been in court, and in the company of each other, he might ask questions like the following, for reasons which will be obvious:

Q: 'How did you travel to the court this morning?'
Q: 'Who was with you?'
Q: 'Where did you have lunch to-day?'
Q: 'Who was there?'
Q: 'Was X not there as well?'
Q: 'Did you know that X was in court all morning?'
Q: 'Why did you miss her out?'
Q: 'Did you speak to X at lunch?'
Q: 'What did you talk about?'
Q: 'Did you discuss this case?'
Q: 'What was said about the case?'
Q: 'Did you discuss the evidence which you are giving now?'
Q: 'Has your evidence been influenced in any way by that discussion?'
Q: 'Why did you not discuss the case?'
Q: 'Have you not been told about the evidence which Constable Bell gave this morning?'
Q: 'If you weren't told about that evidence can you explain how you came to use Mr Bell's very words a moment ago?'

The last question illustrates a common tactic, viz to scrutinise evidence for signs of special knowledge followed by a request to the witness to explain this odd happening.

In cross-examining lying defence witnesses about whether they have discussed their evidence, the objective is not the expectation that they will admit that it is false and that they prepared it collusively; the realistic aim is to demonstrate their bad faith by eliciting evasive denials, and exposing the inconsistencies and improbabilities in their evidence. This will tend to undermine trust in them, and will taint their evidence when it is challenged on objective grounds.

There is, of course, no reason why a defence advocate cannot employ similar tactics with prosecution witnesses, including police officers. They are necessarily in constant association with each other, and their duties oblige them to exchange information. There is nothing wrong with this, if it is done in the course of making enquiries, detecting and apprehending suspects, and preparing for trial.

This offers a legitimate line of enquiry by the defence about the possibility that their evidence may be influenced, unintentionally, eg discovering that a suspect had a lengthy criminal record, might remove the doubts of a police officer who identified him visually while committing an offence, before he escaped.

However, it is very different if, while a trial is running, police witnesses meet and discuss their evidence in ways which could influence subsequent testimony. If this has occurred, a defence advocate might employ some of the tactics discussed above, especially if the challenge takes the form of attacking the truthfulness of police officers.

CHAPTER 10

Re-examination

I INTRODUCTION

An advocate has the right to re-examine his witness on topics which were raised in cross-examination. The aim of re-examination is to undo the harm caused by cross-examination and to restore the effect of the evidence-in-chief.

The main legal rules are the above restriction of topics and, with a few exceptions, the veto on leading questions.

Generally, the opportunities and risks of re-examination are not as well understood as they should be. Inexperienced advocates do not conduct re-examinations with conspicuous skill and they may damage their own cases.

If re-examination is well done, it can have a significant restorative effect on evidence which has been damaged to a certain extent, but not in all cases. Dramatic results should not be expected. If, however, re-examination is done badly, it can greatly intensify the damage caused by cross-examination.

Inevitably, re-examination on any point will draw attention to the advocate's view that it is necessary. It will highlight a gain made by the cross-examiner which is causing concern to his opponent.

Drawing attention to this point is unavoidable and harmless if re-examination repairs the damage and restores the status of the evidence-in-chief. But the risk is that it may not achieve that objective. If it fails to do so, it will only make the adverse evidence more compelling and more prominent and therefore worse. For this reason, caution and good judgment are always needed before deciding to conduct a re-examination.

It is better not to re-examine at all than to do it badly and to fail in this way. This applies not only to re-examination as a whole, but also to particular topics within it if it is undertaken at all.

Consequently, in order to create a favourable impression of lack of concern and invulnerability, many advocates prefer, where possible, to avoid re-examination, and to derive some added benefit from their way of announcing this. Instead of saying 'No re-examination, My Lord', they may embellish their decision with words like 'I have no need to re-examine, My Lord', which presents some marginal propaganda.

II PERMITTED TOPICS

In re-examination, questions may only be asked about topics which arise from cross-examination.

A cross-examiner may be expected to object at once if his opponent makes any attempt to contravene this fundamental rule of law which is designed to prevent unfairness. If new matter is allowed, the cross-examiner would have had no opportunity to deal with it. (It is only in exceptional circumstances that a court would admit new matter in re-examination, with a further opportunity to cross-examine on it.)

If objection is taken, but is opposed, the court must hear arguments and decide whether or not the proposed line of evidence arises from cross-examination.

This will present no difficulty if the topic was raised expressly therein, but problems arise about lines of cross-examination which only imply but do not express something.

In principle, only a line of evidence relevant to the issues would be admitted in cross-examination, and presumably any line of evidence proposed in re-examination would also be relevant to the issues. But although these two lines of evidence may have some meaningful connection with each other, in the overall context of the trial this may be too remote and too unspecific to justify the admission of the proposed evidence.

While the distinction between matters raised in cross-examination and those which were not can hardly be absolute, the scope of re-examination will depend on whether a given court interprets the rule narrowly or liberally, in the particular circumstances.

However, some types of evidence are certainly inadmissible in re-examination, especially using it to supplement examination-in-chief. An advocate cannot now introduce matters which he omitted, deliberately, or inadvertently, or where he did not obtain the answer which he wanted, or just in order to emphasise something.

Advocates sometimes omit lines of evidence in examination-in-chief expecting that they will be raised by their opponents in cross-examination. They foresee some tactical benefit from this, perhaps because the cross-examiner will be surprised and unprepared for the evidence which he elicits. They intend, then, to exploit that evidence in re-examination.

This opportunity may never arise. The opponent may not cross-examine at all or, if he does so, he may omit the desired topic. This may happen through inadvertence, or else because the opponent knows the facts, and understands the tactics. The opponent's best course of action may be to refrain from cross-examination, and thus block the testimony altogether.

It is dangerous to withhold important evidence in examination-in-chief on the assumption that it can be brought out in re-examination. All the material evidence which supports a party's case should be elicited in examination-in-chief.

III LEADING QUESTIONS

In re-examination, the general rule excludes leading questions, but there are exceptions; also the rule is not always applied strictly.

Leading questions are only prohibited on disputed facts and are permitted about uncontested matters. Also, they are often asked about facts where agreement is foreseen, although not yet agreed. A quick word between advocates in court, or a lack of objection, will facilitate this.

When a witness reaches the stage of re-examination, especially in a well-advanced trial, the area of agreed facts will be defined, expressly or by implication, and will be much expanded. So, despite the general veto, there may be great scope for leading questions on undisputed facts.

The following is an example of a leading question about uncontested facts:

> Q: 'On 30 June last year, in the evening, did you serve the accused with drinks in the Horseshoe Bar where you worked?'

This elicits a good deal of information about undisputed facts, rapidly. It is efficient and eliminates a series of time-wasting, non-leading questions like the following:

> Q: 'Where were you on the evening of 30 June last year?'
> Q: 'What were you doing there?'
> Q: 'Did you see anyone then, whom you now see in court?'

Q: 'Would you point him out please?' and so on.

If some facts are agreed and others are disputed, leading and non-leading questions may be combined.

In the above example, there may be a dispute about whether or not, when the accused was served with drinks, he was holding a pool cue, which was later used as a weapon in an assault on the witness. Here, non-leading questions might run as follows.

Q: 'Where was the accused when you served him?'
Q: 'What did you serve him with?'
Q: 'Can you remember in which hand he took the glass?'
Q: 'What was he doing with the other hand?'

If answer is that the accused was holding something, the next non-leading, question would be,

Q: 'What was he holding?'

Another exception to the prohibition of leading questions is that an advocate may use them to elicit denials from his own witness, as follows:

Q: 'Mr Butler, on that occasion did you strike the waiter on the head with a pool cue?'

Sometimes, by framing a question in terms of alternatives, a leading question is apparently converted into a non-leading question:

Q: Were you the driver, or a passenger in the car?'

Essentially, this is still a leading question, since it confines the witness to admitting that he was in the car, in one capacity or another.

But depending on the context, it is possible that this question might not evoke any objection.

Leading questions are useful in re-examination for rapidly referring the witness to the real point in dispute, or to something which he said in cross-examination, without a long, cumbersome, non-leading preamble.

Advocates should object if, in re-examination, their opponent starts to ask inadmissible leading questions which would harm their case. They should do this as quickly as they can, since merely asking the question conveys the desired answer to the witness and may be suggestive to a jury.

Some advocates rarely object to leading, hoping for the opponent's reciprocal indulgence or to avoid giving the jury a bad impression.

Many experienced advocates continue to ask leading questions without restriction, until stopped by an objection from the opponent.

Even where leading questions are allowed, an advocate may avoid them, if he wishes to emphasise certain agreed facts.

Leading weakens the impact of evidence. It suggests concern about what a witness might say, if his evidence were not controlled and edited, and that the the advocate, not the witness, is testifying.

IV WHEN TO RE-EXAMINE

A comparison of the risks with the possible gains explains why re-examination is not a routine procedure. It is conducted infrequently and, if at all, very briefly.

Unnecessary or weak re-examination simply strengthens the opponent's case, highlights adverse points and suggests that they are important. It lets a witness repeat and elaborate on harmful evidence. It may turn a molehill into a mountain and create unnecessary obstacles. On the other hand, ignoring unhelpful points in cross-examination reduces the attention paid to them and suggests that they are unimportant.

An advocate must decide whether to re-examine at all and, if so, on which topics. The decision can be difficult and requires good practical judgment in the particular circumstances of the trial.

The decision depends, partly, on the theory of the case in the pre-trial strategic outline which should be prepared as a draft final speech. This was discussed previously. The notes of the evidence-in-chief should be marked for re-examination in appropriate areas.

Re-examination should not be conducted where the challenge had no material effect or left the main points undisturbed, or where the damage done was only slight, remote or potential. Every point need not be covered if the essentials are established.

Again, if the evidence was really savaged by the cross-examiner, and serious harm was done, re-examination may be unable to remedy this. Perhaps the situation can only be salvaged, if at all, by other evidence. Re-examination is more appropriate where only moderate damage has been sustained.

Re-examination is not designed to cure any omission or to alter or emphasise anything in the evidence-in-chief.

An advocate should only re-examine with a clear purpose and reasonable prospects. The essential objective is restorative, ie to repair damage caused by cross-examination.

It may be done for clarification to cure confusion and disorder due to cross-examination.

Again, in re-examination, evidence may be qualified and explained, and reasons may be provided, which puts answers in cross-examination in a more favourable light. At this stage, unlike others, how and why questions may be helpful. Damage may be rectified by setting facts in a new context.

Some topics raised in cross-examination may need to be developed so that the expanded evidence removes problems and doubts.

Re-examination can correct a one-sided impression caused by selection of favourable facts, controlled questioning and editing.

A witness may be rehabilitated, if his credit was impaired by attacks on his character or conduct.

Inconsistencies may be explained or reconciled.

If cross-examination renders a line of enquiry admissible, which would have been inadmissible in examination-in-chief, this opportunity may be exploited.

But valuable though such goals of re-examination may be, an advocate should only undertake it if he is reasonably sure that they are attainable.

V HOW TO RE-EXAMINE

A General

Some general principles apply to all re-examination.

The mere fact of re-examining on a topic is a recognition that some damage has been sustained in that area. So steps should be taken to counteract this impression.

In re-examining, an advocate should always maintain an image of confidence and lack of concern, and should show no dissatisfaction with adverse answers.

Again, since an advocate re-examines his own witness, co-operation may be expected. The witness should be treated accordingly. Moreover it would not be in the advocate's interest to discredit him. The witness must be relied on for his evidence-in-chief.

Further, where damage is irremediable, the less the reference made to it the better. When this is seen, the re-examination, or that part of it, should be ended at once. In any event re-examination should always be as brief as possible.

Lines of re-examination will be specific to the kind of damage done, and how it was caused.

B Countering constructive cross-examination

If an opponent, by constructive cross-examination, elicits evidence helpful to his case, in the form of new and material facts, or by insinuating new meanings for agreed facts, this would be damaging to the adversary and difficult to rectify by re-examination.

New facts may create an impression of deliberate non-disclosure in examination-in-chief. If there is a helpful explanation for this omission, it should certainly be brought out in re-examination.

Difficulties of law and tactics would face an advocate who tried to dispute new facts revealed by his witness in cross-examination. He would be in the dilemma of opposing his own witness about these facts, while relying on him for others. Here, some damage may be beyond restoration.

Where the cross-examiner insinuated new meanings for undisputed facts, attempts to reverse them will employ the same methods by adjusting the evidence here and there, until it yields or is consistent with the original interpretation, which was presented in the evidence-in-chief. This may not be wholly successful. Alternative possibilities, once realised, tend to persist in one's mind.

C Countering destructive cross-examination

Where the harm done by cross-examination was the result of a challenge, for reasons already explained it is usually best to ignore slight damage rather than to focus on a potential weakness and make it significant.

But if the damage is severe, eg exposure of a witness as a liar, or the demonstration that a story is absurd, it may be beyond rectification and then it would be better to abandon the attempt. Persistence may only make matters worse. The only hope may lie in other evidence, or legal arguments.

It is where only moderate harm has been caused by cross-examination, that re-examination has its main prospect of success.

Here, lines of re-examination depend on several variables including the nature of the damage done, how it was caused, whether mistake or lying is alleged, and whether the crime or identity is the real issue.

To enumerate the exact methods of counteracting every type of destructive cross-examination would duplicate and invert previous text. A few principles should enable specific applications to be worked out in practice.

Confidence in the accuracy of evidence may have been put at risk by a challenge to the witness as mistaken or untruthful, or by criticism of the quality of his evidence, or both. One line implies the other. The witness's state of mind, ie his being mistaken or untruthful must be reflected in inaccurate evidence, and vice versa. But one approach or the other is usually emphasised.

Where the witness was the main target, a key to the line and prospects of re-examination is how far this attack may have impaired the court's trust in him.

It is difficult to restore trust once it is lost, but it will not be extinguished merely by exposing an honest mistake in an isolated part of the witness's evidence, which leaves the rest, and his integrity, intact. Here, the remedial aim of re-examination would be to underline the witness's sincerity, and the objective grounds for holding that this part of his evidence is accurate.

If a general challenge to the reliability of the witness's powers of observation or the efficiency of his memory was built up, any disputed part of his evidence may be suspect. Re-examination would be aimed at restoring confidence in his faculties.

Moreover, every effort should be made to show that even if only limited reliance can be placed in the witness generally, he is not necessarily wrong in this instance. Support for his evidence should be derived from other witnesses if possible.

However, the worst prospect for re-examination is where cross-examination raises such doubts about whether a witness is lying, that the whole of his disputed evidence is tainted with distrust. The grounds of attack may have been the witness's attributes, eg bad character, motives for lying, or striking defects in the evidence, eg inconsistency or improbability. In combination, such factors may be devastating.

Re-examination about bad character or motivation seldom helps. If such harmful facts emerged in cross-examination, they may be beyond dispute.

However, it is the inference about veracity to be drawn from these facts which counts, not the facts themselves. In re-examination, the witness will deny that he is untruthful. It is better to re-examine on such topics, only formally and briefly, and to leave the significance of character or motives for final argument, in the context of all the evidence, some of which may support the witness.

It would be worthwhile to re-examine in order to refute alleged self-contradiction, where this is the basis for claiming that the witness is lying. The advocate may try to clarify, explain, or reconcile statements to show that even if they were vague, ambiguous or seemed incompatible, they were not really inconsistent. Unless this can be done, the inconsistency will remain as a serious obstacle.

An attempt to discredit the witness may depend on the improbability of his evidence, ranging from single facts to his whole story. A skilful advocate can exploit this in cross-examination, especially with a weak witness. However, a skilful opponent may also be able to achieve something in argument about improbability, in his final speech. He would lay a foundation for this in re-examination. Improbable does not mean impossible, and what is unlikely may still be true.

Gross exaggeration of the improbability and how this was achieved by the cross-examiner, may be obvious to the court, and this can offer an opportunity for correcting the cross-examination, which should be taken in re-examination. There is often a reasonable prospect of restoring the balance, by means of patient reconstruction in the desired direction.

Of course if the evidence has been exposed as patently absurd and ridiculous, re-examination should not be expected to defeat this.

If the real issue in the trial is whether or not the crime was committed, it is likely to be an intangible conduct-crime, or to depend on some intangible element. As explained in chapter 2, result-crimes are usually proved, without dispute, by compelling physical evidence, whereas intangible criminal situations are often contested, and the verdict depends on eyewitness evidence of the main incident.

If it was claimed in cross-examination that various obstacles to observation or distorting influences on memory had led the witness into error about the commission of the crime, such contentions are often exaggerated and arguable. Difficulties of observation, forgetting, and suggestive influences often cause inaccuracy about the peripheral details, but do not necessarily create mistakes about the essential facts of a crime.

Where this kind of cross-examination may have done any damage, there is generally scope for restorative re-examination.

Apart from such further evidence about the facts as may be elicited, the witness may be guided into confirming his adherence to his account. If he is trusted, his confidence, and assurance that the facts are as he states, are likely to be more persuasive than the impediments to observation or recollection. Both in his examination-in-chief and in re-examination, the advocate who called the witness should be careful to maintain this trust by eliciting the evidence in a reasonable way, conceding difficulties if this is appropriate.

Intangible crimes or questions of fact easily lend themselves to lying. Nothing is left after the incident to point to the facts, one way or another. It is largely the word of one set of witnesses against another set, or even of one person against another. The scope for re-examination to offset a challenge to the truthfulness of a witness has been discussed above.

Where the real issue in the trial is the visual identification of the accused as the offender, by Crown witnesses and about which doubts have been created, a prosecutor will have difficulty in restoring sufficient confidence in that evidence by re-examination, in view of the burden of proof beyond reasonable doubt which he must discharge for conviction.

While trust in the witness, and in a witness's self-assessment, are important tests in distinguishing accuracy from error, correct visual identification is not guaranteed by a witness's confidence alone. A sincere witness, who is quite sure of his identification may still be mistaken.

Accordingly, even if a re-examined witness reaffirms his certainty in a visual identification, that alone may not remove doubts which arose from cross-examination. A prosecutor may have to depend on support for the identification from other witnesses or other kinds of evidence, eg circumstantial or forensic evidence, or admissions by the accused.

It has been seen that there are limited opportunities for effective re-examination. The evidence obtained in examination-in-chief or in cross-examination is usually more important. But where re-examination is in fact undertaken, it should be kept as short as possible.

After each re-examination has been concluded, advocates should ask judges or magistrates if they wish to ask any questions. If they do, it would be proper practice for each party to have an opportunity to ask further questions arising from those put by the bench.

CHAPTER 11

Cross-examination: closing speeches

This chapter reviews various general features of closing speeches and highlights aspects which are directly related to cross-examination.

I SPEECH AS STRATEGIC PLAN

The need to draft the closing speech before the trial has already been discussed. It should be an outline of an advocate's theory of the case which integrates all the issues of fact and law, and the evidence which he anticipates.

The draft should include flexible guidelines for cross-examination of the witnesses who are expected to testify, set out as bold and easily located headings, but there should be no verbatim lists of questions. During the trial, this would be a blueprint for the tactics to be employed. The draft speech will be altered in accordance with the evidence as it comes out, and will integrate its salient points.

It is often impossible to predict when a speech will have to be presented. By using this method, an advocate will be prepared to do this at any time.

II FORM OF CLOSING SPEECH

There is no standard way of organising a closing speech. A sound analysis derived from classical rhetoric would divide it as follows:

A   Introduction
B   Argument
C   Peroration

The Introduction creates rapport between the advocate and the tribunal of fact and gives an overall view of the argument to be presented.

The Argument presents the advocate's theory of the case in fact and in law, interwoven with the evidence.

The Peroration is intended to drive the argument home by arousing feelings and calling for action.

The material to be presented in each division is discussed in the next section.

III CONTENT OF CLOSING SPEECH

The content of a closing speech depends on many variables, eg the case, the evidence and the court.

In abstraction from particular trials, patterns for an ideal speech cannot be formulated. But the general principles suggested here apply in most situations and can be modified to fit the context.

A Introduction

The first step is for the advocate to create rapport with the tribunal of fact, bearing in mind, whether it is composed of jurors or magistrates, that they are lay persons.

He should, of course, have been building that helpful relationship throughout the trial. It is an intrinsic part of the persuasive process. But he will not easily transform himself from a tiger in cross-examination into a sycophantic lamb when addressing the jury.

Lawyers have never been popular. One common view is that they are smart, cunning, hypocritical and untrustworthy, especially defence lawyers, who will try all sorts of tricks to get their clients off. Lawyers may also be resented because of their air of superiority, and the bullying of witnesses with whom some jurors may identify. An advocate must overcome such prejudices to present himself as an honest guide who is there to help the court. If they trust him, his words will have added potency.

Although an advocate must not state his opinions, he conducts the case as if he believed in it. His image in the eyes of the court may be expected to influence the reception of his speech.

When this is understood, practitioners can work out how to present themselves in particular cases; this does not start in the introduction to the closing speech, but that is an important stage.

It is good to begin the speech in a non-contentious way, with sincere comments with which everyone will agree, eg 'Ladies and

Gentlemen, this is a distressing case. We all feel sorry for the terrible ordeal which Mrs Butler suffered at the hands of an attacker'.

This, of course, is what the jury are thinking and feeling, and to acknowledge it creates a bond, and displays the advocate as a reasonable person.

He might then say that his case is that the attacker was not Mr Bell. (He should always use his client's name, not the dehumanising phrases, 'the defendant' or 'the accused'). He would then present an overview of his argument without detail.

Summarising and outlining points before dealing with them gives an impressive display of their cumulative impact. The less there are, the more easily they are absorbed, although in theory the more there are the stronger the case will be.

For maximum persuasive effect, a balance must be struck between essential arguments, and those which may be omitted to give the speech more impact.

The Introduction should include a concise, non-technical, explanation of the meaning of the presumption of innocence, the Crown's burden of proof, and the standard of proof required for conviction. It must be said that the defence need not prove anything, since a reasonable doubt about the essentials of the Crown case is sufficient for an acquittal.

At the start of a speech, the tribunal's attention is probably at a peak. It is important to maintain it at that level. This involves matters of style, which are considered below.

B Argument

The first stage in presenting an argument is to define the issues. In criminal trials they are usually issues of fact, which depend on conflicting evidence. Disputes about law are less common. By crystallising the respective cases of the prosecution and then the defence, in a non-contentious way, these issues will be brought into focus. An advocate say for the defence will then present his argument on those issues.

If he has been conducting his case well, the court should already be familiar with his theory of the case, the story which he is telling, and its main themes. It was recommended that the court should constantly be reminded of these matters.

Now is the time for a systematic presentation of his total, integrated, view of the essential facts, interwoven with the evidence and law, as persuasively as possible, although concisely.

This should not be a one-sided account, emphasising only what is favourable and ignoring whatever is adverse. It is equally important to deal with the two aspects of his opponent's case: (1) he should confront directly his opponent's main contentions which are directed against his own case or may create doubts for the court and (2) he must also try to demolish or at least weaken his opponent's positive case.

Brevity is desirable in every aspect of advocacy. Arguments should be condensed into a few essential points which, if accepted, mean that the case must succeed. The fewer the points, the easier it will be to assimilate them, see their interrelationship, and recall them when deciding on the verdict.

References to disputed evidence should be organised for easy recollection, perhaps in the order in which it was given.

The advocate need not refer to a great deal of evidence, or quote it verbatim or at length. What is necessary is to state the point of the evidence of important witnesses.

He may criticise evidence, pointing out its flaws, inconsistencies and improbabilities, but he should not state any personal opinion about its accuracy.

He must certainly deal with any disputed evidence which is adverse to his case. It may ease the way to a helpful assessment if conflicting evidence can be reconciled. Otherwise it is open to the advocate to contend that a damaging witness was mistaken or untruthful. In any event he might be able to argue that even if the evidence was accurate, it did not mean what the opponent contends.

A defence advocate might comment approvingly that the defendant gave evidence, although he had no duty to do so, pointing out how well he withstood an excellent and thorough cross-examination. It is best not to comment if the accused did not testify.

The speech may include very brief, careful and non-technical explanations of points of law, stressing that these are matters for the bench. By anticipating a judge's directions to a jury, an advocate may gain their approval, when they receive these directions later.

A dilemma can arise at the heart of a closing speech. Which is more persuasive for the court — an all-out adversarial approach to disputed evidence and issues, leaving judgment to them, or a quasi-judicial approach, marked by concessions?

There is no simple answer. The proper balance always calls for good judgment in the particular circumstances, which includes the unpredictable reactions of the tribunal

Less experienced advocates seem to adopt the more adversarial approach. In some ways this may strengthen their arguments. In others, it may be counterproductive if they lose their credibility as honest guides.

A court is always impressed by reasonable concessions; they gain respect for the advocate and tend to place him on the judicial level of thinking. This image is more persuasive than one of inflexible partiality and dogmatism.

In nearly every trial, the defence could make one type of concession without damaging their case, namely if they admit the main branch of the charge which is undisputed. As was shown in chapter 2, the real issue is whether the crime was committed, or the identity of the accused as the offender, but hardly ever both. Yet it is surprising how rarely the uncontested issue is formally conceded.

Even in relation to the real issue which remains in dispute, certain facts may be unquestionable, eg if they were the subject of compelling evidence led by the opponent, or admissions which he obtained in cross-examination. Again, much court time could be saved by admitting such matters as bundles of documents, signatures and figures, which can easily be proved anyway. Nothing is gained by not conceding these facts, while to concede them may enhance an advocate's status and promote acceptance of other parts of his case.

It is suggested that in every case therefore, there will be many facts which could be conceded without weakening one's argument in the slightest.

Good advocates will concede these facts and will derive the benefit of doing so.

This reasonable approach is in accordance with the best traditions but, regrettably, not with the universal practice of advocacy. It brings both intellectual honesty and the will to win into focus so that they coincide.

C   Peroration

In classical rhetoric the Peroration was a rousing appeal to feelings and action. In this form it is inappropriate to pleading in a criminal court.

However, one cannot exclude the feelings of jurors merely by telling them to do so, but the expression of an advocate's feelings has no place in forensic pleading.

The call to action at the end of a closing speech takes the form of a request for the desired verdict. This may come at the end of a very concise summary of the argument, as a natural outcome.

IV   CROSS-EXAMINATION ASPECTS OF SPEECH

The closing speech has particular links with some elements of cross-examination.

The speech may complete the process where the cross-examiner refrained from asking a final explicit question to avoid the risk of an unwanted answer. In his closing speech he can invite the court to infer the desired facts.

A related situation is where the cross-examiner, obtained the wanted answer but dropped that line of enquiry to prevent the witness from retracting or qualifying it, or to avoid alerting his opponent to its significance. Otherwise his opponent might have tried to meet the adverse evidence by re-examining or by calling further evidence. This risk being over, the cross-examiner can develop the favourable implications of the answer in his speech.

A further way of completing cross-examination in the speech is to combine and assemble apparently minor elements in the cross-examination of several witnesses, to striking effect, ie to turn molehills into mountains.

The significance of isolated items of evidence elicited in cross-examination may be enhanced in the speech by integrating them into the cross-examiner's whole case as a coherent story.

Inconsistency which was exposed in evidence of one or several of the opponent's witnesses and left unexplained can be exploited in the speech.

Defence cross-examiners often challenge Crown eyewitnesses to a crime as mistaken, supported by alleged inconsistencies; comparisons will be made in the closing speech. If so, it is ineffective, to exaggerate minor discrepancies between witnesses which simply arise from the universal fallibility of observation and memory. Inaccuracy about secondary or peripheral facts commonly arises from this or from diversion of attention to central facts. It does not mean the court cannot rely on these witnesses to report the main facts properly. Testimony is often accurate about essentials, but not about details.

On the other hand, material inconsistencies which emerged in cross-examination should be emphasised in the speech, and they may well cast doubt on accuracy.

The extent to which a court trusts or distrusts a witness is crucial. Doubts about credibility are removed if the witness's sincerity is accepted. Other evaluations, namely whether the witness is mistaken or reliable, will be affected by his self-assessment, ie his degree of confidence in the accuracy of what he reports.

This self-assessment may be a significant guide where conflicts of evidence arise, and arguments about difficulties of observation or memory, one way or another, are inconclusive. The witness was there and, if he is regarded as honest and reliable, his assurances may have weight.

It follows that closing speeches should develop any evidence from which confidence in the witness, or defects, as the case may be, can be derived.

A witness's self-assessment is particularly important where issues arise about whether visual identifications are mistaken. Since certain miscarriages of justice occurred, and the *Turnbull* rules were formulated, courts are now more receptive than ever to defence contentions that Crown witnesses may have misidentified the accused.

Defence cross-examination will try to expose sources of error in observation or memory which could have led to mistaken identification, or which make the evidence too unreliable to prove guilt beyond reasonable doubt. Apart from extreme situations, where a judge may withdraw the case from the jury, such challenges may only raise, but not resolve, doubts.

Here, trust or distrust in the witnesses' self-assessment may be important. But for a witness, uncertainty is possible in distinguishing visual recognition from mere resemblance. Recognition, if accurate, proves identity. Resemblance is merely an element of evidence pointing to it. Some witnesses are confused about this, and their evidence may be ambiguous, eg 'It looks like him.'

It is also necessary to bear in mind that an honest but mistaken witness may believe that his identification evidence is accurate, and that his sincerity may be convincing, although misapplied. Advocates should be prepared to meet this difficulty in their speeches.

Facts related to the identification may help, eg the exact words used in identifying the suspect at a parade, any hints of doubt or assertions of certainty, or possible influence by bias, discussion, delay, or dubious police procedure. This is material both for cross-examination and for presentation in the closing speech.

There may also be incriminating evidence in the form of alleged admissions by the accused to the police. It is uphill work for the defence in cross-examination, or in the speech, to challenge several officers as mistaken, when each of them has noted a full confession in his notebook. If the objection has merit, it would suggest a joint hallucination.

If they are not mistaken, they must either be lying or else the confessions were actually made. Such issues may generate copious arguments.

Frequently, visual identification evidence is supported by, or even replaced by, circumstantial evidence from which an inference as to the accused's implication may be drawn.

The factual basis of circumstantial evidence may have resisted challenge in cross-examination, especially if it consisted of a number of separate and neutral facts spoken to by independent witnesses. But even so, it is still open to a defence advocate to argue in his speech that there is, at least, reasonable doubt about the possible incriminating inference which may be drawn.

However, a defence closing speech will not simply advance the defence cross-examination. It will also emphasise defence evidence, if given. This may include the accused's denial of guilt, explanations of incriminating evidence, or perhaps alibi evidence.

A defence speech should also place major emphasis on the Crown's burden of proof for conviction, the necessary standard of proof, and that the accused, who is presumed to be innocent, is entitled to the benefit of any reasonable doubt and should therefore be acquitted.

Cross-examination of witnesses as untruthful generally combines an attack on their credit with a challenge to their evidence as being inconsistent or improbable. To create distrust and expose implausibility are the cross-examiner's aims. The material which he elicits can be organised and presented in his speech to greater effect.

Sometimes, for reasons which were discussed, an advocate may be reluctant to charge a witness with lying explicitly, while he is actually under cross-examination. A defence advocate may lack confidence in the challenge or fear that the defendant will lose his 'shield' if imputations are made against Crown witnesses, or he may have doubts about the advisability of such tactics. If so, in the closing speech he has another opportunity of specifying that the allegation is that the witness was lying and was not just mistaken.

A speech is also an opening for arguing that inconsistency previously exposed by cross-examination was an indication of untruthfulness, and not mistake. If this is successful, it could taint the disputed evidence of one or more witnesses more widely than the immediate area of inconsistency,

Evidence which was challenged as improbable in cross-examination is an excellent subject for development in the closing speech.

The alleged improbability may apply to a single element in the opponent's case, to a group of facts or to his whole story.

The test is that of ordinary experience, and there is scope for extending initial improbability by argument to the point of absurdity and ridicule, thus destroying credibility.

Cross-examination may have exposed the facts on which scientific or technical opinions were given by expert witnesses. These opinions can be challenged in the speech.

V STYLE

Style in advocacy is very much a personal matter, and there are wide individual variations. Only limited guidance may be given.

The popular image of high drama with flights of oratory and rhetoric, which demonstrate the advocate's brilliance, is neither the typical picture of the modern courtroom nor the standard at which to aim.

It would be more appropriate to employ a pleasant, courteous, conversational style with an objective, realistic and business-like approach.

Since jurors and magistrates are lay persons, language should be clear, simple, and free from pomposity or circumlocutions of which lawyers are often guilty. Plain everyday language should be used, but not slang, and the approach should in no way be condescending.

During his speech an advocate should look at members of the tribunal, one by one, making very brief eye contact, but without staring at any individual. This enhances his communication to the tribunal and sometimes he may be able to gauge their response to what he is saying, and adjust it.

Whether the advocate makes gestures or uses 'body language' as some would suggest may be left to individuals. Such aids are better if they are spontaneous, but muted.

The same applies to such matters as tone of voice, volume, pitch. pace and so on. Advocates may find guidance on such matters elsewhere.

Monotony should be avoided, partly by keeping some animation and variation of expression in one's voice. Some thought should also be given to ensuring a high level of attention by making the presentation interesting, eg by relating arguments to the human story which is put forward. It should be possible to keep this interesting, without ornate flourishes. The general approach to the tribunal should be one of empathy. The advocate should try to see the case from their point of view, identifying their problems and confronting and helping them to overcome their doubts. This is an exercise in persuading lay people, not a scientific thesis. It should not be too abstract.

In referring to evidence, the advocate should not state his own opinions. He may defer to the tribunal's role as judges of the facts by using phrases like, 'You may think' or 'It may be your impression that.' He should never mislead the tribunal by misquoting what witnesses said, or paraphrasing it to give it a different gloss.

Repetition should be avoided where it is unnecessary, as it usually is, unless it is done deliberately for emphasis.

The final recommendation applies to the whole of advocacy and is stated in the form which it advises. Brevity!

Index